100 IRISH STORIES
OF THE
GREAT WAR

IRELAND'S EXPERIENCE OF THE 1914–1918 CONFLICT

Steven Moore

COLOURPOINT

To Susan McAllister, my eternal friend

Published 2016 by Colourpoint Books
an imprint of Colourpoint Creative Ltd
Colourpoint House, Jubilee Business Park
21 Jubilee Road, Newtownards, BT23 4YH
Tel: 028 9182 6339
Fax: 028 9182 1900
E-mail: sales@colourpoint.co.uk
Web: www.colourpoint.co.uk

First Edition
First Impression

Text © Steven Moore, 2016
Illustrations © Various, as acknowledged in captions

A catalogue record for this book is available from the British Library.

Designed by April Sky Design, Newtownards
Tel: 028 9182 7195
Web: www.aprilsky.co.uk

Printed by GPS Colour Graphics, Belfast

ISBN 978-1-78073-076-9

Front cover: (Upper) The German Uhlans had a reputation for being particularly brutal, with
many allegations of their cruelty made during the first months of the war.
(A Popular History of the Great War)
(Lower) Soldiers launching an attack at Gallipoli. Despite the differences in the landscape, the
techniques followed, including mad dashes across No-Man's-Land, were much the same as on
the Western Front. *(A Popular History of the Great War)*

Frontispiece: Irishmen are buried in cemeteries across the world, such was the extent of their
contribution to the war effort. This headstone, in a French graveyard, shows that though
the remains of this soldier could not be identified by name or regiment, there was sufficient
evidence to indicate they were those of an Irishman. *(Author)*

CONTENTS

ACKNOWLEDGEMENTS

Ireland, as is befitting an island that is so steeped in its history, is blessed with an abundance of museums, libraries and institutions that are generous with their time and resources. Amanda Moreno, of the Royal Irish Regiment Museums Group, was infinitely patient and helpful, providing both images she had personally taken and introducing me to the curators at the Royal Ulster Rifles Museum in Belfast, the Royal Irish Fusiliers Museum in Armagh and the Royal Inniskilling Fusiliers Museum in Enniskillen, to each of whom I would like to express my appreciation. I have been greatly assisted, as always, by Carol Walker, director of the Somme Museum, and the late Noel Kane, archivist and tour guide; by the staff of the National Archives of Ireland; the University College Dublin; Belfast Central Library, and particularly its Newspaper Library; the Public Record Office of Northern Ireland; and the Irish Linen Centre and Lisburn Museum. Beyond these shores my gratitude goes to the Archives of the Catholic Archdiocese of Perth in Australia; Tommy Matches, of Orkney; Sarah Wearne, of Abingdon School, England; the Australian War Memorial; the City of Vancouver Archives; the Library and Archives of Canada, Gerry Thomas of the Holyhead Maritime Museum, Wales; and the Commonwealth War Graves Commission.

When putting together these 100 stories I am sure I have spoken to, or emailed, at least as many people in search of information and illustrations and visited countless websites across the world whose creators and contributors were not always obvious. As much as I would like to name them all, many will have to remain unsung heroes but have, nonetheless, my sincere thanks. Those I can thank by name include Brian Curragh, originally from Northern Ireland but now living in England; Trevor Adair, of G Heyn, Belfast; Mary Robinson, of Holywood Presbyterian Church; Don Morfe, of the American Medal of Honor Historical Society; Archdeacon Gary Hastings of St Nicholas' Parish Church, Galway; Lester Morrow, Comber; David Johnston, Bangor; work colleagues Chris McCullough and Norman Hamilton; Iain McFarlaine of London; Niall O'Siochain; and Michael Melching, Germany; William Stockdale, Newtownards; and my long-suffering wife Heather.

Those to who I owe the most, of course, are the soldiers, sailors, airmen, nurses and volunteers that appear in the pages that follow and all those of that generation they represent. Perhaps it would not be out of place either, in closing, to thank a generation of journalists, particularly across the Irish newspapers, whose diligence and hard work in recording the events and experiences of 1914–18 at such a personal level contributed so much to this work.

As always, any errors that may have slipped into this work I, alone, take responsibility.

Steven Moore

About the author:

Steven Moore, formerly News Editor with the *News Letter*, the oldest English language daily newspaper in the world, and currently Deputy Editor of *Farm Week*, the leading agriculture newspaper in Northern Ireland, was born and educated in north Belfast, but has lived in Bangor, County Down, since 1982.

He is also the author of *Hanged at Crumlin Road Gaol: The Story of Capital Punishment in Belfast, Chocolate Soldiers: The Story of the Young Citizen Volunteers and 14th Royal Irish Rifles during the Great War* and *The Irish on the Somme: A battlefield guide to the Irish Regiments in the Great War and the Monuments to their Memory.*

"It's a long way to Tipperary,
It's a long way to go.
It's a long way to Tipperary
To the sweetest girl I know!
Goodbye Piccadilly,
Farewell Leicester Square!
It's a long long way to Tipperary,
But my heart's right there."

WAR WITH GERMANY.

Declaration Last Night.

OPENING OF HOSTILITIES.

British Mine Layer Sunk.

KING'S MESSAGE TO THE NAVY.

Scenes of Excitement in London.

Britain last night declared war against Germany. The country was prepared for this by the announcement of the Prime Minister in the House of Commons earlier in the day that an ultimatum had been presented, and a reply demanded by midnight. The demand of his Majesty's Government was that the neutrality of Belgium should be respected; but it was evident, from the tone of the Prime Minister's remarks, that, in view of the statement that German troops had already crossed the frontier, and that Belgium had been warned that opposition would be answered by force, there was little hope of a satisfactory answer.

INTRODUCTION

A LONG WAY TO TIPPERARY

It is a commonly held maxim that where there is a fight there will be an Irishman. Some use it disparagingly, of course, conjuring up a stereotype of the "fighting Irish" of the bar brawl or street quarrel and implying that trouble somehow always follows in their wake. Like all such generalisations, there is an element of truth and certainly as a people, regardless of class, creed or religious affiliation, the Irish have never been inclined to shirk a fight. It would be preferable to think, however, that the true essence of the saying refers to the Irishman's military prowess, where they have proved to be a breed apart. For centuries, the Irish soldier and sailor were the backbone of the British Army and Royal Navy. During the First World War they could be found in just about every battalion, on every ship and in the air as members of the fledging air force. Irishmen and women served in every theatre of the war, were involved in virtually every battle, and represented a wide array of nations. Author Rudyard Kipling, who lost his 18-year-old son Lieutenant John Kipling of the 2nd Irish Guards in September 1915, perhaps put it best when he wrote the lines: "For where there are Irish there's bound to be fighting".

This book sets out to tell 100 stories of the Irish during the Great War, one for every year that has passed since the beginning of the greatest conflict ever witnessed up to that time. It is a symbolic number, of course, for every man, woman and child of that era would surely have had a tale to tell such was the magnitude of events going on around them. It aims to be a snapshot of how Ireland and its people were affected by, and had an effect upon, the Great War. Irishmen and women served throughout the world, in vast numbers on the Western Front and Gallipoli, but also in the less well remembered battlegrounds such as the Middle East and Africa. Most served in the British forces but were also represented in not insignificant numbers in the ranks of the Commonwealth armies of Australia, New Zealand, Canada and South Africa and even turned up in some of the Allied nations, including the American, Russian and Serbian forces.

Opposite: How the Belfast *News Letter* reported the declaration of war on Germany.

Just how many Irish fought during the Great War of 1914–18 is a debate that has raged for decades and is still unresolved. Adding to the difficulties of those who have attempted to put a figure on Ireland's contribution has been defining just when a person can be deemed to be Irish. Obviously there is no issue with those native to Ireland, but what about those born elsewhere whose parents or grandparents were Irish and who still felt themselves to be first and foremost Irish? An extreme example was Patrick Mahon, who thought himself Irish though he most likely had never set foot in Ireland. His family had originally come from County Clare but had been part of the "wild geese" that had left centuries before to offer their services to the French army. A well respected soldier who had served on attachment with the Russian army for a spell, during which time he had attended the coronation of the last Tsar, Lieutenant Colonel Mahon was also the author of a number of military books. He was killed on 22 August 1914, at Sainte-Marie-aux-Mines in Alsace as he commanded the artillery of the 71st French Division, being struck by a piece of shrapnel as he attempted to save his guns from the advancing Germans. Mahon is surely too far removed to be considered truly Irish, yet one newspaper reported:

"He never forgot his Irish connection, never concealed his love of the old land, and was so imbued with the spirit of Irish nationality that he adopted as the pseudonym for his writings the thoroughly Irish name of 'Art Roe,' making that honoured name as well known in France and as popular among Frenchmen as Samuel L Clemess made in America his assumed name of Mark Twain."

Then there is the "English" Victoria Cross (VC) winner Flight Sub Lieutenant Rex Warneford, the first pilot to destroy a German airship. Flying near Ghent, Belgium, on 7 June 1915, he had chased the heavily-defended Zeppelin across the skies for miles. He reported: "When close above him (at 7,000ft) I dropped my bombs, and whilst releasing the last, there was an explosion which lifted my machine and turned it over. The aeroplane was out of control for a short period, but went into a nose dive, and the control was regained." The King, on hearing of his achievement, immediately awarded him the VC. Just ten days later he was killed in a crash after picking up a new plane. Warneford had been born in India in 1891 of parents who were also both born on the sub-continent. However, his grandparents on his mother's side were both from

County Down, so a claim for him being Irish could just as easily be made as for him being 'English,' which comes through his grandparent's lineage on his father's side.

It was an Irishman that fired the first shot by the British army in the First World War, or so it is widely held. Drummer Edward Thomas, of the 4th Royal Irish Dragoon Guards, also played a part in the first cavalry charge of the conflict – the first engagement by British soldiers on continental Europe since the Battle of Waterloo, 99 years earlier. Led by Captain Hornby, the cavalrymen's sabres drew the first blood early on 22 August 1914, close to Mons. Thomas recalled:

"My troop was ordered to follow on in support, and we galloped on through the little village of Casteau. Then it was we could see the 1st Troop using their swords and scattering the Uhlans left and right. We caught them up. Captain Hornby gave the order '4th Troop, dismounted action!' We found cover for our horses by the side of the chateau wall. Bullets were flying past us and all round us, and possibly because I was rather noted for my quick movements and athletic ability in those days I was first in action.

I could see a German cavalry officer some four hundred yards away standing mounted in full view of me, gesticulating to the left and to the right as he disposed of his dismounted men and ordered them to take up their fire positions to engage us. Immediately I saw him I took aim, pulled the trigger and automatically, almost as it seemed instantaneously, he fell to the ground, obviously wounded, but whether he was killed or not is a matter that I do not think was ever cleared up or ever became capable of proof."

Ernest Edward Thomas was a career soldier who had joined the Royal Horse Artillery as a drummer at the age of 14. By 1914, at the age of 29 and with 15 years of service behind him, he was a member of the 4th Royal Irish Dragoon Guards. He was promoted to sergeant in 1915 and transferred to the Machine Gun Corps the following year before finally returning to the 4th Dragoons. He survived the war and left the army in 1923. Thomas is widely heralded as being Irish, yet his military documents give his place of birth as Colchester, England. His Irish credentials, therefore, despite being generally accepted, are ill-defined.

Another "Irishman" born in England was Jack Judge, who wrote the famous First World War song *It's a Long Way to Tipperary*. However, though born in Birmingham his heritage was unquestionably Irish, his father coming from County Mayo and both grandparents on his mother's side being from Ireland. The song was apparently written overnight and then performed for the first time on 31 January 1912, at the Grand Theatre, Manchester, as a result of a wager. It became a huge success, selling more than a million copies of the music sheet. Judge himself is said to have performed it in front of soldiers from the 2nd Connaught Rangers in Dublin during one of his many visits to the city and they in turn carried the tune to the Western Front, where it became the unofficial battle anthem of the British army.

Women were excluded from the fighting forces but played an instrumental part in keeping the war machine moving. At home they took over many of the roles previously held by men who had enlisted and were quick to embrace the new challenges that arose in the shell factories. Women volunteers, some medically trained and others keen amateurs, tended the sick and wounded right up to within firing distance of the German guns. Most were with the British forces but others spread their wings further. A correspondent of *The Times* recorded:

"In a hospital not far from Paris there is a little diet kitchen of which it is pleasant to think, for it shines with cleanliness and gives forth the most delicious scents. It is in charge of a girl from the North of Ireland, who studied cooking for a year before the war began, thinking she might need to use it for quite a different war. Now she spends her days in sending up the daintiest and lightest of dishes to very ill French soldiers, and gallons of cooling drinks are brewed by her during the day for the whole hospital. When convoys of wounded men come in after 24 hours in the train, she makes warm drinks to soothe them to sleep after they have been bathed and tended by the doctors and nurses, and who shall affirm that her ministrations are of less importance than those of the surgeon or the chemist?"

Others came much closer to the fighting than they would ever have wished, while one Irish woman, Flora Sandes, went further again, joining the Serbian army.

Big families were the norm in 1914 and it was not unusual to have three, four, five or even more sons serving in the forces. The Rev J Wright, rector of Dunganstown, County Wicklow, had four boys serving: one in the Royal Fleet Reserve, one in the Royal Naval Air Service, and two in the army with the King's Own Lancasters and Seaforth Highlanders. In November 1915, he received a letter from the Privy Purse Office at Buckingham Palace which read:

"Sir – I have the honour to inform you that the King has heard with much interest that you have at the present moment four sons serving in the army and navy. I am commanded to express to you the King's congratulations, and to assure you that his Majesty much appreciates the spirit of patriotism which prompted this example in one family of loyalty and devotion to their Sovereign and Empire."

Such personal Royal approval was fairly unusual though another kind of communication was all too common – the black edged telegrams that arrived at the homes of countless families telling them of the death of a loved one, followed by letters and telegrams of condolence.

The pages that follow are not meant to be a history of the First World War as such, though the reader will be able to follow the course of the fighting in a broad sense. Rather it is intended to give a taste of the Irish experience of the conflict. Many of the stories contain graphic first-hand accounts, often using letters sent home to loved ones or memories scribbled down on the pages of journals as the base material; others are taken from newspapers, the language of which helps get across the mood of the period; and some are the tales that a book of this nature could not omit, such as the first and last Victoria Cross winners, those shot at dawn, air heroes, accounts from the major battles or the sinking of the RMS *Leinster*. Others, it is hoped, will introduce the reader to less trampled areas of the 1914–18 period.

"The first thing you feel in war at the start is the awful horror of it all, but after a week of it you get used to it and don't mind the smell or the smoke, the horrible sights and the terrible sounds of the guns. You get used to seeing men beside you talking to you one minute, and the next lying there just warm corpses. You get used to the terrible wounds and suffering around you, and you get so used to the cold, damp trenches that you cannot sleep afterwards in a dry bed of straw."

Private Edward Hallinan, of Ballina, County Mayo,
2nd Connaught Rangers, October 1914

1914

OFF TO WAR

It took 37 days from the murder of Austrian heir to the throne Archduke Franz Ferdinand in the Serbian capital Sarajevo on 28 June 1914, to Britain's declaration of war on Germany. A full four weeks passed before the Austro-Hungarian Empire confirmed its intention to "punish" the Serbs by marching its armies into the small Balkan state. Things then moved rapidly. On 1 August, Vienna's staunchest supporter Germany declared war on Russia, Serbia's principal ally, and on 3 August on France, which was bound by treaty to come to Russia's aid. Britain, which had an understanding with France, hesitated with its Liberal Cabinet split over whether or not it was legally, or morally, obliged to enter the war. The Germans, however, by invading Belgium as a prelude to an attack on France, forced its hand and at 11.00 pm on 4 August 1914, the United Kingdom declared war.

Ireland in 1914 had been on the brink of its own civil war. The Third Home Rule Bill was about to become law; both the Ulster Volunteer Force (UVF) and Irish Volunteers had managed to smuggle in substantial quantities of arms; Ulster Unionists, led by the Dublin barrister Sir Edward Carson, were prepared to set up their own Provisional Government rather than accept being ruled by Dublin; and John Redmond's nationalist MPs, courtesy of holding the balance of power at Westminster, were pulling the Government's strings. The Great War, however, changed everything. Both Carson and Redmond, the former after receiving assurances that Home Rule would not be implemented until peace returned, threw their weight behind the recruiting campaign in Ireland, each believing that their support would ultimately promote their causes.

The Germans had a long-standing campaign strategy, the Schlieffen Plan, which required them to rapidly sweep aside the small Belgium army. King Albert I, however, its supreme commander, had other ideas. At the Battle of Liege, the first major conflict, the Belgians held up the mighty Imperial German Army for twelve days, costing it dearly in time and lives. After the

Opposite: Refugees from Belgium fled to France by whatever means they could, with the lucky ones, such as this group driving through the streets of Paris, able to avail of horse-drawn wagons. *(From the Times History of the War 1914, published 1915)*

fall of Liege the Belgian army was forced back to Antwerp. Miss Mary J Fallon, from Salthill, Galway, was still in the city when the Germans arrived at its gates and witnessed an enemy airship drop a bomb that damaged houses and killed at least one man. She managed to escape by finding a space on one of the last boats to get away. The French, who had launched their own advances into Germany further south, had their first major clash in the north at Charleroi, coming out second best and leading on to the Battle of Mons on 23 August, the first time the British Expeditionary Force (BEF) was engaged.

There were an estimated 20,000 Irishmen serving in the regular British army at the declaration of war, with another 30,000 on the reserve list. While most were serving with Irish regiments, others were members of English, Scots and Welsh units. When the BEF set sail for France that August it included the 1st Irish Guards, 2nd Royal Dublin Fusiliers, 2nd Royal Munster Fusiliers, 2nd Royal Irish Rifles, 2nd Royal Inniskilling Fusiliers, 1st Royal Irish Fusiliers, 2nd Connaught Rangers, 2nd Royal Irish Regiment, 2nd Leinster Regiment, 4th Royal Irish Dragoon Guards, 8th King's Royal Irish Hussars, 5th Royal Irish Lancers, South Irish Horse and North Irish Horse.

Outnumbered by 160,000 German troops to the BEF's 70,000, and outgunned two to one in artillery, the British were forced to retreat from Mons, though not before the quick-firing infantry had inflicted heavy losses on the advancing Germans. At Le Cateau on 26 August the BEF suffered some 8,000 casualties as the rearguard attempted to hold the line and allow the main force to escape, with the Dublin and Munster Fusiliers among those suffering heavy casualties in the early battles. Sergeant James P O'Farrell, of the Royal Irish Fusiliers, noted:

"Cambrai and Le Cateau will live in my memory more vividly than anything else in this poor old world of ours. From that day at Le Cateau everything has been one long jumbled up nightmare of night attacks, marches that seemed to have no end, and constant fighting. There is nothing more pregnant with the highest excitement, and everything that fires the blood and imagination, than a good stiff fight, with the bullets and shrapnel whizzing and ripping and the shells bursting around you. But the aftermath, when you think of the horror of it all, the unnecessary sacrifice of life, the huddled-up bodies that lie in such significant heaps after a battle – sons just like I am, with, perhaps, the same home ties, and little sisters and brothers looking forward to our return – it makes one very sad. The person responsible deserves the greatest punishment that could be meted out to him. If the Kaiser is really responsible for this war, no punishment is too severe for him."

Squadrons of the North Irish House (NIH), along with its sister regiment the South Irish Horse (SIH), were the only reserve units included in the original British Expeditionary Force, with the NIH becoming the first non-regular unit of the army to see action. During the course of the war the regiment grew to two battalions, one of which was later disbanded to provide infantry reserves and the other converted to a cyclist unit.

The Battle of the Marne, fought from 5 September, finally reversed the German advance, throwing them back from the gates of Paris. After retreating some 40 miles, the Germans began to dig in north of the River Aisne. Trench warfare had begun, and with it a new phase of the war as both armies attempted to outflank the other in what became known as the Race to the Sea. By the end of the year, the front lines that were to remain largely unchanged for the next four years had been established, running from the border with Switzerland to the Belgian coast.

The BEF, under the command of Irishman Sir John French, arrived at Ypres, in Belgium, in October 1914, manning a 35-mile stretch of line. A German offensive in Flanders was launched on 20 October with the aim of capturing the ports of Dunkirk, Calais and Boulogne but was frustrated when the Belgian army opened up the sea sluices to create a two-mile wide 20-mile strip of flooded land. The focus then moved to Ypres, which the enemy overlooked on three sides, with the onslaught continuing until 22 November when the winter weather finally forced a halt to hostilities. Bombardier S Kirgan, from Ballymoney, County Antrim, fought with the No 1 Siege Battery, Royal Garrison Artillery, around Aisne, Antwerp, Dixmude and Ypres. "We had a horrible time," he told his wife in a letter home to Townhead Street:

"I would not like to mention all. Well, I was 57 days there when I got hit with a 'coal box'. The shell burst about thirty yards from my detachment, killing the officer, a sergeant, and a gunner, while I was wounded in the right leg with a piece of shrapnel which hit the gun wheel first, afterwards going into my leg. When it struck the wheel it broke the axle, so I escaped luckily from more serious damage. I was removed to a farm until night set in, when I was conveyed to hospital. It was three days before I got my wound dressed by a doctor, and he found a piece of shell about the size of a shilling piece working right into the bone."

Germany's navy was the pride and joy of the Kaiser, who hoped it might be able to take on the might of the Royal Navy. The first naval battle took place at Heligoland Bight on 28 August when the British made a successful raid on enemy shipping. However, the German fleet was the clear winner at the Battle of Coronel, off the coast of Chile, on 1 November, during which Admiral Sir Christopher Cradock's squadron was destroyed. In response, the Royal Navy sent out a powerful task force to hunt down Admiral Spee, and on 8 December, at the Battle of the Falkland Islands, it reaped revenge, sinking the prized German battleships *Scharnhorst*, Spee's flagship, and the *Gneisenau*.

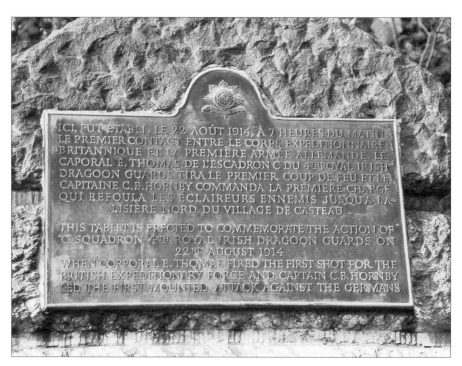

A plaque marks the spot where the first shots of the war were fired on 22 August 1914. (*Courtesy of Amanda Moreno, of the Royal Irish Regiment Museums Group*)

FLEEING THE BRUTAL HUN:
The Irish at Courtrai

For weeks the small Irish community of Courtrai hoped against hope that the war would not reach it though, from the moment the German army had crossed into neutral Belgium on 4 August 1914, most knew it was only a matter of time. The little colony, consisting of several hundred families with most from the north, was primarily an extension of the flax and linen trades back home in Ireland. From the Middle Ages Courtrai, or Kortrijk as it is known today, had been a major centre for flax and wool, growing on the back of the industry into one of the wealthiest cities in Europe. Indeed, much of the flax grown in the vicinity of Courtrai that year was already steeping back in Ulster. Its links with Ireland had been forged over many decades and extended through generations of its inhabitants. While some Irish families had packed up and left within days of the war commencing, others had waited until the German army was just miles away. A handful, given their marriage ties or circumstances, decided to brave it out and awaited the enemy's arrival.

On Sunday, 23 August 1914, the residents of the city awoke to the rumble of heavy guns being fired in the distance. The war was finally on their doorstep. One of the last to leave was Jack McCaw, who waited until the German cavalry was probing the countryside nearby before fleeing to the house of his brother-in-law, Dr Sam McComb, on the Antrim Road in Belfast, where he spoke of his experiences.

"The Uhlans have been making frequent raids on the country districts around Courtrai. They are equipped to the teeth, each man carrying repeating revolvers, a Mauser rifle and a lance. They ride the finest horses procurable on the continent, and dash along with reckless abandon. Their officers speak Flemish and French fluently, and their knowledge of the topography and physical feature of the country has made me come to the conclusion that for years back they have had quite an established system of espionage in vogue. Germans who have been living in different parts of Belgium are now with the imperial forces. Only the other day one of these rode into a small town where he had been doing business, and where he had been treated with confidence and consideration. He was immediately recognized as a leader in the enemy's forces, and someone shouted out 'My God, that is the horse dealer'. The people whose territory he invaded were those on whom he had existed. All round the outskirts these batches of Germans have been giving trouble. They have occasional skirmishes with the French cavalry. I know of one in which two Uhlans were shot and four arrested. One of the latter seized a revolver from the belt of his captor and attempted to shoot him, but was intercepted in time. Another Uhlan blew his own brains out. Whenever any of these fellows are taken prisoners the first question they ask is 'Are we going to be shot?'"

With the Germans already in control of the railway line further north, Mr McCaw had been forced to take a tram from Courtrai to Newport. The bridges there had already been blown up to slow down the enemy's advance, and so he had to cross the canals on a series of planks. He then made his way to Ostend where he was able to catch a boat to Folkestone.

Another to wait until the last minute before fleeing the town had been Jerome Lennie Walker, or Jim to his friends. The 25-year-old had opted to stand his ground while the remainder of his family fled and worked alongside the Red Cross, using his car to ferry about aid and people. With the Germans virtually on top of Courtrai, he had travelled to Ypres, remaining there throughout the early bombardments when he was forced to shelter in a cellar for weeks at a time. During the breaks in the fighting Walker helped in the removal of 3,000 inmates from the lunatic asylum to Paris. Despite having such poor eyesight that he was virtually blind without his glasses, he sought a commission in the army on his return to Belfast and, as a gifted linguist, was given a position on the divisional staff. However, he was determined to take the fight to the enemy and managed to get himself transferred to the 14th Royal Irish Rifles where, on 6 May 1916, he had the misfortune of being the first officer of that battalion to be killed and to be among the first Ulster casualties in Thiepval Wood, where so many were to die later during the Battle of the Somme.

ARRESTED AS A GERMAN SPY:
The Rev Francis Maginn

The Rev Francis Maginn was a highly respected man. Born at Mallow, County Cork, in 1861, the Church of Ireland missionary he had been left deaf from the effects of scarlet fever at the age of five, but had gone on to become a powerful advocate for fellow sufferers. A co-founder of the British Deaf Association (known then as the British Deaf And Dumb Association) and Superintendent of the Ulster Institute for the Deaf, he was a most unlikely spy – yet just days after Britain's declaration of war on Germany he found himself under arrest on just such a charge.

The outbreak of hostilities had unleashed a frenzy of accusations and arrests throughout the British Isles. In Ireland, the Royal Irish Constabulary was attempting to keep all foreigners under observation, particularly those of German and Austrian extraction, and arrests soon followed. In the first few days of August, for example, a German living and working at the Whitespots lead mines, situated between Bangor and Newtownards, County Down, was detained. Paul George Wetsen was charged under the Official Secrets Act of having "unlawfully and feloniously obtained and communicated to other persons at present unknown certain sketches, plans and information, which were calculated to be, and might be, useful to an enemy". He was ultimately cleared when it emerged the drawings and rough plans were of no significance though, rather than going free, he was interned like dozens of his fellow countrymen. Joining him were the likes of John Rockmann, a German who had been living in Britain for the past 28 years, most latterly at Madrid Street in Belfast, and who was a British subject. He had been accused of being in a prohibited place after police stopped him at Belfast docks; and three German hairdressers arrested in Newry, one of whom was married to an Irish woman and had lived in Ireland for the past 20 years, half of that time in the County Down town.

It was in such an atmosphere of suspicion and distrust of anyone who appeared in anyway different that Mr Maginn had begun a train journey through Scotland. He was waiting at the station in Elgin for an onward connection when a detachment of soldiers, members of the 1st Battalion Seaforth Highlanders, arrived on the platform. Mr Maginn, who often depended on the use of pencil and paper to communicate, takes up the story:

"I was standing near the soldiers, and sympathising with a soldier who was in difficulties how to fill in the cartridges into the holes in the bandolier. I felt inclined to help him; a kind gentleman did so. I saw the gentleman handling the rifle, and asking the soldier about it. Previous to that I lost my pencil, and was looking for it about the platform. Probably they imagined I was examining the rifles and ammunition. I asked the gentleman for a loan of his pencil, and asked him if the rifle was a Mauser, being ignorant of firearms. I never handled a gun in my life, and would not know how to shoot a haystack."

At the mention of a Mauser, a German rifle, an officer immediately came over and examined his papers. Concluding that he 'looked foreign,' and seeing reference to Officer de l'Academie Francaise on his documents (an honour conferred on him by the French government for his work with the deaf and dumb), he ordered his arrest and sent off a dispatch rider to fetch the local constabulary. Fortunately, one of the first police officers to arrive on the scene had a sister who was deaf and dumb and was able to converse using sign language. A superintendent and the chief constable were next to arrive, the latter looking over the reverend's papers before ordering his immediate release. "He good humouredly asked me whether it was for gun-running in Ireland that I wanted the information. I could not help laughing at such an idea," recalled Mr Maginn.

The clergyman appeared to have a knack at being in the wrong place at the wrong time:

"By the way, I may explain that I was out the night of the Larne gun-running, and saw a large number of motor cars passing through Belfast. I did not understand what it was, for very few did, so well was the secret kept. I also happened to go up to Dublin from Belfast that Sunday of the awful shooting in Bachelor's Walk. I and my wife were in that street, and had we arrived there only fifteen minutes sooner we might have been shot. It was for these reasons I wanted to know the kind of rifles. I was told they had Mausers at Larne. I never saw a Mauser in my life."

ARRIVAL OF THE FIRST AIRMAN:
Hubert Dunsterville Harvey-Kelly

At 8.20 am on 11 August 1914, the wheels of the first British war plane to arrive on the Western Front touched down on French soil. At the controls of the BE2a was Hubert Dunsterville Harvey-Kelly, whose family hailed from Roscommon and Westmeath. There to meet him were a number of Royal Flying Corps (RFC) personnel who had travelled by ship and train. The former Royal Irish Regiment soldier had been on attachment to No 2 Squadron of the RFC, based in Scotland, and had flown from Montrose to Dover in a series of hops before his final flight of one hour and 55 minutes took him into the history books. Within the next few days dozens of further planes would arrive in France, some piloted across and others carried on transports.

Lieutenant Harvey-Kelly was to notch up another first two weeks later when he and two comrades brought down the first enemy aircraft. On 25 August he spotted a single German Taube flying over the French lines. Despite being unarmed, Harvey-Kelly swooped down on the enemy craft, and closed right up to his tail. The German pilot immediately dived in a bid to shake off his pursuer but to no avail. The other two British pilots then closed up, flying either side of the Taube and boxing it in. The German pilot decided his best chance of escape was on the ground and landed his aircraft before running off into nearby woodland. The British pilots also landed and gave chase but couldn't find their quarry so returned to the skies after setting light to the enemy plane.

Harvey-Kelly, promoted to squadron commander, awarded the Distinguished Service Order (DSO) and mentioned in dispatches during his flying career, died on 29 April 1917 – a good innings for a pilot by the standard of the day – from injuries sustained in a dog-fight near Arras, northern France.

Another Irishman early into the fray was Francis, 6th Earl of Annesley, though the shortness of his service was sadly more typical, as apparently was his cavalier attitude, though this was tinged with an underlying deeper realisation of the dangers faced. A member of the Royal Naval Air Service (RNAS), he wrote home to Castlewellan, County Down, outlining a couple of days of his activity. On 21 October 1914, he was "having a dull time". He mused:

"The battle is still raging round five miles from here, and I have only got to it one afternoon, and that to take ammunition out. Yesterday troops from the Aisne passed through, all with beards, and caked in mud. The South Irish Horse came through too, and one of them I spoke to said that he had seen all the North Irish Horse a short time before. We had two marines killed and one wounded in the armoured cars yesterday, both by shrapnel. Marrix, the man who destroyed the Zeppelin, had 14 bullet holes through the wings of his aeroplane yesterday. What a life, isn't it? Yet we laugh about it, and treat it as a joke, but I am certain it makes us all think a little harder."

The following day he was lucky to escape with his life when his airplane's engine failed, though his main concern appeared to be the risk of being taken prisoner. He wrote:

"In the air yesterday we got shot at a lot when 2,500 feet up, so we rose to 5,000 feet. Clouds very low, and we were, of course, right among them, and could see nothing, not even the tips of our wings. Suddenly our engine gave out, and we glided down about 2,000 feet, and found we were still within range of German shrapnel. Luckily we had the wind with us, and glided a mile over the German lines, landing in a turnip field. Turned over very neatly. We did not know that we were in a friendly country. We waited, with shells bursting round us for ten minutes, when four French cavalry rode up to us. What a relief that they were French and not Germans!"

He added, by way of a footnote: "We saw war vessels off Ostend shelling the Germans. I shall never forget it as long as I live. This flying under shell and rifle fire must beat most things for pure and unadulterated excitement. Went for a joy ride this afternoon, and watched the battle – a little too long for comfort, as a shell burst behind us in the road."

The sub-lieutenant, who had succeed his father as the 6th Earl Annesley in 1908, marrying the following year, arrived home in Castlewellan less than a fortnight later for an unscheduled leave, setting off for the south of England again the following evening. His family never heard from him again. Several days later the Admiralty issued a statement reporting him missing. It read:

"The Secretary of the Admiralty announced that Flight-Lieutenant Charles Francis Beevor, RN, with Sub-Lieutenant the Earl of Annesley,

RNVR, as a passenger, left Eastchurch to fly abroad at 3.15 on Thursday, 5th November. The machine never reached her destination. Careful search has been made with aeroplanes, seaplanes and patrol ships, but no tidings of the missing airmen have yet been received."

Lord Annesley was 30 years of age. His body was never found and he is commemorated on the Chatham Naval Memorial.

Lieutenant Hubert Dunsterville Harvey-Kelly had led the way by flying his machine across the Channel to France. Most of the Royal Flying Corps personel and equipment that followed, however, was transported by sea.
(From the Times History of the War 1914, published 1915)

THE FIRST IRISH VICTORIA CROSS WINNER:
Maurice James Dease

Lieutenant Maurice James Dease was a true hero. Despite being wounded a number of times he remained at his post until fatally injured. Together with Private Sidney Godley, both of whom were awarded the Victoria Cross, he ensured his surviving men escaped the advancing Germans during the retreat from Mons, the first full-scale British encounter with the enemy. Lieutenant Dease's citation records:

"On 23rd August 1914 at Mons, Belgium, Nimy Bridge was being defended by a single company of Royal Fusiliers and a machine-gun section with Lieutenant Dease in command. The gunfire was intense, and the casualties were heavy, but the Lieutenant went on firing in spite of his wounds, until he was hit for the 5th time and was carried away to a place of safety where he died."

Maurice Dease was born on 28 September 1889, to Edmund and Katherine Dease at Gaulstown, Coole, County Westmeath. The family had lived in the area for at least 600 years, with an ancestor, Dr William Dease, a founding member of the Royal College of Surgeons in Dublin. Maurice's mother was related to the Murray family from Cork, associated with the Cork Distilleries Company.

Dease had been a soldier for four years, and was serving with the 4th Royal Fusiliers in August 1914. Nimy Railway Bridge, on the Conde Canal, was a key objective of the enemy as the waterway provided a natural barrier. Likewise, the British were equally determined to hold the line and deny the Germans the strategic crossing point for as long as possible. As machine-gun officer, Dease deployed his two guns close to the bridge where they could do the most damage. Constantly he ran back and forth between the two guns to ensure they kept up their rate of fire and were well supplied with ammunition. As soon as one machine-gunner was killed, another was sent in his place. The Germans, aware that it was the gun teams that were holding up their progress, concentrated their fire on them. Eventually the decision to withdraw the Royal Fusiliers was taken, with the two machine-guns used to cover the men as they pulled out. Dease took over one of the machine-guns himself and, aged 24 and despite having been wounded a number of times, kept the enemy at bay until fatally wounded. Godley, from East Grinstead in England, had joined the army in 1909 and was aged 25 in 1914. He had to remove the bodies of three previous gunners to get at his weapon but managed to hold the bridge for a further two hours after Dease was killed. Finally running out of ammunition, he threw the working parts of his machine-gun into the Conde Canal so it would be of no use to the enemy. Badly wounded in the head and back, the later wound inflicted by shrapnel from a shell that had exploded yards away from him, he crawled to the main road where he was helped to a first aid post by Belgium civilians. As his injuries were being attended the Germans arrived, making him a prisoner of war. He learned of his award of the Victoria Cross while in a POW camp at Doberitz. Sidney Godley died in Essex in June 1957, at the age of 67.

In 1939, a quarter-of-a-century after the Battle of Mons, some 50 men of the Royal Fusiliers attended a ceremony at the opening of a new bridge at Nimy during which a plaque honouring the heroism of Lieutenant Dease and Private Godley was unveiled. The following year, as a result of the Second World War, it was removed again and hidden away for safekeeping, not being returned to the bridge until 1961.

Lieutenant Dease, who was buried at St Symphorien Military Cemetery, 2 kms east of Mons, is also remembered at Westminster Cathedral, Wayside Cross in Woodchester, Stroud, Gloucestershire, and on the War Memorial at Wimbledon College chapel. His Victoria Cross is displayed at the Royal Fusiliers Museum in the Tower of London. In 2012 the museum purchased a painting of the VC hero, originally commissioned by his brother and painted by leading artist William Carter from photographs.

WITNESS TO A GERMAN ATROCITY:
Corporal Jim Heaney

At Le Cateau on 26 August 1914, some 68,000 BEF soldiers faced approximately 160,000 Germans of the 1st Army. The decision to make a stand was accompanied by confusion, with orders and counter-orders being issued right up to the last moment instructing units by turns to dig in or to continue the retreat. The 4th Division, having arrived at Le Cateau by train two days before, was thrown into the fray on the extreme left, with the Royal Inniskilling Fusiliers, part of its 12th Brigade, holding a segment of line near Esnes. Among their number was Corporal Jim Heaney, who owed his survival to the courage of French women who literally put themselves between him and German soldiers intent on mass murder.

From Stannus Place in Lisburn, County Antrim, he was a well known figure in athletics circles, having won the North of Ireland cross-country championships held in Belfast's Belvoir Park in 1913 and being selected to represent Ireland. However, his fleetness of foot wasn't enough to outrun the Germans. His platoon was in a forward position throughout the day, and though later reinforced, suffered many casualties, though not without making the enemy pay heavily. The German 7th Jagers, attempting to outflank the British lines, were caught crossing a cornfield by the fusiliers, and were forced back with heavy losses. Later the enemy launched a determined infantry attack on the battalion's position, again attempting to work round its flank, but this was also repelled. By 5.00 pm, when orders arrived with the 4th Division instructing it to withdraw and continue the retreat towards St Quentin, the Inniskillings had been forced back into Esnes and the whole line was under heavy German bombardment. The action at Le Cateau cost the British 8,500 casualties and 38 guns but bought vital time. The withdrawal was carried out without the Germans realising the main force was leaving the battlefield and giving the BEF some much needed breathing space.

Corporal Heaney, however, had been wounded by shrapnel in both legs and his left hand, the latter wound ultimately resulting in two fingers having to be amputated, and was left lying on the field of battle. He told the *Belfast Telegraph*:

"I was picked up by a number of French women and brought to a little village school-house. The main body of the building already contained eighty British wounded, and I and some eleven others were consequently placed in what I think was a cloak-room, where our injuries were attended to, and where we received every kindness. Indeed, I could not speak too highly of the treatment we received at the hands of these daughters of France."

Later that evening, as the corporal lay on his makeshift stretcher, he heard the doors of the school house being smashed open, sparking cries of fear and panic from the women and children attending the soldiers. A group of Germans consisting of both cavalry and infantry soldiers entered the building and, according to Corporal Heaney, began murdering the wounded using swords and bayonets. Only the begging of the women, who threw themselves at the enemy's feet, brought the slaughter to an end.

The British wounded still alive were taken to Cambrai, some four miles away, being blindfolded so they couldn't see the enemy dispositions. Corporal Heaney was treated in a French hospital there for a month before, along with other prisoners of war, being moved to a camp at Cassel. After 17 months of captivity he was repatriated.

Another member of the Royal Inniskilling Fusiliers wounded at the battle, and latter repatriated because of the severity of his wounds, was Belfast man Private J Pritchard, who had his own story of German cruelty. Found by the enemy after lying in the open for two days, he was taken to a French farmhouse were German wounded were being attended but was left lying there for another two days without receiving treatment. Next he was loaded on to a cart for a torturous journey. He recalled:

"We had two days before we came to another hospital, and our wounds were smelling so badly we asked to get dressed. But instead they poked us with the rifles and told us their own people came first. They were trying to get information from us, and they said if they found we were wrong we would be shot. Our food was in the morning one glass of coffee, dinner one saucer of soup, supper a cup of coffee, no sugar or milk, and a little black bread. We were put in the carts again for a three-days' ride, and then put into dark wagons. We did not know where we were going to as they kept everything dark to all prisoners."

At Cologne Station the wounded were left lying on the platform for two hours in pouring rain being jeered by a crowd of German civilians that had gathered to see this first batch of British prisoners. He went on:

"As soon as the doctor saw my hand he told me I would get lockjaw, and that I would get my leg off in half an hour's time … In the dressing-room they were as rough as they could be with us, but we made it up amongst ourselves not to give in to them. They told us that we were dogs, devils, and that we were too wicked to die."

The German Uhlans had a reputation for being particularly brutal, with many allegations of cruelty made during the first months of the war.
(*A Popular History of the Great War, published 1933*)

ESCAPING ACROSS THE SEA:
William Parker

William Parker must have cut a bizarre figure as he approached the guard at Shorncliffe Camp near Folkestone, on the English coast. Unshaven and unwashed, and dressed in an old suit that had been given to him by a French farmer, with a collar and tie donated by a sympathetic fellow passenger as he crossed the Channel, he more resembled a tramp than a British soldier. Presenting himself to the commanding officer, he told a tale of being taken prisoner by the Germans, of making good his escape during which he shot one of his captors, then making his way across hundreds of miles of open country until finally turning up at the French coast.

A member of the 2nd Royal Inniskilling Fusiliers, Drummer William Ephraim Parker, from Enniskillen in County Fermanagh, was 29 in 1914. Speaking in Belfast as he passed through on his way to his regimental depot in Omagh, County Tyrone, and then wearing clothes donated by old friend James Orr, who only hours previously had himself enlisted in the Royal Irish Rifles, he told a *Belfast Telegraph* reporter:

> "It was at Mons that we were first in action, and although the regiment suffered some losses we inflicted very heavy losses on the Germans, whose advance en masse made them easy targets; but when they were isolated it was very difficult to distinguish them because of the colour of their uniforms … The fighting was continuous and during the operations at Cambrai I got a shot in my water bottle. I was on outpost duty, and during the battle several of the picket were killed. The Germans threw two army corps on us, being about ten to one. They attacked in great numbers, and we were working on the defensive to keep them off our pickets. The Germans knew about this, and made flank attacks on each side, employing great numbers of Uhlans in the effort to crush the British. During this fight the Inniskillings lost pretty heavily."

Isolated after the men around him were killed, Parker was rushed by four Uhlans, who took him prisoner. However, after a short walk in the darkness the group came to lines of barbed wire that only allowed them to pass through in single file. Parker seized his chance and slipped under the head of the last horse, grabbed the German's rifle and fired at him, the shot knocking him off his horse. Running into the darkness, only pausing briefly to fire several more shots in the general direction of the enemy horsemen, he made good his escape.

He was now alone, however, in a strange land, unable to speak any French, and no idea in which direction he should head. Around dawn he came across a farmhouse, his arrival causing alarm among the occupants. However, they gave him a change of clothes, disposing of his uniform, and allowed him to hide in the house attic for several days. On one occasion, having tired of his hiding place, he was wandering about the house when he spotted a group of German soldiers approaching. Hiding between a wall and the frame of a bed, he had to undergo several uncomfortable minutes as the enemy troops made their way from room to room, but remained undetected. Suitably chastened, he spent the next three days and nights in the attic before deciding to make a run for it with the hope of either reaching Boulogne or making contact with the retreating British lines.

At the village of Caudry he was aided by a priest, who not only provided him with written directions, listing the villages he had to pass through, but wrote him a note asking any French citizens he met to help him on his way. At Douai he was nearly captured again, but was saved by locals who put him on the road to Arras – where he was arrested as a German spy. With the help of an interpreter, and by showing his British army identity disc, he convinced his captors to release him and was again on his way, this time with documentation provided by the city's chief of police. At St Pol he boarded a train to Boulogne, arriving six days after first being taken prisoner. Parker reported to the British Consul there, who advised him to cross over to Shorncliffe, providing him with a pass to travel. The *Belfast Telegraph* reporter concluded:

"Parker's one desire is to be refitted and sent to the front immediately. He tells his story without any brag or bravado, and it must be said that he has shown admirable qualities of courage and endurance. He confirms the reports of other soldiers that the Germans are afraid of our cavalry, and that their infantry are massed in such a manner that they fell victims in hundreds to our rifle and artillery fire."

The drummer got his wish and was soon returned to the front where, on 7 November 1914, he was killed. He has no known grave and is remembered on the Ploegsteert Memorial. His old friend, James Orr, was also to die during the war. He was killed at the Battle of the Somme while serving with the 13th Royal Irish Rifles and is commemorated on the Thiepval Memorial.

Drummer William Parker's narrow escape from captivity proved tragic in the end as he was killed a few months later. *(From the Belfast Telegraph)*

FIRST VICTIM OF FRIENDLY FIRE:
Irene Ethel McGeown

The war was less than three weeks old when Irene Ethel McGeown became the first Irish civilian victim of "friendly fire", shot in the back of the head by a soldier whose sole intention had been merely to warn. The 33-year-old had been holidaying with her family in north Down when tragedy struck. On Monday, 24 August 1914, she set off by car from Bangor for Donaghadee, with her brother-in-law, Alfred Chapman, at the wheel with her sister, Laura Evelyn Chapman, next to him. Irene was sitting in the back with two friends, a Miss Branagh and a Miss Burke. Her brother Clarence waved her off shortly after 8.00 pm, as he had done each evening during the previous week.

The car, with two acetylene and two oil side-lights burning for illumination, with another at the back, reached Orlock, just a few miles from its destination, a little after 8.30 pm, just as dusk was turning to night. As Mr Chapman, a clothing manufacturer, approached the naval signaling station he noticed several people on the left side of the road, but, he was later to claim at the inquest into his sister-in-law's death, didn't see any soldiers. As he passed the base he heard someone shout out "halt", but not seeing a sentry, continued on his way up the hill at an estimated 10 miles an hour.

Nineteen-year-old Rifleman George Williamson, of the 4th battalion Royal Irish Rifles, had strict orders not to allow anyone to pass the station after nightfall without being challenged. Those who failed to stop were to be fired upon. His instructions, issued under the Defence of the Realm Act, charged the army with securing public safety with all of Belfast having been made a prohibited area. As the station at Orlock was part of the city's defences, it too came under military law. The sentry had already stopped a couple of cyclists that evening to check their papers, and they were standing with him when the car sped past. He called out "halt", repeating the order three more times before stepping out into the road and raising his rifle to his shoulder. With the car now some 85 yards away and showing no signs of slowing down, he pulled the trigger with the intention of firing above the vehicle. He could offer no satisfactory explanation as to how, instead, his bullet smashed through the back window, striking Irene in the head.

Mr Chapman, on hearing the shot, immediately brought the car to a halt. It was apparent that Irene had been seriously injured, with blood pouring from a head wound.

Both soldiers and civilians ran to the car to help and, at the suggestion of one, the wounded woman was taken to the nearby farm of a Mr Aird. Mr Chapman then drove off to fetch Dr Nesbitt from Donaghadee, and on his return found two other doctors, Mitchell and Craig, on the scene. Also there was Lieutenant William E Howard, the officer in charge of the troops at the Orlock signal station. He had been visiting Mr Aird when he heard the shot and had attempted to aid Irene, who was unconscious.

The bullet, it was later confirmed, had struck her at the base of the skull, passed through her brain and exited through the top of her skull, taking much of the bone with it. Despite the extent of her injuries, Irene, who had been taken to Bangor Cottage Hospital, lingered on before dying early on Wednesday, 26 August. An inquest was held at the hospital later that day with coroner Dr Samuel Wallace presiding. The jury, without retiring, returned a verdict in accordance with the medical evidence, attaching no blame to anyone, and adding that the sentry had fired the shot in the execution of his duty.

Irene, who was originally from Lisburn where her father had run a stationer's shop and photographic business in Market Square, was buried from her home, 34 Wolseley Street, Belfast, on Friday, 28 August, to the City Cemetery. Although meant to be a private family affair, crowds of people gathered along the roadway to pay their respects and the blinds of houses along the route were drawn in sympathy. Some 36 wreaths covered the coffin on its bier, including many from the military authorities. A clutch of senior officers were among the mourners. At the graveside the service was conducted by the Rev William Colquhoyn of Fitzroy Avenue Presbyterian Church. Today she shares a grave with her brother-in-law and sister, Alfred Chapman and Laura Evelyn Chapman.

FIRST SHIP SUNK BY A SUBMARINE:
Staff-Surgeon Thomas Aubrey Smyth

Shortly before 4.00 pm on Saturday, 5 September 1914, the cruiser HMS *Pathfinder* was making its way back from its patrol of the Scottish coast when it became the first ship in history to be struck by a submarine torpedo. Commissioned in 1904, the *Pathfinder* was initially part of the Atlantic Fleet before being attached to the Home Fleet. In March 1914, under the orders of Winston Churchill, she had sailed into Belfast Lough as part of the plan to flood Ulster with troops to suppress the threatened resistance to Home Rule. However, as with the army officers at the Curragh Camp who were refusing to move against the loyalists in the north, the captain of the *Pathfinder* told his admiral that "I have no intention of going against Ulster should the occasion arise". Instead he met socially with the local Ulster Volunteer Force commanders and allowed his officers to meet with unionist leader Sir Edward Carson, much to Churchill's annoyance.

At the beginning of the First World War the *Pathfinder* was part of the 8th Destroyer Flotilla based at Rosyth in the Firth of Forth. Struck by a single torpedo off St Abbs Head, Berwickshire, fired by the German U-21, the initial explosion was followed by a second, much more damaging blast, as a magazine exploded. HMS *Pathfinder* sank within minutes. From a crew of approximately 270, just 18 men survived, including Staff-Surgeon Thomas Aubrey Smyth. Two days later, writing to his mother at her home, Bedeque House, Dromore, County Down, from his bed in the Royal Naval Hospital in Edinburgh, he described his miraculous escape:

> "The explosion blew a great hole in the side of the ship. I was at the time in the ward-room, but ran up on deck immediately, and it was then evident by the way the bow was down in the water that she would sink rapidly. I should say the whole thing occurred in about 10 minutes which time was spent in throwing overboard the few articles which would float (the reason there was not more of these was that in preparation for war all unnecessary woodwork was got rid of to prevent fire.) I was then thrown forward by the slope of the deck, and got jammed beneath a gun (which I expect was the cause of my bruising), and while in this position was carried down some way by the sinking ship, but fortunately after a time I became released and after what seemed interminable ages I came to

the surface, and after swimming a short time I was able to get an oar and some other floating material with the help of which I was just able to keep on the surface. After holding on for a long time – I believe it was an hour and a half – I must have become unconscious for I have no recollection of being picked out of the water. You see we were alone when it happened, so it took a long time for the reserve torpedo boats to come out and it was too quick to get any of our own boats out, besides most of the few we had were splintered to pieces."

Staff-Surgeon Smyth had studied at Edinburgh University before volunteering in 1901 as a civilian surgeon in the Boer War, where he served for nine months before being invalided home with enteric fever. After attending the Royal Naval College he had served on the *Canopus*, *Research*, *Vernon* and *Rainbow* before finally joining the *Pathfinder*.

U-21's commander, Otto Hersing, noted the significance of his "kill" in his captain's log of that day. He wrote: "I believe I have shed the first blood using submarines within this war. Though High Command believes this will be a swift and honourable war, I think otherwise. The recent enemies we have encountered show that it will be a bloody and deadly war." He said the *Pathfinder* had been spotted through the periscope by his second in command around 3.00 pm.

"I rushed to the bridge and told the helmsman to submerge. It was a British light cruiser and it seems it was equipped with cannons and machine-guns and probably depth charges. When we reached 50 metres, we fired one torpedo and destroyed the vessel. We soon surfaced and saw about 100 people. We believe there was a crew of about 600-plus people thus this would seem that the British just had a very heavy loss of life."

Hersing, who survived the war, remained commander of U-21 up until August, 1918. The U-boat itself, however, sank in 1919 while being towed across the North Sea.

The first Royal Navy ship lost during the war was HMS *Amphion*, which only hours before, on 5 August 1914, had, with HMS *Lance*, been credited with firing the first shots at sea to sink a German mine layer, the *Konigin Luise*, which had been dropping its deadly cargo off the Thames Estuary. Unfortunately, at 6.45 am the following day, as the *Amphion* made for its home port of Harwick, it struck one of the German mines, then a second less than 20 minutes later. Among the crew lost was Seaman George Charles McConaghy, from Limavady, County Londonderry, while the survivors included Midshipman Edward Steven Fogarty Fegan, born in England of Irish parents, who in November 1940, as captain of HMS *Jervis Bay*, earned the Victoria Cross for engaging the German pocket battleship *Admiral Scheer* despite being vastly outgunned.

A number of Irish sailors were among the crew members lost when the *Pathfinder* was sunk, including Belfast men William Swann, James Hillis and Charles Gorman. *(From the Belfast Telegraph)*

Captain Francis Martin Leake commanded HMS *Pathfinder*. *(From the Belfast Telegraph)*

WOMEN OUTRAGED AND YOUNG GIRLS VIOLATED:
Rifleman S Curtis

When the German advance was finally brought to a halt no-one was more pleased than Rifleman S Curtis, of the 1st Rifle Brigade. He had kept a diary throughout the early months of the war in which he regularly expressed his opinion that the British should be advancing, not falling back. On 6 September he got his wish as the Allies went on the offensive. During the Battle of the Marne the enemy was pushed back from within 30 miles of Paris to east of the River Aisne, a withdrawal of some 40 miles. Rifleman Curtis wrote on 7–8 September:

"We have been retiring for twelve days, covering 345 miles. This morning we were in sight of Paris, 14 miles away, but glad to say we have left it behind us. We had no sooner marched off this morning than the Germans commenced firing at us. They seemed surprised at us facing them again. They say they thought of going into Paris. They did not seem to like being driven back. In any case we have driven them away from Paris 19.5 miles, and landed them at Noyon. On the 8th September Noyon was deserted, and we found that disgraceful acts had been committed by the Germans. Men have been shot, women outraged and afterwards killed, and young girls violated. It is pitiful to see them. There are women with the clothes torn off them, their bodies ripped up, and their homes looted. We have had a great success."

Curtis, who had formerly worked in the Belfast shipyards before joining the army, had been west of the small French town of Le Cateau on night of 25 August 1914, when General Horace Smith-Dorrien, commanding the British II Corps, had ordered his troops to stand and fight. The combination of sustained and accurate rifle fire by the infantry and the firing at point-blank range over open sights by the artillery held up the German advance and inflicted a heavy toll on the enemy, though at considerable cost to the British troops. On that occasion, Curtis recorded:

"We have had a terrible time since Sunday morning last at Mons. We are back in France again. To-day it has been worse than hell ever could be; to us it has been worse by far than Mons. I wonder how the other division has been doing. We have suffered awfully. From 3 o'clock this morning up till an hour or so ago – 9.30 pm – it has been absolute slaughter. We have been compelled to shoot women and children in order to get at the enemy hiding behind them. We found to our disgust and their disgrace that hundreds of women and kiddies were being marched in front of them, being forced on by the cowards' bayonets. Children were on the backs of their mothers, and many a poor woman who thought she was carrying her baby in safety found at the first opportunity she had of looking that the child had died from bayonet wounds. That was how they faced us – behind human cover. But they paid very dearly for it. Of course, the women had to go first, but we aimed low, so as to catch them in the shins and feet. I know of only two women who were killed outright, but scores were wounded in the legs. As soon as the women went we altered our aim a little higher, and it told its own story. They were firing at us, too, and caused awful damage. There are terrible sights at St Quentin. Many Royal Irish Rifles from the Shankill Road are here. There will be many widows and orphans as a result of this day's fighting, yet we are on the winning side up till now. Hope they will let us have a few hours' rest tonight."

Rifleman Curtis continued:

"During last night not much happened, except the outpost firing a shot now and again. We left St Quentin at 4.30 on the morning of 27th August, and have had a very hard march of 29½ miles. Don't quite understand why we have come this way. We are on the road to Paris; therefore we are retiring instead of advancing. Surely we are not running away. We have not had any casualties today. Nothing of importance happened, but dozens of refugees are in a pitiful plight on the road to Paris – old men and women with children strapped on their backs and a few knick-knacks in a shawl. We marched off from Charlesville at 4.30 on the morning of the 28th August. Still going on the Paris road. Halted at 6.30 and took up a position against the German cavalry, killing 28 horses and 38 men, and capturing 166 horses and 174 men. Kept on march till 9.20 pm, 26½ miles since morning's fight."

The First Battle of the Marne ended on 10 September with heavy casualties suffered by all sides. The French incurred 250,000 losses, the Germans a similar number, and the British around 12,750.

RALLYING TO THE GREEN FLAG:
The Irish Guards at the Marne

Michael MacDonagh was an Irish writer and parliamentary journalist with *The Times*, London. He wrote a number of political books including works on the lives of Daniel O'Connell and William O'Brien, and works on the Home Rule Movement and Catholic Emancipation. During the war he produced two books, including, in 1916, *The Irish at the Front* quoted below. His writing is typical of his day, with a strong patriotic flavour. He relates how, at the Battle of the Marne, fought from 5–12 September 1914, a "green flag" of Ireland had rallied the Irish Guards and helped the Allies push the Germans back from the doors of Paris:

"Between the different British regiments there was an emulation to outshine each other. It was a splendid vanity, for everything done to realise it tended to the confusion of the common enemy. This phase of the war was therefore crowded with incidents showing the bravery of the soldiers of all the nationalities within the United Kingdom. From the Irish point of view the most remarkably dramatic was the rallying of the Irish Guards round the green flag.

'It is only a square piece of cloth, but its colour is green, and on it is the Harp of Ireland and inscribed in a wreath are the words: "Eire go bragh," once bright and clear, but now faded and obliterated almost beyond recognition. That is the flag the Irish Guards obtained when they received information that they were for the Front, and from the moment they set foot on foreign soil that treasured emblem of Irish nationality has been displayed at the head of the battalion, the pride and admiration of the regiment.'

So writes Corporal Michael O'Mara of the Irish Guards. The first occasion upon which the flag was produced was when the Marne was crossed, and on September 9th the Irish Guards had to advance for miles across rather open country, swept by shot and shell, to dislodge the Germans from a commanding position south of the Aisne.

The Irish as soldiers have two qualities which, though widely different in nature, are really each the concomitant of the other. The first is imperturbability, springing from indifference to danger, of which the Retreat from Mons supplied some choice examples, as I have recorded.

This attribute is displayed while they are waiting for the shock of an advancing attack, or for the command to launch themselves upon a foe shooting at them from behind entrenchments. The clash comes or the order to charge is given; and then it is that, showing the other quality, they give vent to the fire and force of their passionate temperament, which, as often as not, impels them to attempt strokes more daring and rash than the occasion quite demands. In the course of the advance between the Marne and the Aisne on September 9th the changeful fortunes of the conflict seemed to make the final issue doubtful. The line of the advance of the Irish Guards was a hill upon which the Germans were strongly posted with several machine-guns, each pouring forth a terrible stream of 600 bullets a minute. Men were dropping on all sides.

Then it was that the towering form of an Irish Guardsman was seen running well on in front of the first line flourishing the green flag, which he had tied round the barrel of his rifle, and shouting "Ireland for Ever." The men roared at the sight. On they swept, with redoubled speed, after the darling flag, in one of their furious, overmastering Irish charges, made all the more terrible by their vengeful yells. A thunderstorm was raging at the time. The gleam on their bayonets may have been the flash of the lightning, but it was more suggestive of a glint of the flame of love of country that glowed in their eyes. 'It was all over in ten minutes,' writes Private HP Mulloney to his sweetheart in Ireland. 'They absolutely stood dumbfounded, with white faces and knees trembling. I shouldn't like to stand in front of that charge myself. Our men were drenched to the skin, but we didn't care; it only made us twice as wild. Such dare-devil pluck I was glad to see. "Back for those guns," roared an officer, "or I'll have every one of you slaughtered." The men didn't want telling twice. We proceeded to line up the prisoners and collect the spoils, which amounted to about 150 prisoners, six Maxim guns, and 38,000 rounds of ammunition.'

Even in these rude passages we find expressed the rapture of the Irish Guardsmen with the tumult and the passion of the fight. The hill was surmounted and the machine-guns taken. Afterwards the advance was continued for five miles, over a country covered with dead Germans and horses, and blazing homesteads. The Irish rested for a time in a field, and then pushed on again until they reached the banks of the Marne. They captured 600 Germans, including many officers and eight machine-guns. But if the advance was swift, sure, and triumphant a bitter price had to be paid for it, as is the way of war, for many a fine and stalwart Irish youth found his grave between the rivers. The man who produced the green flag was Corporal JJ Cunningham from Dublin. He bought it in London before the Irish Guards left for the Front. It became a prized possession of the regiment."

The Irish Guards, inspired by the waving of their 'Green Flag,' captured 150 prisoners and dismantled and took away half-a-dozen German Maxim guns.
(From the Times History of the War 1914, published 1915)

WITNESS TO A TRIPLE SINKING:
Stoker William Neill

If the sinking of HMS *Pathfinder* early in the war had been an indication that the submarine, considered by many to be of limited use in war, could be an effective weapon, the undeniable proof came on 22 September 1914, with the destruction of three British ships in one attack. The U-boat involved, U-9, had left its base in Heligoland the month before as part of the first war patrol of its kind. In the early hours of that day it came across a three ship North Sea patrol of old style armoured cruisers made up of HMS *Aboukir*, HMS *Hogue* and HMS *Cressy*. They were slow moving but capable of dealing with the frequently adverse weather conditions, though thought to be so vulnerable that they had been nicknamed the "live bait squadron".

At 6.25 am the submarine fired its first torpedo, striking the *Aboukir* on its port side. The order to abandon ship followed shortly afterwards and the two accompanying vessels, believing a mine had done the damage, closed in to rescue survivors. Half an hour after the first explosion, the *Aboukir* rolled over and sank. At about the same time U-9 fired two torpedoes at the *Hogue* from only 300 yards, with it sinking in just 10 minutes though not before getting a few shots off at the U-boat when it briefly came to the surface. The *Cressy*, which had stopped engines to pull survivors out of the water, immediately got underway again as its gunners attempted to strike the periscope of the approaching U-9. Two more torpedoes were fired, one hitting the *Cressy* on her starboard side. Coming in again for the kill, the submarine fired its last torpedo and 15 minutes later the *Cressy* also disappeared under the waves. Almost 1,500 men died though another 837 were rescued by other ships, both merchant and Royal Navy, which quickly arrived on the scene.

Among the survivors was 23-year-old William Neill, a stoker on HMS *Cressy*. From the Limestone Road, Belfast, his elder brother Charles, also a stoker, was among the victims of the sinking. William had served five years in the Royal Navy, with stints on the battleships HMS *Inflexible* and HMS *Glory* and the destroyer HMS *Grasshopper*. The Neill brothers had been undergoing their annual training as reserve men at Chatham when war was declared and were immediately made permanent members of the crew. He recalled:

"We were in our hammocks when we were informed that the *Aboukir* was sinking. At first I thought this was merely a joke, or a ruse to get us up early. Having dressed and stowed my hammock, I went to the upper deck, and saw right enough that the *Aboukir* was sinking. We were steaming towards her to render assistance, and throwing over mess room tables and stools to support those of her crew who got into the water, when the *Hogue* was also torpedoed, and we saw that she was sinking too. Before the latter disappeared, the *Cressy* was struck forward, and would no doubt have kept afloat had she not afterwards been torpedoed amidships. We kept our guns going until the dynamos stopped after the second explosion, and had the satisfaction of disposing of one submarine at least – and probably two – a performance which our fellows greeted with a rousing cheer."

In fact, the *Cressy's* gunfire was totally ineffective and the U-boat was undamaged. Bertram WL Nicholson, commander of HMS *Cressy*, reported:

"Almost directly after the *Hogue* was hit we observed a periscope on our port bow about 300 yards off. Fire was immediately opened and the engines were put full speed ahead with the intention of running her down. Our gunner, Mr Dougherty, positively asserts that he hit the periscope and that the submarine sank. An officer who was standing alongside the gunner thinks that the shell struck only floating timber, of which there was much about, but it was evidently the impression of the men on deck, who cheered and clapped heartily, that the submarine had been hit."

Stoker Neill added: "Large numbers of the crews followed the last movements of the ships by crawling right over the side and on to the bottom before they disappeared; and it was the suction that accounted for a great many of the men going."

Another survivor was Able Seaman James Anderson, a Royal Navy Reservist from Fairhill, Galway, who spent three hours in the water clutching a plank. He was finally picked up by a Dutch trawler and transferred to a British cruiser, which landed him in Harwich.

Commander Otto Weddigen, in charge of U-9, became a national hero in Germany and was presented with the Iron Cross First Class by the Kaiser himself. He was killed on 18 March 1915, when his new command, U-29, was rammed by HMS *Dreadnought*.

BATTLE IN THE STREETS OF GALWAY:
Split within nationalism

The declaration of war had done much to take the heat out of the Home Rule crisis but produced a wider split within nationalism. The Irish Volunteers divided over calls to join the British military, with the National Volunteers emerging as a result. It was Sinn Féin, however, viewed by many as not merely anti-British but actively pro-German, that aroused the most resentment early in the war.

In October 1914, the "War Correspondent" of the *Galway Express* got his first taste of combat on home soil:

"It has been my fortune to witness the first battle fought in that historic city since through Kaiser Bill's dictum, the fertile plains of fair Belgium commenced to be soaked with the blood of murdered heroes; and though Galway's first engagement lacks the halo which surrounds the Allies' conflict 'on far foreign fields,' the motives, which roused the fiery Irish blood of the city, prompted that same desire which actuates our brethren in the greater war. To-night the conventional calm which settles on the city with the advent of night was rudely broken by the clash of arms – real instruments of destruction. For the past few days posters were displayed on the hoardings announcing a meeting of the Irish Volunteers who were sympathetic towards the old Provisional Committee's manifesto – in effect, inviting those who applauded the actions of the Huns who murdered innocent women and children, burned and desecrate churches, etc, to come and join. The meeting was announced for 8 o'clock to-night, at the hall in Williamsgate St, but before the time had arrived an increasingly large crowd swelled the street outside, and as the few – we will come to their numbers later on – entered the hall they were heartily groaned.

At this initial stage of the proceedings it was clearly evident that Galway's 13,000 souls were not to be found on the wrong side of the fence, and certainly the ardour of the pro-Germans, alias Sinn Féiners, must have been effectually dampened by the preliminary hostile display. The meeting proceeded inside, the reporters being refused admittance. The passage to the hall was 'guarded' by a young fellow with a rifle, to which a bayonet was attached. But that individual very shortly perceived the wisdom of the old maxim that discretion is the better part of valour, for he quickly disappeared into the body of the hall where the solemn conclave sat. The huge concourse outside was brimful of good humour, and many and varied were the jocose remarks made about, and the dubious compliments paid to, the Sinn Féiners."

The mob commenced to throw stones and bottles at the building until it was realised those inside were about to emerge:

"They marched out of the hall two deep, the first four couples being armed with rifles and fixed bayonets, while the remainder of the group bore wooden guns… That the affair would develop into an active engagement was not anticipated by anyone. Armed in all the panoply which artificial courage, rifles, and wooded guns could bestow, the eighteen stalwarts marched down Shop Street. The crowd, not one of whom had as much as a stick, followed closely after. As the "four corners" were approached, the vanguard of the crowd came up on the rear of the Sinn Féin army. The result was instantaneous. A very brief scuffle, and a young Volunteer was found to be in possession of one of the wooden rifles, which he took from a Castlegar brave who immediately took to his heels. Complete disorder ensued in the rear guard of the enemy as the middle of Shop Street was approached and some of the crowd again rushed the enemy. Short scuffle No 2 and some more wooden guns changed hands, while the ranks of the enemy became broken, and about half-a-dozen ran out in front of the men with the fixed bayonets.

Their arrant cowardice evoked jeers and cheers from the now thoroughly excited crowd, and the bayonet men, apparently with an effort to retrieve their position and instil some spark of courage into their followers who chose to demonstrate the effectuality of a pair of legs in a hasty retreat, turned around opposite Mr O'Gorman's shop. For a brief space the sparkle of the steel swayed some of the crowd, but not for long. Another rush was made, and those who still held wooden rifles, and who, apparently, were fighting a rear-guard action, were disarmed while you would be saying 'Jack Robinson'. Matters began to look ugly. The Volunteers who had got possession of the wooden instruments proceeded to utilise them.

Then one incident occurred which aroused the wrath of the crowd.

In the van was a brave Galway soldier, who has returned wounded from the Battle of Mons – Pte Joe McGowan of the RE's. He had no weapon of any description, but he received a stroke from the butt of a Sinn Féin rifle on the head, which temporarily disconcerted him. He who, however, had faced the Germans when the latter were 20 to 1, was not going to be terrorised by the sight of a Tweedledum with the enemy's rifle, and amid enthusiastic cheering a short and sharp engagement ensued outside O'Gorman's. Some bottles were thrown, but they spent themselves harmlessly on the roadway. The Volunteers who had become possessed of the wooden guns made good use of them on the craniums, etc, of the enemy. Some of the latter then took advantage of that important medium known as Shanks' Mare, and were next seen running for all they were worth round by St Nicholas' Church."

MAKING A STAND AT YPRES:
Sergeant Joseph Lowry

Following their reverse at the Marne, and with winter approaching, the Germans began digging in as a stalemate was reached. At the same time both armies were still attempting to outflank the other to the north. This so-called Race to the Sea ended on the coast, with lines of trenches now stretching from the border with Switzerland to the North Sea. Following the fall of Antwerp the BEF had withdrawn to the west, forming a 35-mile line in front of Ypres with the remnants of the Belgium army to the north and the French to the south. Strategically located on the route to the Channel ports, the city offered the Germans their best prospect of a final breakthrough. On 20 October they launched what was to become known as the First Battle of Ypres only to be halted when the sea sluices were opened, creating a two-mile wide waterway between Dixmude and Nieuport. The Germans renewed their attack on 31 October, this time against the British forces manning the salient in front of Ypres. The line held, though it took every available man to plug a gap created on 11 November during an assault by two crack German units. Eleven days later, as the winter really began to bite, the fighting came to a close.

County Armagh man Sergeant Joseph Lowry, from Glenanne, Loughgilly, had been through most of the fighting to date. The 30-year-old had enlisted in the Gordon Highlanders in 1903, serving in India for seven years before returning home in January 1911. In the months up to his mobilisation he had been involved in training the Loughgilly company of the Ulster Volunteer Force. Writing home from his hospital bed in Marseilles, he said:

"You can have absolutely no idea of the conditions under which we have lived these last few months. I was not in one battle but a succession of battles, day in and day out, from the 12th of October up to the 24th November, when I had to give in with my feet, but, thank God, my heart was good and is yet. We started fighting outside Ypres (3 miles) on the 5th November, but before then we were on the same battle front in France, so I have fought in both countries. You know the line extends for a great distance, and a very thin line it was as far as we were concerned, but although they tried hard with their very pick they only succeeded once in getting through by sheer force of numbers. Not till every man was killed in that immediate neighbourhood did they break through, and then commenced a slaughter which I hope I will never witness again. It was hand to hand, and the strongest with rifle and bayonet won. They took some of ours prisoners, and we did the same. (This was Saturday night, 24th October.) Next morning there were over a thousand of their dead in front of our trenches and over 200 were picked up on a road just behind the trenches."

Sergeant Lowry described how, under the command of Quartermaster Sergeant Smith, he had been part of an advance party that ambushed a German column, claiming they killed some 200 with only a handful escaping:

"We were lined up on the roadside and this party came marching down the road just the same as our Volunteers used to do, laughing and chatting, intending to round up some more prisoners, but they did not dream of where we were, and we waited until they were opposite us (about three yards distant) and then – you may talk about hell being loose. It was terrible. Only a few escaped. The dead were actually falling on us. This stopped their little game, and they discreetly withdrew, and were such remnants as were left – went back to our trenches."

Lowry and Smith, though the latter had been wounded, volunteered to check if the Germans were still holding a line of trenches earlier vacated by the Scots.

"Smith immediately called on me, and the two of us went back and located the trenches which were empty save for three Germans. Smith, wounded though he was, accounted for one, and I for the other two. I can't describe the sensation of putting a bayonet through another man, but it certainly means if you don't the other fellow will, and I can't say that it has ever troubled me very much. I seem to have had a charmed life up to date, for all my chums and those who came out with me have either been wounded, captured, or killed, and I devoutly thank God for His blessings to me and my wife and children."

Another member of the 2nd Gordon Highlanders, Drummer William Kenny, was awarded the Victoria Cross. Born to a military family from Drogheda, County Louth, the 34-year-old had already come under the notice of his superiors for earlier deeds when at Kruiseik, on the Menin Road, he had repeatedly risked his life to save others. His citation read:

"For conspicuous bravery on 23rd October, 1914, near Ypres, in rescuing wounded men on five occasions under very heavy fire in the most fearless manner, and for twice previously saving machine-guns by carrying them out of action. On numerous occasions Drummer Kenny conveyed urgent messages under very dangerous circumstances over fire-swept ground."

Damage at Armentieres, south of Ypres, after German assaults in October and November 1914. The Gordon Highlanders fought with the BEF, holding the line at Ypres during the 'Race to the Sea'.
(From A Popular History of the Great War, published 1933)

FIRST MP TO DIE:
Captain Arthur Edward Bruce O'Neill

Captain Arthur Edward Bruce O'Neill holds the unfortunate distinction of being the first of twenty-four Members of Parliament to die during the First World War. The 38-year-old, who served in the 2nd Life Guards, a cavalry regiment, was killed on 6 November 1914.

Captain O'Neill, of Shane's Castle, Antrim, had commanded the North Antrim Regiment of the Ulster Volunteer Force before returning to the colours on the outbreak of war. The 2nd Life Guards was in reserve on 6 November 1914, but received urgent orders that afternoon to support the French after they had been driven out of their trenches. Dismounting under fire, with the 1st Life Guards on their right, the battalion took up position on a ridge close to the village of Zillbeke. According to one of the surviving officers, the battalion advanced under heavy rifle fire on the village then charged.

"We cleared the village at the point of the bayonet, killing about 30 Germans and capturing 20. I was the only officer left after this attack, as our commanding officer, Major Dawnay, a most gallant man, was killed sitting next me in the trench by a shrapnel shell. We also lost Captain O'Neill, killed, and Mr Johnson and Mr Hobson, wounded, during this attack."

The officer, who was writing to the sister of Second Lieutenant W Petersen, the third officer of the 2nd Life Guards killed that day, went on:

"Your dear brother died with two other officers of the regiment, Major Dawnay, commanding, and Captain Arthur O'Neill, in driving the Germans back; they accomplished the work, and in doing so actually saved most likely a great defeat of our arms; the fact is recognised by the General."

Due to Captain O'Neill's death, his son, Shane, succeeded to barony in 1928 on the death of his grandfather. A Lieutenant Colonel with the North Irish Horse, he too was killed on 24 October 1944, during the Italian campaign, at the age of 37 – just a year younger than his father when he died. Another son, Terence O'Neill, went on to become Prime Minister of Northern Ireland.

Captain O'Neill's body was never recovered and he is commemorated on the Menin Gate Memorial in Ypres. His Commonwealth War Graves Commission entry records:

"Member of Parliament for Mid-Antrim and the first MP to be killed during the Great War. Son of 2nd Baron O'Neill and Lady O'Neill, of Shanes Castle, Antrim, Ireland; husband of Lady Annabel O'Neill (now Lady Annabel Dodds). His son Lieutenant Colonel Shane Edward Robert O'Neill fell in the 1939–1945 War."

The ferocity of the fighting around Ypres can be gauged from the comments of Trooper Albert Courtney, who was serving with the 1st Life Guards. The Belfast man was wounded in the battle on 29 October and, but for the courage shown by two comrades, probably wouldn't have lived to tell the tale. The former Inniskilling Dragoons trooper had only left the army earlier that year on his return from India and had been working as a nurse in the Royal Victoria Hospital when he was called up again as a reservist. He recalled:

"We got an order to retire in single file, and when I got to the vicinity of a farm house one shell burst behind me and another in front, with the result that I was struck with shrapnel both in the left lung and in the back. I lay prostrate and could hardly breathe. Indeed, I thought I was done for completely, when (George) Ford and another brave fellow came to my assistance. Knowing the grave danger they were running, I told them to go on, but not withstanding the terrible risk they were running, for the Maxim bullets were coming fast, they picked me up and carried me – under fire all the time – to a doctor a good half-mile away. The medico, who was attending to patients behind a haystack, dressed my wounds, and afterwards, with the assistance of a number of others, carried me two miles to a horse ambulance, in which I was taken a further three miles to a motor ambulance. In the latter I was brought into the town of Ypres, and after further treatment there, was taken three hours later to Boulogne."

After ten days in an Australian voluntary hospital he was evacuated to England and later allowed to return home on sick leave.

GERMANY'S IRISH BRIGADE:
Sir Roger Casement

Former British diplomat turned Irish nationalist Sir Roger Casement had been in the United States when war was declared. With encouragement from Irish-American groups he travelled to Berlin on the last day of October 1914, where he persuaded the German Secretary for Foreign Affairs to draw up a paper guaranteeing home rule for Ireland in the event of an Axis victory and give permission to recruit an Irish Brigade from prisoners of war. From December 1914 and into the early months of 1915 some 2,200 Irish, predominantly Roman Catholic, POWs were moved to Limburg Camp, near Cologne. On 6 December Casement visited the camp, staying for a number of days and receiving a largely cool reception.

Two soldiers of the Royal Army Medical Corps, from different sides of Belfast and the political divide, found themselves being courted. Private Andrew McClay, from Bell's Row, Whitehouse, had been captured on 27 August 1914, as he attended to German wounded. Put on a cattle waggon, he was sent on a rail journey of hundreds of miles to Sennelager Camp, close to Paderborn, Germany. Repatriated the following year as part of an exchange of prisoners, he rejoiced in being "home in time for the Twelfth," adding:

> "I should also mention here that at an early stage of our internment we were paraded, and all of Irish nationality were ordered to fall out. Those who did so were subsequently paraded by themselves, and I learned all who were Catholics were sent to a separate camp, where they were told an Irish Brigade was being formed in Berlin, and they were invited to join it."

Returned home at around the same time was Corporal John Robinson, from Ross Street in the Falls Road area of Belfast, who had 10 years service under his belt when he was wounded and taken prisoner at Le Cateau. The rumours had abounded for days before the order went round for all Irish Catholics to parade, he recalled. "Seven hundred men filled with curiosity responded, but not all were Irishmen, nor were all Catholics – there were some Shankill Road men, for such were the hardships that men would have done anything to escape from the camp, even for a short period." The camp commandant addressed them, his first words being: "Well, boys, remember

Bachelor's Walk," the scene of the shooting in Dublin days before the outbreak of war during which members of the Scottish Borders opened fire on Irish Volunteers bringing smuggled weapons into the city. He then asked: "Don't you want Home Rule?" with the reply coming "We do, but we can get it on our own". Those on the parade were given anti-English propaganda and allocated separate accommodation, with sentries with revolvers and bayonets overcoming their initial reluctance to being parted from their comrades. Three days before Christmas the "Irelanders" were transferred to Limburg Camp, where a green flag with the shamrock and harp, minus the Crown, was flying.

On 5 January 1915, Casement returned and made a recruitment speech to the men, being shouted down and jostled. There were calls of "how much are the Germans paying you?" and at one stage Casement, who repeatedly had to call out for the men to stand back, had to use his walking stick to force them away. On 15 May 1915, Casement tried again, telling the men:

"You have been told, I daresay, that I am trying to form an Irish Brigade to fight for Germany; that I am a German agent; and that an attempt is being made to suborn you, or tempt you to do something dishonest and insincere for the sake of the German government and not for the welfare of Ireland. Well, you may believe me, or disbelieve me, and nothing I could say would convince you as to my own motives, but I can convince you, and I owe to yourselves as well as to myself to convince you that the effort to form an Irish Brigade is based on Irish interests only, and is a sincere and honest one, so far as my actions with the German government is concerned and so far as their action in the matter goes. An Irish Brigade, if it be formed today, will rest on a clear and definite agreement wherein the German government is pledged to aid the cause of Irish independence by force of arms, and above all, to aid Irish men to themselves fight for their own freedom."

The handful of men who did join the Irish Brigade initially moved around the camp attempting to encourage others to make the move, while the Catholic priests urged them to transfer their allegiance. Corporal Robinson, who was offered another stripe to join, was told by one of them that he was a "fool" for not taking the opportunity. In total, only 56 men out of some 2,200 Irishmen at Limburg joined Casement's brigade, which was based at

Zossen Camp from July 1916. On 21 April 1916, Casement – accompanied by two volunteers from the Irish Brigade – arrived off Tralee Bay in Kerry in a German submarine. He was arrested less than 12 hours after coming ashore by the Royal Irish Constabulary. Tried and convicted of treason, Casement was executed in August 1916.

Private Andrew McClay, from Bell's Row, Whitehouse, had been captured as he attended to German wounded.
(From the Belfast Telegraph)

Corporal John Robinson, from Ross Street in the Falls Road area of Belfast, was an old soldier of ten years standing.
(From the Belfast Telegraph)

REAPING REVENGE AT THE FALKLANDS:
First-Class Stoker William Rea

At the Battle of Coronel, fought off the coast of Chile on 1 November 1914, the Royal Navy suffered a bloodied nose when a German squadron, including the armoured cruisers *Scharnhorst* and *Gneisenau*, sank the cruisers HMS *Good Hope* and HMS *Monmouth* with the loss of more than 1,600 men. Ten days later, the battlecruisers HMS *Invincible* and HMS *Inflexible* slipped out of Devonport en route to the Falkland Islands and intent on reaping revenge. They were joined by the armoured cruisers HMS *Carnarvon*, HMS *Kent* and HMS *Cornwall*, and the light cruisers HMS *Bristol*, HMS *Glasgow* and the HMS *Otranto*. The convoy had arrived at the Falklands on 7 December mooring up at Port Stanley to take on coal.

Within hours the *Gneisenau*, accompanied by the *Nurnberg*, approached the islands with the intention of attacking the wireless station, but turned to flee on spotting the battlecruisers. The German ships met up with the rest of their squadron and headed south-easterly with the *Scharnhorst* in the centre and the *Dresden* and *Leipzig* astern. The faster British ships gave chase and shortly before 1.30 pm were close enough to open fire. In the subsequent battle the *Invincible* engaged the *Scharnhorst* and *Inflexible* attacked the *Gneisenau*, while the smaller cruisers broke off to fight their own battle. Holed below the waterline and suffering major damage to its upper structure, *Scharnhorst* sank shortly after 4.00 pm with all 860 men, including Admiral Graf Maximilian von Spee, going down with their ship. The *Gneisenau*, *Leipzig*, and *Nurnberg* all suffered the same fate while the *Dresden*, which managed to escape initially, was hunted down and destroyed. All told, some 2,200 German sailors died in the action.

On board HMS *Invincible* was First-Class Stoker William Rea, from Cairns' Buildings, Ballysillan, Belfast. On 10 December, having returned to Port Stanley, he sat down and wrote an account of the battle to send to his wife. The letter was the first communication she had received from him since the outbreak of war. He wrote:

"I can let you know where we are as there is no secret about it now. We have had a stroke of good luck, and have done what it might have taken us months to do – found the German fleet. We arrived in Port Stanley on Monday, and on Tuesday morning, as we had started to coal the ship before going to sea again, we got word from one of our light cruisers that the German fleet was approaching the islands. We had no steam, but in an hour's time were on our way at full speed, and we had scarcely got outside when we sighted the enemy's fire ships. They were apparently trying to work the same move as they did with the *Good Hope* and *Monmouth*.

A chase started, and we gained on them steadily until noon, when we were almost within range. We got our dinner, and the bugle sounded 'Action-Stations,' and in a few minutes we were in it. Then followed a lively afternoon. The shells fell hot and fast, and every now and again would crash into us, tearing through the sides and decks as if they were tin, and setting her on fire almost every time. The fire was hard to keep under, and the action lasted all the afternoon until six o'clock, when the last of the two big cruisers, *Scharnhorst* and *Gneisenau*, went under.

We stood by to save as many lives as possible, but had only one boat left, and it was difficult to do much. Still we managed to save a few, but, as there were over 1,000 on board, it was only a few. A good many of them died during the night, as the bitterly cold water was more than anybody could stand long. It was a pitiful sight, but it was us or them, and we got the better this time. To look round the ship after the action you would think it an impossibility that we had no one killed or seriously injured. It was my birthday, but I forgot all about it until afterwards. It was this job that spoiled your holiday in Portsmouth, but the *Good Hope* and *Monmouth* are avenged."

First-Class Stoker Rea, who was aged 37, was on board HMS *Invincible* during the Battle of Jutland, 31 May 1916, and died along with more than 1,000 shipmates when his ship was sunk. He is commemorated on the Portsmouth Naval Memorial.

PUSHING THE GERMANS OUT OF AFRICA:
Private George Haskis

Walfisch Bay, once part of the Cape Colony under British rule and ceded to South Africa from 1903, was surrounded by German colonies in Africa and was quickly overrun at the beginning of the war. It offered a sheltered port but little else in the way of infrastructure apart from an assortment of shanty huts and a hinterland of sand dunes. Nonetheless, it was felt to be sufficiently important enough to warrant sending a landing force that included the South African Irish Brigade.

On Christmas Day, 1914, three days after setting sail from Capetown on a ship appropriately named *Galway Castle*, the brigade arrived in Walfisch Bay. On board was Private George Haskis, originally from Belfast but then serving with General Botha's Irish volunteers. Writing to his mother in Meadowbank Street in the city, having at last found time to let her know he was "still alive and well," he gave an account of his adventures:

> "There were about six ships altogether came round at the one time, and we were accompanied by two cruisers, in case any of the enemy's ships should be knocking about. However we arrived here safe, and without any opposition whatever. The buildings here consist of a few old dirty tin shanties, and one store which is closed up, the owner apparently having left when the Germans came here. Our regiment being the first to land, we promptly hoisted the Irish flag (green, with the Union Jack in top corner), with a round of cheering."

The flag had been a gift of the Botha family to the Irish Brigade and accompanied it throughout the war. Christmas dinner for the new arrivals consisted of coffee and biscuits, much to Haskis' disdain, with another three days before they got to sample the traditional plum pudding, when "one about the size of a cup was divided between three men, although each man was supposed to receive one each".

With the arrival of further regiments a proper camp was established, or as Haskis put it, "the place is looking a little more civilised". He went on:

> "Most of the natives here are Hottentots. They are a funny looking lot altogether. They will give one a lot for a pipe full of tobacco, and even the

young girls smoke. We have sent them all inland to make room for our own boys whom we have brought with us."

The 'Hottentots,' today considered to be a disparaging term, refers to the Khoikhoi, who have their origins in the Botswana area of Africa though began migrating to the southern regions from at least the 5th century.

The Germans, who had occupied the bay for a time, had withdrawn shortly before taking the best of the local natives with them, leaving behind only the old men, women and children, which were in turn expelled by the South Africans to allow more room for their own men. Private Haskis went on:

"We are camped quite close to the beach, and are able to get down for a wash. There was great scarcity of fresh water when we first arrived, and one had to have a permit before one could procure any, but conditions are improving every day, and we are able to get a better supply now. We have had a busy time since our arrival; the first day (Xmas) we had to start and dig trenches in case of an attack from the enemy. They are not very far from here so we always have to be on the alert. We all sleep out in the open. I can assure you, mother, I much prefer it to sleeping in tents as it is not cold at night. We feel the cold mostly early in the morning, especially at 4.30 am when we occupy the trenches. There is nothing but sand as far as the eye can see, and regular mountains of it, and not a blade of grass to be seen anywhere. We are right in the desert. It is an awful experience to be caught in a sandstorm. A lot of our chaps including myself were out on picket duty about a mile outside the camp, right on top of the sandhills, and we experienced a slight storm, and a Johannesburg dust storm is not a patch on it."

In the event, there was to be little fighting in southern Africa with the Germans deprived of their colonies with comparative ease. Following the war South Africa continued to rule the area until it transferred control to the Cape Province in 1977. It was ceded to Namibia in 1994.

INTRODUCTION
Lord French, who led the British
Expeditionary Force to France,
is commemorated in St George's
Church, Ypres. *(Author)*

1914: OFF TO WAR
The murder of Archduke Franz Ferdinand, heir to the Austrian Imperial throne, while on a visit to Sarajevo was the spark that ignited the Great War.
(A Popular History of the Great War, published 1933)

1914: OFF TO WAR
The call to arms, with the return to the colours of all former non-commissioned officers being urgently required to help swell the ranks at the front and to train the New Armies being formed. *(News Letter)*

1914: OFF TO WAR
Germans who had been living in the north of Ireland were rounded up before being
marched through Belfast to be taken by train to Dublin and internment.
(Belfast Telegraph)

1914: OFF TO WAR
Men of the North Irish Horse (NIH), seen here riding through Belfast in 1914, were
part of the British Expeditionary Force sent to France. Along with its sister regiment,
the South Irish Horse, the NIH was the first Territorial unit deployed.
(Belfast Telegraph)

FLEEING THE BRUTAL HUN
The remains of Jerome Lennie Walker today lie in Authuille Military Cemetery, some three miles north of Albert in the Somme department of France. The 27-year-old had been one of the last of the small Irish community of Courtrai, Belgium, to flee the advancing Germans in 1914. *(Author)*

ARRESTED AS A GERMAN SPY
The Rev Francis Maginn, deaf from the age of five and a Church of Ireland missionary, would have made for a very unlikely German spy. *(Courtesy of Action On Hearing Loss)*

ARRIVAL OF THE FIRST AIRMAN
A soldier stands guard over one of the first improvised airstrips set up by the Royal Flying Corps in France in 1914.
(The Times History of the War 1914, published 1915)

THE FIRST IRISH VICTORIA CROSS WINNER
Lieutenant Maurice James Dease, from County Westmeath, was the first man in the Great War to exhibit the outstanding self-sacrifice and courage necessary to win the Victoria Cross.
(Courtesy of the Somme Museum)

WITNESS TO A GERMAN ATROCITY
The battle at Le Cateau was a desperate affair as the British, retreating from
Mons, attempted to halt the advance of overwhelming enemy numbers,
resulting in the loss of many men killed, wounded and taken prisoner.
(*The Times History of the War 1914, published 1915*)

WOMEN OUTRAGED AND YOUNG GIRLS VIOLATED
Rifleman S Curtis was scathing of the German soldiers' behaviour, accusing them of,
among other crimes, forcing women and children to march in front of them as human
shields. (*The Times History of the War 1914, published 1915*)

RALLYING TO THE GREEN FLAG
A French postcard celebrating the Battle of Marne, during which the tide of war turned for the first time. *(Author's collection)*

RALLYING TO THE GREEN FLAG
The Germans blew up bridges as they retreated, making it more difficult for the British and French to push home their success at the Marne.
(A Popular History of the Great War, published 1933)

WITNESS TO A TRIPLE SINKING
A sketch, by US Navy artist Henry Reuterdahl, showing the loss of the HMS *Hogue*.
The *Cressy* can be seen in the background.
(Collier's Photographic History of the European war, 1916)

WITNESS TO A TRIPLE SINKING
HMS *Cressy*, in coming to the assistance of the stricken *Aboukir*, left itself open to
attack. Despite its claims to have engaged the U-boat, its gunfire was ineffective.
(A Popular History of the Great War, published 1933)

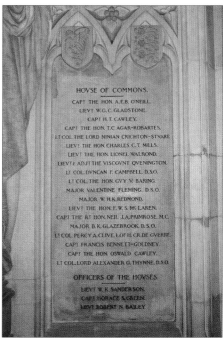

FIRST MP TO DIE

A memorial at the Palace of Westminster in London commemorates the Members of Parliament and their sons lost during the Great War, with Captain O'Neill heading the list. *(Courtesy of Brian Curragh)*

REAPING REVENGE AT THE FALKLANDS

This photograph, taken by an officer onboard one of the ships of the British fleet, shows boats from the *Inflexible* and *Invincible* picking up survivors from the *Gneisenau*. *(The Times History of the War 1914, published 1915)*

PART OF ADMIRAL STURDEE'S FLEET.
Top : H.M.S. "Invincible"; centre left: H.M.S. "Canopus"; centre right : H.M.S. "Glasgow";
bottom : H.M.S. "Inflexible."

REAPING REVENGE AT THE FALKLANDS
Some of the British ships involved in the battle, HMS *Invincible*, HMS *Canopus*,
HMS *Glasgow* and HMS *Inflexible*.
(*The Times History of the War 1914, published 1915*)

ADMIRAL GRAF VON SPEE AND HIS FLEET.
Top, "Scharnhorst"; centre left, "Leipzig"; centre right, "Nürnberg"; bottom, "Gneisenau."

REAPING REVENGE AT THE FALKLANDS
The main German force included the *Scharnhorst*, *Leipzig*, *Nurnberg* and *Gneisenau*.
(The Times History of the War 1914, published 1915)

PUSHING THE GERMANS OUT OF AFRICA
The *Galway Castle* lands the first South African troops, including Belfast man Private George Haskis, at Walfisch Bay on Christmas Day, 1914.
(*From* With Botha in the Field, *published 1915*)

THE CHRISTMAS TRUCE OF 1914
Lisburn man Willie Walsh, of the 1st Royal Irish Rifles, was instrumental on the
British side for the Christmas ceasefire of 1914.
(*The Times History of the War 1914, published 1915*)

1915: DEADLOCK ON ALL FRONTS
Holt liner *Diomed*, sailing out of Liverpool on its way to Shanghai, tried to outrun a German U-boat only to be caught and sunk off the Scilly Isles on 22 August 1915.

FIRST IRISHMEN SHOT AT DAWN
Twenty-six soldiers serving with Irish regiments were executed during the Great War. This photograph, however, involving the Royal Irish Fusiliers, was set up for the camera with the 'German spy' being Private Bailey, the Officers' Mess cook.
(Courtesy of the Royal Irish Fusiliers Museum)

NURSING FRIEND AND FOE ALIKE
Pau hospital, in southern France, was funded by public contributions from Ulster and staffed by nurses from the Ulster Volunteer Force Nursing Corps.
Front row (l–r), Dr Leonard Brown, Dr Woodroffe, Miss Sinclair, Dr Pradignac, Miss Ballantine;
Second row (l–r), Sister McCullagh, Sergeant Downer, RAMC, Sister Rolston, Sister Patrick, Nurse Cunningham, Nurse McCrory, Sister Kilpatrick, Lieutenant Gouet, Sister Steen;
Back row (l–r), Nurse Dickson, Nurse Tupper, Nurse Forde, Nurse Thompson, and Nurse Auchinleck. *(Belfast Telegraph)*

NURSING FRIEND AND FOE ALIKE
Lord French's sister, Mrs RM Harley, had been part of the hospital committee at Pau and had ensured the staff received everything they needed for the efficient running of the facility. She was killed by shell fire in March, 1917. *(The Great War Magazine, published 1915–1919)*

THE FIRST POISON GAS ATTACKS
The Canadian troops, despite heavy casualties, defended stoutly in the face of a
German gas and infantry attack. *(A Popular History of the Great War, published 1933)*

THE FIRST POISON GAS ATTACKS
Belfast man Private David Smith, of the Canadians, needed further
treatment for a loss of sight following the gas attack. *(Belfast Telegraph)*

THE CHRISTMAS TRUCE OF 1914:
Rifleman Willie Walsh

Even after months of death and suffering, the Christmas spirit was still alive among the dirty and wet men facing each out across the muddy No-Man's-Land in December 1914. Along much of the British front, running from south of St Eloi to the La Bassée Canal at Givenchy, a calm descended as the fierce fighting of previous days died down. The mutual singing of festive carols began early on St Stephen's Day but even so, the Tommies were still amazed to see Christmas trees, decorated with candles and paper lanterns, appear on the enemy parapets. Local truces evolved, often with the simple aim of allowing each side to recover its dead and lay them to rest in peace, while in other locations the two sides met out in the open to talk and exchange tokens of their temporary friendship. Among the Irish units that took part in the truce were the 2nd Royal Dublin Fusiliers, 1st Royal Irish Fusiliers, 2nd Leinster Regiment and 1st Royal Irish Rifles.

Lisburn man Willie Walsh, of the 1st Rifles, had been instrumental on the British side in forging a ceasefire on his section of front. Writing to his father David at Hill Street in the town, he told him how the festive period had been one of "peace and quiet". He went on:

"On Christmas Eve night the Germans put up lights on the top of their trenches as a greeting, and shouted over to us in English 'A happy Christmas to you,' and we responded by repeating the same. They then challenged us to send over one man halfway, and they would do likewise; so I got out of our trench and walked over. I was met by a young German soldier, who shook hands with me, put his arms around my neck, and brought me right over to their trench. They came out, gathered round me like bees to shake hands, and gave a cheer of joy. We exchanged greetings, after which they gave me boxes of cigarettes, cigars, and some chocolate, and I gave them all my cigarettes. A German officer, probably thinking I was seeing too much of their trenches, approached and, shaking hands with me, wished me a happy Christmas, after which he said I must return. When parting he said, 'I beg of you not to fire and we won't'. I promised that we would not. He gave me a German field postcard, with his name and address. The translation is 'In memento of Christmas, 1914–15; Alwin Obermeier, Petershagen, Westfallen

(Weber).' I then returned to our trenches, and as soon as the boys saw me they cheered for all they were worth. Not a shot was heard that night nor on Christmas Day. Both sides took their turn at singing the whole night through. Immediately after 'Stand to arms!' a voice broke the silence by shouting 'Good morning,' and the Germans returned the compliment. The distance between us is only 200 yards. They walked about all day in front of the trenches, and we did the same. They would meet our fellows half way and have a chat and exchange things as mementoes. They gave us what we call the 'German brown bread'. It is a brown colour like our own wheaten. I had some of it, and it was all right. I asked one fellow how he liked the war, and he said he didn't like it at all. He expected it would be over soon. They looked very clean and well cared for. As soon as dusk drew near both sides returned to their trenches, singing as fresh as ever until the danger rocket was fired at twelve o'clock, when all resumed their old positions. We are again blazing away at each other as hard as ever."

William Walsh was unfortunately killed on 20 March 1916, at the age of 28, and is buried at Rue-du-Bois Military Cemetery, Fleurbaix, in northern France.

Lieutenant Davis Williamson, of the Royal field Artillery, told a similar story in a letter written on Christmas Day to his father and delivered to his home at Forthill, Castlecaulfield, County Tyrone.

"There was a sort of truce arranged today between some of our fellows and the Germans in front of them. Although the regiments to right and left kept firing spasmodically all day the others went across, and they and the Germans exchanged tobacco and talked and sauntered about between the two lines of trenches. It was the queerest sight in the world to see two lots of men who a few hours before were intent on killing each other (and will be again tomorrow) talking together as if they were the greatest friends in the world. They even arranged a football match, and since I started writing this letter a telephone message has come through to say that the Germans had won by three goals to two. We all had Christmas cards from the King and Queen this morning, and this afternoon each received a little box from Princess Mary, with tobacco and pipe inside. It is very cold here now, but frosty. It is much better, however, than the rain. Indeed, the country has a really Christmas look this morning with the hoar-frost covering everything."

By Boxing Day most had resumed their normal trench caution though the live-and-let-live attitude continued in places for several more days with reduced firing, though without the fraternisation.

Another officer, Lieutenant Thomas of the Royal Munster Fusiliers, had a totally different, but very pleasant, Christmas in a German hospital. He had been wounded in the throat on 27 August 1914, and taken prisoner. His injury meant he was unable to speak until an operation performed by German surgeons. In a letter to his cousin Francis Maginn, the superintendent of the Belfast Mission Hall for the Adult Deaf and Dumb, he recorded:

"You will, I expect, be surprised to hear that I am quite gay here in spite of everything. We have a Christmas tree, beautifully decorated, and last night every man got a lovely big parcel of apples, oranges, cakes, nuts and cigars – I believe from the Kaiser. Some nurses came in and sang Christmas carols, then we had carols in French, Russian and Polish; the French and German sounded very nice, but the Russian and Polish are awfully funny. I'm enclosing the label that was on my parcel. It means "A Happy Christmas," and it will do as a Christmas card to you. There was also a card with a verse from the Bible in English, something like our Christmas cards."

"My regiment is going forward to attack the Hun tomorrow morning (24th) at dawn, and, if possible, give him about turn to Berlin. Now, by the time you receive this I will be lying in a soldier's grave somewhere in France. Keep yourself cool and calm, and when my son William grows a bit older just let him know the part his father took in the great war, 1914–15, and when he is able to look after my DC Medal and whatever other ones are given you for me give them to him. I tried hard to get a leave home this month, but could not get one, as I knew that sooner or later this trench fighting would have to stop. Well, darling, I am going forward in the fight for freedom with a good heart and putting my trust in God for the Allies to be victorious."

Sergeant William Shearer, DCM, Shankill Road, Belfast
2nd Royal Irish Rifles, killed 25 November 1915

1915

DEADLOCK ON ALL FRONTS

The deadlock that had characterised the final months of the previous year continued into 1915. The Germans, engaged in a war on two fronts, were of the opinion that they would have to conclude hostilities in Russia, where they were confident of success, before being able to bring sufficient manpower to the Western Front to make a significant difference. For the French, of course, having the German army occupy a large swathe of its territory was abhorrent and they were determined to take the fight to the enemy, with largely disastrous results. The British had the smallest standing army of the main combatants, with the BEF already having been devastated by the early battles. It had a "new army" in training but it wouldn't be ready to take the field until later in 1915. In the meantime, Lord Kitchener, the Secretary for War and another Irishman, was looking to establish a second front. On 2 January 1915, he wrote to Sir John French, commanding the BEF: "The German lines in France may be looked upon as a fortress that cannot be carried by assault and also that cannot be completely invested, with the result that the lines may be held by an investing force while operations proceed elsewhere." That second front, it was ultimately decided, was to be Gallipoli where the objective was to knock Turkey out of the war and open a more practical line of communication with Russia.

The focus at the beginning of the year was much nearer to home. In December 1914 the German navy had bombarded the English coastal towns of Scarborough, Whitby and Hartlepool. An attempt to repeat the stunt the following month went wrong, however, with a British convoy intercepting the enemy ships at Dogger Bank on 24 January. A short engagement followed, with the British emerging the victors though the majority of the German fleet was able to slip away unscathed. The significance of the battle, however, was its boost to British morale and the decision of the Kaiser to order his fleet to avoid further risks. The submarine war went on unabated, however, and it was an attack by U-20 on the British ocean liner RMS *Lusitania*, on 7 May, that caused the most controversy. A number of those on board were American

Opposite: Earl Kitchener, on a visit to the French trenches in 1915,
watches the affects of a bombardment on the German lines.
(From A Popular History of the Great War, published 1933)

and the attack on an unarmed civilian ship did much to change public and political opinion in the United States.

Another man to witness the might of the U-boat was John Davidson, from Duncairn Gardens in Belfast. Ship's carpenter aboard the Holt liner *Diomed*, sunk by U-38 60 miles off the Scilly Isles on 22 August 1915, as it sailed from Liverpool to Shanghai, he recalled how the ship had tried to outrun the submarine whilst being fired upon by its deck gun:

"But it was all of no avail. After a race of about two and a half hours the Union Jack was lowered as a signal of surrender. At this time nearly all the lifeboats had been smashed to smithereens. The deck houses were reduced to matchwood. The captain was killed outright, the young man at the wheel had his head blown off, and the third steward was also killed. The chief officer, Mr Richardson, was shot through both his legs with a cigarette in his mouth; he crawled along the deck on his hands and knees and gave his orders as if nothing had happened; but the steering gear, I imagine, went wrong. Eventually when there was nothing else for it he sent down the bell signal to the engineers and fireman below to save their lives.

How did the crew escape? I can only tell you how I escaped. Out of the fleet of lifeboats only two were sufficiently intact to be of any service; I got into the first one launched. It was crowded, but it only remained afloat for five minutes. The shells had made havoc with her sides. We couldn't bail the water out of her, and she capsized and foundered. We struggled in the sea for a considerable time – I could not say exactly how long – until we were picked up by the second lifeboat. This boat was also pierced with shot and shell, and we were up to our knees in water all the time. However we managed to keep her upright until a torpedo boat destroyer came along and picked us up."

Davidson, apart from wrenching his shoulder, escaped unharmed. Among the other casualties was Able Seaman James White, a 25-year-old from Wexford. He is commemorated on the Tower Hill Memorial at Trinity Square, London, which remembers those of the Merchant Navy and fishing fleets lost during the war.

On land, the French were first to go on the attack in 1915 in the Artois region but, due to the redirection of resources to Gallipoli, the British forces were not ready to take offensive action at the same time, as previously planned. However, on 10 March the BEF attacked the German lines at Neuve Chapelle, seeking to take the village of Aubers and push towards Lille. After initial success, the advance was halted after three days with the arrival of enemy reinforcements. Gunner R Markwell, from Belfast, was serving with the 5th Battery of the Royal Field Artillery. He wrote:

"At Neuve Chapelle I passed through fire and water… I could not describe this battle for you. It is beyond all the efforts of description that any human being could employ. Sir John French did convey in his dispatch a graphic idea of the scene, but only those who witnessed the fight can have any true or real conception of what it was like. Mons was not in it with this engagement, neither was Ypres, nor yet the Marne."

On 22 April the Germans launched what was to be their only major offensive of 1915 on the Western Front. The Second Battle of Ypres, during which the enemy used poison gas for the first time, forced an Allied withdrawal of more than two miles towards Ypres. The fighting rumbled on and off until the end of May, with the Germans making further gains to the north but the Allied lines held, though at St Julian the 2nd Royal Dublin Fusiliers was all but annihilated. The Ypres salient was reduced to some three miles across and five miles deep.

At Festubert from 15–27 May, the British advanced close to a kilometre, taking the village, before being fought to a halt in driving rain with the loss of some 16,000 casualties. The next major action wasn't launched until the autumn when the British attacked Loos while the French attempted to advance at Champagne and Vimy Ridge in Arras. Following a four day bombardment, the Battle of Loos began on 25 September but was called off just three days later. Despite outnumbering the Germans by up to seven to one in some places, its success was very limited and costly with the British commanders blaming the shortage of artillery shells for its failure – a claim that sparked a political row at home. The battle at Loos was renewed briefly on 13 October with further heavy losses.

The first of the New Armies had begun arriving towards the middle of the year. Some 80,000 men had volunteered in Ireland in the first 12 months of the war, with the 10th (Irish) Division formed in August 1914, the 16th (Irish) Division in September, and the 36th (Ulster) Division in October, all part of

Kitchener's New Armies. Both the 16th and 36th divisions were dispatched to France in 1915, with Private Charles Connolly, of Abbeyview, Westgate, Drogheda, serving with the 14th Royal Irish Rifles, recording his first time in the frontline:

"Our platoon was brought through endless communication trenches, the passage being very tiring owing to our slipping about in the mud and falling into holes. At length we reached a regular maze of trenches, following our guide like sheep. We were pushed into a dug-out, and being worn-out just fell down and slept as we were. However we were knocked up to stand to arms just before daybreak. I was rather surprised to find that we were in the first-line fire trench. We looked over the parapet one at a time, and in the dull light could dimly discern the German lines at a short distance. As the light increased so did the firing. It is startling at first, especially the artillery fire, but before long you become so used to it that you don't even notice it. We were rather unfortunate in getting wet weather for the first few days, the rain turning the trenches into an indescribable state of soft, slimy mud.

That afternoon we were put to digging some trenches, and to tell the truth I never got it so hard before. The part we were in was only half dug, and did not afford sufficient cover from rifle or machine-gun fire, so it was a case of getting down every minute. But that was not the only trouble. The trench was filled with water, almost two feet deep. We were separated some distance from one another, and after toiling for some time an officer came splashing along and asked me if I were enjoying myself, to which I replied, 'I don't think.'

The first evening I thought very exciting and well worth experiencing. We got orders to open fire, and for the first time got our chance of pouring lead at the Huns. However, the Germans were not asleep, and soon the bullets cracked round us in all directions, and we were obliged to keep down."

The 10th (Irish) Division was held back from the Western Front so it could take part in the Gallipoli campaign.

FIRST IRISHMEN SHOT AT DAWN:
Albert Smythe and Thomas Cummings

Shortly after 8.00 am on Thursday, 28 January 1915, Irish Guardsmen Albert Smythe and Thomas Cummings were brought under armed escort to their place of execution. Bound hand and foot, their eyes covered by blindfolds, they stood side by side to meet their fate. Within minutes, a party of their comrades had ensured they were the first Irishmen of the Great War to join the shot-at-dawns – killed by their own side for desertion.

Throughout the war more than 3,000 British soldiers were sentenced to death by Field General Courts-Martial, with some 11 per cent actually carried out. Of the 26 soldiers executed while serving with Irish regiments, 23 were found guilty of desertion; one of striking an officer; one for quitting his post; and one for disobedience.

Both Smythe and Cummings had been detained on 15 January when a military policeman, accompanied by a gendarme, had called at a farmhouse following a tip off from the mayor of Choques, who had been informed by neighbours that two strangers had been staying there for the past three weeks. Inside a locked barn they found the pair and placed them under arrest.

Private Smythe had joined the army in 1909, being promoted to a lance corporal the following year only to lose the stripe again for drunkenness. He transferred to the 3rd Dragoon Guards but soon deserted, though he gave himself up again. Allowed to remain in the army, he was made a machine-gunner in the 1st Irish Guards. A major, providing a character reference at his court-martial on 19 January, concluded: "I have known this man all his service personally and since he obtained the King's Pardon during peace he did very well – but since he came on active service he has not done well."

Smythe went missing from his battalion on 1 November 1914. On that evening he had volunteered to act as stretcher-bearer to evacuate some of the wounded. As he made his way between the dressing station and the front the group he was with came under fire and became separated in the dark. He told the court:

"I went forward but got separated from my mate as we were under fire. I lost my way but found a French battalion with whom I stopped six weeks. I first started for Hazebrouck but on the outskirts of that town found that my battalion was at La Bassee so tried to go there and on my way stopped at the farm, where I was apprehended. I was just resting there."

Private Cummings, from Belfast, was accused of going missing from the battalion on 6 November, a day on which it had endured heavy fighting, suffering many casualties. His story at his court-martial was strikingly similar to Smythe's – that he had become separated from his comrades during the engagement and lost his way. "I wandered about for a long time and eventually came upon some French troops," he said.

"I spent about two days with the French troops and then tried to find my battalion. I have been walking about the country ever since and could not find it. I had been staying at the farm where the military mounted police found me for about three days. The day before the military mounted police found me I had heard that my battalion was at La Bassee and that evening I had intended starting off to rejoin it."

Cummings, who had enlisted in 1904, had spent his army career as a signaller before entering the army reserve in 1912 with an exemplary character. He was recalled to the colours at the outbreak of the war. "I knew him well and have always considered him an excellent man," a major told his court-martial. It was to no avail with the sentences against both men confirmed by a chain of officers right up to the BEF commander Sir John French. The executed men were buried side-by-side nearby but their graves could not be found after the war and today their names are commemorated on the Le Touret Memorial to the missing, between Bethune and Armentieres, Pas de Calais, France.

The regulations permitting such executions were repealed in 1928 and 1930. In 2006, more than 90 years after the deaths of privates Smythe and Cummings, the British government announced it was to grant all 306 soldiers executed during the Great War for cowardice or desertion posthumous pardons.

NURSING FRIEND AND FOE ALIKE:
An Irish hospital in France

The Ulster Volunteer Force, as part of its preparations for possible conflict over Home Rule, had a well established nursing corps which it offered to the War Office in 1914. The unionists of north Tyrone, however, went further, funding and largely staffing a complete hospital at Pau, in the south of France. In early October 1914, having had its offer accepted by the French government, the first consignment of staff and materials left from Liverpool.

The British Journal of Nursing reported:

"They are taking £250 worth of instruments and surgical stores for a 50-bed hospital for three months and are supplying the beds and bedding. The hospital is being financed by a North of Ireland committee under the presidency of the Duchess of Abercorn."

The initial staff consisted of the matron, a Miss McCord from County Down, who had formerly been with a London hospital; St John nursing sisters Johnson, Cobbett and Jennings; sisters Stevens, Jameson, Shimmin and Sullivan, all from Dungannon, M Ferran of Belfast, Wright from Strabane, and Patrick of Castlederg; probationers Alexander, Dickson, Harkness, Moore, and Thompson were, like most of the nursing staff, members of the Tyrone UVF Medical and Nursing Corps. The orderlies were Sergeant Buss, Corporal Downer, both from Londonderry, Hunter of Belfast, and Strabane man Lowry, all said to be UVF members; with a Miss Ballantine in charge of the stores and a Miss Sinclair the administration. Dr Norman Darling, a Harley Street surgeon and doctor to the Spanish royal family, was in overall charge assisted by doctors Woodroffe and Clarke, both Irish.

Miss Sinclair, writing home in early 1915, said a shortage of tradesmen had hampered the preparation of the building, Villa Beaupré on Avenue Thiers (now Avenue du General de Gaulle):

"We spent three very long weary weeks getting the house ready. It had not been occupied for a long time, so needed a lot of cleaning as well as carpentering and plumbing work. It was a most disheartening business. Things never move very fast in this part of the world, and just now, of course, all workmen are at the war except the very old and the very young, and they have more to do than they can possibly get through, as all the hospitals here are clamouring for them beside their private customers. Every time we got the house clean a plumber or an electrician or someone came along and dirtied all the stairs and passages again. All the floors are polished, and they had to be washed time after time, and then polished. Then, when we thought we were fairly right, something went wrong with the chimneys…"

The hospital was inspected by the French authorities, who apparently were much impressed. "Our operating theatre and sterilizing room are much admired, with their nice glass and white enamel fittings. The instruments, too, are a source of great interest. We also have a very nice laboratory and dispensary," noted Miss Sinclair. An incinerator built in the backyard of the hospital to burn the medical waste was so well received the authorities ordered that all the medical facilities in the area construct similar burners.

The doctors, matron and theatre sister lived on the premises with the remainder of the staff being temporarily housed in hotels while work went on to convert a house opposite, that had formerly belonged to a German who had fled on the outbreak of war, into a nurses' home. A committee of influential women, including the daughter of the town's mayor, Sir John French's sister and the wife of the British Consul, ensured the French cooperated fully, including supplying furniture and equipment from the local hotels and big houses. The hospital had eight wards, named after Allied generals including French, Roberts, Kitchener and Gough, and fifty-four beds. In addition, the medical team helped look after a smaller hospital located in a former monastery at nearby Lescar and called each morning at the Sacrecoeur Convent, to the rear of their facilities at Pau, which had been converted into a hospital for wounded Germans. Miss Sinclair added:

"If the people who have been kind enough to help this hospital could see their 'guests' I am sure they would feel, as we all do, thankful to have the opportunity of doing something to help these men who have suffered so much, and who are so wonderfully brave and gay in spite of it all."

At the end of March 1915, the War Office gave notice that voluntary hospitals would no longer be accepted with all the sick and wounded to be moved to large auxiliary military hospitals of between 500–1,000 beds. By this stage, nearly all British doctors and nurses working under the Joint War Committee in France had been recalled, leaving the French doctors, according to the *British Journal of Nursing*, to "deeply lament the loss of their English nurses". However, the Irish staff at Pau appears to have remained until April the following year before being relocated to Lyons. The hospital at Villa Beaupré continued operating with French staff until February 1919.

The hospital at Pau, in southern France, was funded by public contributions from Ulster and staffed by nurses from the Ulster Volunteer Force Nursing Corps.
(From the Belfast Telegraph)

THE FIRST POISON GAS ATTACKS:
Private Samuel Archer

The Germans launched just one major attack during 1915, but it was accompanied by the use of a new and ghastly weapon. What became known as the Second Battle of Ypres began in April and continued into the following month. At dawn on 22 April the Germans released some 168 tons of chlorine gas, using 5,700 canisters, with the sinister greenish-yellow mist creeping over Allied lines being held by French Algerian and territorial troops. The gas caused panic, with the lines being abandoned though not before the chlorine had inflicted an horrendous toll. A seven kilometre gap opened in the lines through which the Germans advanced three kilometres until halted by a hastily organised British counter-attack. On 24 April the Germans advanced again behind a second batch of chlorine gas preceded by a short but fierce heavy bombardment. This time it was Canadian troops on the receiving end and they weren't so easily moved. Despite suffering close to 6,000 casualties, including some 1,000 deaths, they defended stoutly, exacting a high price from the attackers.

Amongst the ranks of the Winnipeg Rifles was Private Samuel Archer, originally from Princes Street in Dromore, County Down. "I suppose you heard about the Germans trying to poison us," he wrote to his parents.

"Well, it did kill some of us. When I saw it coming I stuffed a pocket handkerchief in my mouth, and held my nose, and breathed at lone intervals until it went away. A drink of water afterwards made me all right. The next thing we had to contend with was the Germans coming right for us en masse. Everyone that was able got to their guns, but after a good, fierce battle we beat them back. But such a sacrifice of human life! Men and horses dead, lying in heaps, and time may never be afforded to get them all buried. One thing – we held our ground against fearful odds. No one ever thought of retiring, and we were pretty well thinned out by shellfire. Before the battle the French retired on our left, which made it worse for us. We were almost surrounded, and, but for our Canadian boys in reserve beating them back, they would have been at us on rear and front, and our men (the Canadians) saved the situation, but at an awful cost; but then, it was either death or victory for us – that was the spirit of every man."

Private Archer was wounded on 25 April taking a bullet to his right arm and suffering shrapnel wounds to the thigh. He crawled for what he estimated was half-a-mile to reach a first aid post. "The shells were bursting all around me, and bullets coming in all directions over my head, while the dead were lying everywhere. No matter where you went you could see nothing but dead bodies," he wrote.

"Next came the news of a order that our Army was retiring, and, as we were just about 800 yards from the firing line, there seemed little hope for us poor fellows. An officer came in, and said that any of the men that could walk had better go ahead at once. I got up along with a few others, and thought I would try it. I did not relish the idea of being done to death by the Germans while lying there… The whole way down I came across the dead bodies of my comrades killed by shrapnel, and horses and transports lying in all directions. I would not call this war – it is slaughter."

The British withdrew closer to Ypres and faced further German attacks on 8–13 May and 24–25 May, with the enemy making extensive use of chlorine but only succeeding in securing small gains. The Allies sustained considerably more losses during the battle, amounting to approximately two-thirds of the 105,000 total casualties on all sides, largely due to the gas mists.

The effects of the chlorine gas were still being felt months and even years after first contact. Belfast man Private David Smith, who had moved to Vancouver before the war, was with the Seaforth Highlanders of Canada in trenches between Ypres and Langemarck when the terrified Algerians passed through their lines on 22 April 1915. The Canadians advanced on the evacuated trenches, engaging in fierce hand-to-hand fighting with the Germans. On his return to the support trenches Private Smith's eyes began to trouble him. By the time he was ordered back to billets they were acutely painful and his vision badly affected. He was sent to a dressing station and eventually evacuated to the American Hospital at Paignton, Devonshire, where his sight improved after treatment. However, while back in Belfast in May 1915, and staying with his sister on the Ravenhill Road, his sight deteriorated again, resulting in him being admitted to the military hospital at Victoria Barracks. A month later, with his vision improved sufficiently to allow him to see about 100 yards, he was released from hospital into the Belvoir Park Convalescent Home.

WITNESS TO A 'MIRACLE':
Lieutenant W McM Chesney

On 22 April 1915, the Flemish town of Ypres, known today as Iepers, was under heavy bombardment from the Germans who commanded the high ground on three sides. In the midst of the shelling was an Irish soldier, Lieutenant W McM Chesney, from Kilcurry, Ahoghill, County Antrim, a member of the Royal Army Medical Corps (RAMC) and holder of the Military Medal. The Queen's University graduate was in command of a dressing station in the town's convent during what became known as the Second Battle of Ypres. This was to be the last serious attempt to take the town by the Germans and following its failure they settled for pounding it into dust. On this day, however, in one of the many such stories that abounded during the Great War, a 'miracle' was to take place and Lieutenant Chesney was an unwitting witness. According to the Rev Owen S Watkins, a Wesleyan chaplain, who like the lieutenant was attached to the 14th Field Ambulance, the Belgian peasantry were later to claim that during the bombardment "the Mother of God, dressed as a Red Cross nurse, appeared in the streets of the city, succouring the wounded, and pointing the dying to her own dear Son, Who gave His life for men".

The convent, according to Mr Watkins in a report in the *Methodist Recorder*, was on the Rue de Lille, the "unhealthiest street in Ypres; every house in it was hit, most of them were in flames and the Convent was struck again and again". He went on:

"From dawn until dark Lieutenant Chesney sat in his room waiting for death. A call out into the shell-swept streets to attend to wounded was a positive relief, but as the day crept on these calls became very infrequent, for few living beings were left in the city besides the little band of RAMC. He himself, afterward speaking of his experiences, said, 'The thing that steadied me up like a tonic was the sight of the Sisters – there were three of them left in charge of the place. When a shell hit the building, spewing dust and bricks in the corridors, one of them got up from where she was sitting, fetched a broom, and began sweeping up the mess! Who could feel afraid after that? Once, early in the day, when there was a rush of work, and many injured women and children were brought in, a Belgian Red Cross nurse appeared on the scene, and worked with us. Where she came from I don't know, nor did I learn her name. What became of her is also a mystery, for when there was no more work to do she just disappeared – but she was the bravest woman I ever met, always, of course, excepting the Sisters of the convent'."

By 9.00 pm the situation was so bad the RAMC detachment was ordered out of the town and withdrew through the shattered streets. At the same time another Irishman, Colonel GS Crawford, from Clough, near Ballymena, County Antrim, was commanding the main 14th Field Ambulance, close to the notorious Hill 60 and along the Ypres-Commines canal. The sheer volume of wounded that day, when the Germans used poisonous gas for the first time, was such that even with the Motor Ambulance convoys plying back and forth to clearing hospitals, the nearby women's asylum was still filled to overflowing with the injured and dying. Rev Watkins concluded:

"The strain upon our Commanding Officer, Col. Crawford, was tremendous – hundreds of wounded crowded the building, whilst hour after hour the systematic bombardment of the city proceeded, and the great 17-inch shell ever grew nearer and nearer, until the glass in the windows were broken by the concussion, and great fragments of steel were hitting the front of the building, one huge piece missing Lieutenant Grenfell by inches. What it would mean if one of those huge projectiles were to hurtle into our midst, as it might at any moment, baffled imagination to picture. Constantly Colonel Crawford urged the motors to greater speed. Magnificently the drivers, who had not slept for several days, responded to his appeal, and towards evening we began to hope that in a few hours we should have evacuated, and be ourselves able to trek to safety."

DIGGING IN WITH A BAYONET:
Sergeant Hugh Alexander Wilson

The machine-gun attachment of the Royal Irish Fusiliers went forward as a unit on 25 April 1915, during the Second Battle of Ypres. The men had just made it to a shallow ditch close to the enemy lines when the officer in charge was wounded. That put Sergeant Hugh Alexander Wilson, from Gilford, County Down, in charge. He led the men to a nearby farm house only to discover it offered little cover. "Some of the Dublins were behind the hedge to our left and they were getting slaughtered wholesale, the enemy being only a few yards away," he recorded in his diary.

"This hedge finished a little to the right and so I told the next senior I was going to creep along to see if I could find a position for our guns. The bullets were coming through this hedge like hail, and as I crept along I had to crawl over the dead bodies of some of the Dublins. When I got to the corner I saw that one of ours had been there before for he was lying dead by a tree, so I kept low and had a look around. I could see the Germans bobbing up and shooting just a few yards away and then a party of Dublins charged and it was quite lively watching them shooting and stabbing them. They captured the trenches to our front, but the trenches on our right were still in possession of the enemy. I forgot myself watching this affair, and when I looked round I saw my men all up running to a trench a little to the left. I shouted to them and the other sergeant shouted they had been ordered there. So I was left on my own, and being in command of the guns I had no rifle, and oh I so wished I had one for there was a German bobbing about, that looked an extra good target."

Sergeant Wilson, then aged 30, was an experienced soldier who had joined the Manchester Regiment at 16 and transferred to the Royal Irish Fusiliers in 1908. In an attempt to rejoin his men he now began crawling back along the hedge.

"While I was going along one of the Dublins came along who had been shot through the head, just above the eyes. I lay there looking at him for a good while amazed to know how he was living, but it soon brought me back to myself when he asked to be bandaged up and what was the best way to get back. I said across the open was the only way I knew, but he would be shot again if he tried that way, better to lie here. He would not, however, for he up and ran across and the last I saw of him was going across the fields for all he was worth.

I thought it about time now that I got up, and ran for the trench, little thinking it would be my last run. So I up and ran and had only got a short distance when I felt a sharp stinging blow in my knee, and it came suddenly to me I had been shot. I ran on a few paces more when I found myself unable to do any more, and by good luck I espied a shell hole just in front and with one last effort dived into it. When I got in I found it did not half cover me from view, but my first thought was to see to my wound, for I could feel the blood running from it. I got my bandage out and after a lot of wriggling I managed to somewhat bind it up. My next thought was to get further down in this hole, especially as my feet were showing and I could hear bullets spitting into the ground just by them. I knew that the same German was still having a go at me. There was nothing to dig with only my bayonet, so with bayonet and hands I laboured on, digging it with the bayonet and throwing it out with my hands. At last I had to stop for I had got just under cover and I was getting done up with loss of blood."

Sergeant Wilson, wounded about 8.00 am, wasn't discovered until an officer of the Royal Dublin Fusiliers found him some 12 hours later and attempted to carry him back.

"This was agony but I did not say anything, but when he went a few steps and fell in a ditch with me, I could not help but roar as I came down full on my leg. The Germans heard me I am sure. He said 'poor fellow' and said he would send some men with a stretcher for me, so I was left again. After a while, which seemed eternity, three men came, but no stretcher so they carried me on two rifles on which I sat."

Sergeant Wilson was left with one leg shorter than the other as a result of his injury and was discharged from the army. He died in 1947 at the age of 62.

TEENAGE SURVIVOR OF THE LUSITANIA:
Seaman James Hume

Seaman James Hume, aged just 19, was in his bunk attempting to catch up on his sleep when the *Lusitania* was rocked by an explosion. It was the afternoon of 7 May 1915, and the passenger liner had just been struck by a German torpedo. The Cunard ship had left New York, bound for Liverpool, some six days previously with almost 20,000 passengers and crew on board, many of them American, and was sailing some 12 miles off the southern coast of County Cork when attacked.

Dressed just in his underwear, Hume had rushed up on deck where a scene of confusion greeted him, with crewmen running to and fro and passengers confused and bewildered. Making his way to his allocated boat, he was stopped by a young mother who was desperately searching for a lifejacket. James, from Canmore Street in Belfast, gave her his, helping to tie up the cords and directing her to one of the lifeboats. In gratitude she took a gold watch from her breast and pushed it into his hand despite his protestations. Arriving at his own station, he helped lower the boat down the side of the stricken liner only for it to overturn as the ship lurched.

All along the ship the list was greatly hampering the efforts of the crew to launch the rafts and get them filled with passengers. When he had done all he could, James looked to save himself. By now the ship was well down in the water but such was her scale he was still some 60 feet above the waterline when he climbed on to a rail and dropped into the sea. "All around the ship you could see nothing but heads bobbing up and down in the water, and when I looked back I saw the stern of the vessel in the air. People too terrified to jump were clinging desperately to the sides, and they went down when the ship sank," he recalled. Just 18 minutes after being struck, the *Lusitania* disappeared beneath the waves with the loss of 1,198 lives.

Even those who had made it off the liner were far from safe and James watched in horror as one by one people clinging to the upturned boats were swept away by the buffering of the waves.

"I managed to swim over to a collapsible boat which was floating bottom upwards, the canvas covering being still attached. There were about forty of us clinging to it, including half-a-dozen girls, whom the men folk did their best to support. The boat was continually turning over on its side, however, and one by one the others lost their grip and disappeared. In an effort to keep their spirits up, some of those in other lifeboats began singing, with the chimes of *Rule Britannia* and *Tipperary* floating across the waves."

James, meanwhile, attempted to save the life of a little girl. He recalled:

"A child of about six years was washed up against me, and I endeavoured to support her but lost consciousness, and when I came to my senses I was aboard a fishing boat. I do not know what happened to the child. I was over four hours in the water, and that with nothing on but an undershirt, so you may guess I was nearly frozen. My feet were so cut up that I could scarcely walk."

At Queenstown he was given a coat and trousers some two sizes too big for him and a pair of tennis shoes. He was then taken to Liverpool, where crowds of people had gathered to meet his ship in the hope of finding a loved one onboard. As James came down the gangplank a young woman rushed out of the crowd and threw her arms around his neck and had already kissed him before suddenly drawing back. "Oh, I thought you were my brother," she said.

Another Irishman, going by the name Frank Toner, reputedly not only survived the sinking of the *Lusitania* but the previous *Titanic* and *Empress of Ireland* disasters. From County Dublin, he was working as a fireman and, following the torpedo strike, led a group of men up to the top. Toner reportedly helped women and children into lifeboats. He attempted to avoid the rising waters by climbing one of the masts then swam to an upturned lifeboat where he hung on until rescued by a patrol boat, the *Heron*. His claim of being a triple survivor was never verified though there are suggestions he was serving under an assumed name and that he was really William Clark, a seaman who is known to have survived both the *Titanic* and *Empress of Ireland* sinkings.

The sinking of the *Lusitania* has remained controversial to this day. The loss of so many American passengers helped turn public opinion in the United States against Germany and paved the way for its entry into the war. However, rumours have persisted that the ship was secretly carrying weapons and explosives to Britain for the war effort – a possible cause of a second explosion onboard which hastened its end – which would have contravened international law.

DOING A MAN'S WORK:
Second Lieutenant Albert William Bourke

The Battle of Aubers, on 9 May 1915, was part of a joint British-French initiative to seize the high ground around Vimy Ridge and disrupt German communications on the Douai plain. Delayed by the weather, it was to see the French take on most of the burden, attacking some 15 miles to the south, with the British seeking to take the high ground at Auber Ridge in a pincer movement, and thus depriving the enemy of a significant observation point. It was to prove a total disaster, with no ground taken and some 11,000 casualties suffered.

An intensive bombardment opened up on the British front at 5.00 am. The men of the 1st Royal Irish Rifles, part of the 8th Division, climbed out into No-Man's-Land half-an-hour later in preparation for the coming advance. After 10 minutes, as the barrage lifted, they moved forward. The German barbed wire was found to be largely intact, however, and the German machine-gunners and artillery dominated No-Man's-Land, tearing holes in the ranks of the advancing troops.

Second Lieutenant Albert William Bourke, a member of the Royal Irish Fusiliers on attachment to the 1st Royal Irish Rifles, was at the head of a team of bombers. According to a fellow officer, he was shot in the head during the attack and died instantly, though the fact he was initially buried close to a British first aid post suggests this might not have been the case. By 8.30 am the attack had come to a standstill with only three small footholds established and the men here effectively cut off by the intensity of the fire sweeping the open land. Renewed attacks during the day failed to break the deadlock. The French, by comparison, took a four-mile wide stretch of the German lines and advanced some two miles, though the slowness of bringing in reinforcements meant the success could not be exploited. In the early hours of the next morning, 10 May, the remnants of the 1st Royal Irish Rifles were withdrawn.

On the evening before his death, 23-year-old Lieutenant Bourke, of Cyprus Avenue in east Belfast, was in a strange mood. Though claiming to be in far better form, both physically and mentally, than he had for a while, he was clearly pondering his own fate and how that would affect those left at home. As final preparations were made for the coming battle, he sat down and scribbled a letter to his family. Arriving at the Bourke home after notice of his death had already been received, it read in part:

"Of course we had to pay for these things, but who can grudge the price we pay; certainly the fellows who go down don't. I have been in fairly tight places, and I know the spirit in which the men go in, and I have seen men wounded and killed by my side, and I know the way they go down. Nothing could be finer. I am more than proud to be amongst them, and I know that you are proud of it, too. The news is not really bad. We are only marking time, and I know that the day is coming. Certainly many of the best men God ever made will pay for it with their lives, but old England goes on forever. Only those who have travelled and have been on such trips as this know what England really is. Now, I have no notion of dying, but I am no safer than anybody else, and if I should be killed I should not wish for anything better. I believe it will be doing a man's work as well as I can do it, and I know you will be sorry, but at heart very proud and glad. I am sure you have no doubt of my meeting you in Heaven; in my case I have no doubt whatever. I am sure I don't know why I am writing in this strain. I am not in the least bit morbid; in fact I am in far better form than I have ever been, both bodily and mentally. Whatever may happen will be for the best, and we cannot lose anything either way. I would love to tell you something about my work, so that you could rejoice with me; but I am afraid I can't, so you will just have to be happy, because I am without knowing why."

A memorial service for Lieutenant Bourke was held at Newtownards Road Methodist Church in Belfast, which, along with his parents Charles and Sophia, he had attended since a boy. A special memorial in his memory stands at Le Trou Aid Post Cemetery, Fleurbaix.

TAKING TRENCHES WITH COLD STEEL:
Lance-Corporal John McIntyre

The Battle of Festubert was, in effect, a continuation of the Battle of Aubers and was launched just days after the assault on Neuve Chapelle. On 13 May 1915, some 430 guns and howitzers opened up along a front of some 5,000 yards. At 11.30 pm on 15 May the infantry rushed the German lines. The initial success slowed as tougher opposition was encountered. The village of Festubert was finally taken in renewed assaults from 20–24 May, with the attack called off three days later. All told, the Allies had advanced less than a kilometre and suffered 16,000 casualties.

Among the wounded was Lance-Corporal John McIntyre, of the 2nd Royal Inniskilling Fusiliers. Writing to friends in Dungannon, he explained that both he and his brother Joseph were in hospital:

"Our battalion had a bayonet charge on Saturday night when we took two lines of German trenches at the point of the steel. We were under heavy fire from the time we left our trenches until we reached the Germans, but we fixed them up for the men we lost. I cannot say how many we lost, but I know that a number of my own section fell. Young Willie Dickson, of Dungannon, is killed, and I got a box from his pocket, the only thing I could take as a keepsake. He and I came out here together last September, and went through a lot since. We often talked about the times we had in Dungannon, and wondered if we would ever get back."

The lance-corporal said he had been wounded alongside several friends, lying out in the open until the next day:

"The shell fire was terrific and the shells burst all round us as we lay waiting on our turn. I never saw such fire from the big guns, rifles and machine-guns, and the latter mowed down our men like grass. On Sunday morning, when I revived, I tried to make my way back to the trenches, with the German bullets cutting the ground around me. I took cover behind a dead comrade, and on looking into his face I thought at first, to my horror, that it was my own brother, but on creeping into our trenches he was the first man to speak to me, as he had reached it before me, and had had his wound dressed. I was obliged to stop all that Sunday in the front trench, and German shells nearly did for the lot of us. I saw a dozen of our men killed and wounded by one shell from the enemy's heavy guns. Another killed three of our wounded not more than two yards from where I was lying. It was an awful Sunday."

Lance-Corporal John McIntyre, who despite his injuries helped repel a German counter-attack that day, clearly held the enemy in contempt, adding:

"When we charged with the bayonet in the dark and got into their trenches we made them hop for the dirty tricks they do, and any of them that were left were easily counted. They kill some of our wounded and throw vitriol on others and burn them, and then laugh at the poor fellows' agony. I have seen all this, and also the vitriol bombs they throw at night after a battle to catch the wounded, who are unable to get to safety."

Private R Thornton, who had worked at the Bloomfield Bakery in Belfast before joining the 2nd Royal Inniskilling Fusiliers, took a bullet in the leg. Writing to a friend in the city, he said:

"We started very slowly so as not to let the Germans know, but had only gone 100 yards when the enemy sent off some rockets, but I think they were so much surprised they could hardly believe it was us. They then sent up hundreds and made the night as clear as day. They could see us quite plainly, and opened a terrific shell, rifle and machine-gun fire. We began our rush amidst this shower of hail and shrapnel, the men falling in dozens… Our fellows, shouting and yelling, rushed on, but were pushed back. They came a second time and by this time we were all mad and angry at our losses and thinking of nothing rushed the front line of the enemy with bomb and bayonet. As soon as we gained the front line we rushed off to the second, and had a good deal of fighting to get them out of the second trench."

Passing through the support and communication trenches after being relieved, Private Thornton found them full of the dead and wounded:

"Our stretcher-bearers when carrying the wounded back were killed, and the wounded buried alive, with the trenches being blown in on top of them. It was terrible to see, some fellows sitting with their backs against the side of the trench with their head, arms and legs blown off. The Germans were firing on our wounded and setting fire to them by firing vitriol or some other stuff for their cowardly purpose."

The 'young Willie Dickson' referred to by John McIntyre was the 22-year-old son of Richard and Mary Jane Dickson, of Ballysaggart, Dungannon, County Tyrone. He has no known grave and is commemorated on the Le Touret Memorial.

YOUNGEST KNOWN BATTLE CASUALTY:
Private John Condon

The youngest soldier to die during the First World War, according to the Commonwealth War Graves Commission, was 14-year-old John Condon from County Waterford. It is an assertion that has caused more than its fair share of debate and controversy over the years, sparking claim and counter-claim as to his real age (some maintaining he was older than stated and others that he could have been younger) and even whether or not it is the boy's remains that lie in the grave bearing his headstone.

John Condon was the son of John and May Condon. Born at Ballybricken, County Waterford, having enlisted in the Royal Irish Regiment, he was sent to the 2nd battalion's barracks in Devonport, England, in December, 1914. His comrades in arms, of course, had been on the Western Front since August that year and had been heavily engaged. The battalion's casualties had been such that it was taken out of the line in October in order that its numbers could be built up again. Over the next few months drafts of fresh men were sent across, including the young Conlon.

On 24 May 1915, the enemy released poison gas on a huge scale, with the cloud drifting over the Royal Irish Regiment lines. The battalion's diary noted:

"On the 24th at 2.00 am the battalion stood to arms. At 2.20 the enemy preceded by gas, attacked. A gentle breeze blowing from the north-east brought the full volume of the gas on to that part of the line occupied by the battalion. Although respirators and sprayers were used, many of the ranks were overcome by gas. Shell Trap Farm, which was garrisoned by two platoons of another unit, was captured by the enemy, thus enabling them to enfilade the Royal Irish portion of our line. They walked down our line bombing with hand grenades and, only a few men of the Royal Irish now being left, took it as far as the right of the King's Own. Here the attack was checked."

Among the 379 casualties sustained by the battalion was Private John Condon. His body was not recovered until 1923 when it was laid to rest in Poelcapelle British Cemetery in Belgium.

Exposure to gas was a terrible experience, as the men of Royal Dublin Fusiliers (RDF) could testify. It had been the last of the Irish infantry regiments to be thrown into battle for while all others were represented when the British Expeditionary Force sailed for France in August 1914, the 2nd battalion of the RDF, known as The Old Toughs, remained behind to ward off the threat of a German invasion of Britain. The Dubliners' absence from the firing line, however, was to be short and its involvement intense. On 24 May 1915, it sustained 149 dead and a total casualty list of 645 from a starting strength of 666. Only one officer and 20 other ranks escaped relatively unscathed, including Private James Rogers, of Milbrook, County Kildare.

"The first thing I have any recollection of was a shout of 'The Gas! The Gas!' And it was upon us. A lot of our fellows got badly choked by it, but I was not much affected by it at all. After giving us the gas they began to shell us with high explosives. Part of our fellows on our right had retired, thus leaving our right flank exposed. Most of our officers had been knocked over by the gas and shells, and either killed or wounded. A Scottish regiment came up to reinforce us about 8 o'clock, but they were gassed and had to retire. All our officers and non-commissioned officers had been knocked over except Lieut. Shanks, who was in charge of what was left of us. We held the position until about 11 o'clock, when there were only six or seven of us left. The remainder had all been killed or wounded."

The remaining men slipped away in ones and twos, with Rogers the last to make it back to his own lines. He went on:

"As I came back to headquarters past the dugout I saw a man lying near the trench. I thought I knew the boots – a sort of high-laced boots. I went over and found there was a coat over the man's face. I lifted it off and saw it was the body of Colonel Loveband. He had, as far as I could make out, been shot through the lip, just at the bottom of the nose. I looked at the wound and saw the bullet had gone through the back of the head. He was evidently anxious about us – to see how we were getting on without the reinforcements and wanted to have a look. He came out of the trench and was evidently got by a sniper. His face when I saw him dead seemed as if he was laughing – a sort of smile on his features."

Lieutenant Colonel Arthur Loveband had 29 years service with the Royal

Dublin Fusiliers, and was commanding the regimental depot at Naas when war was declared. After spells with the 3rd RDF at Cork and the 6th battalion at Beresford Barracks, he was sent to the front to take charge of the 2nd battalion. He is commemorated on the Menin Gate Memorial, Ypres. James Rogers survived the war, returning to live in Naas. He died in January, 1947.

Private John Condon, believed to have been aged 14 when killed in Belgium in 1915, is officially recorded as the youngest British soldier to die in the Great War. *(Courtesy of the Royal Ulster Rifles Museum)*

ORDERED TO LEAVE IRELAND:
Herbert Moore Pim

Herbert Moore Pim was a man of extreme, if inconsistent, opinions. Throughout his life he was at times, and to varying degrees, a conservative, liberal, unionist, fascist, British nationalist and would eventually emerge as a staunch imperialist. In 1915, however, he was in a rampant republican phase, preparing for revolution and indulging in anti-war rhetoric that earned him many political enemies and brought him to the attention of the military authorities.

Born at Granville Villas, University Road, Belfast on 6 June 1883, his parents were Robert Pim, later a director of the Alliance Assurance Company, and Caroline, one of the Moore family of Rathmines, Dublin, and later of Dromore. Pim attended Friends School, Lisburn, public schools in England, and finally completed four years studying in France before following his father into the insurance business. A keen writer from a teenager, he published a range of books, from the religious to soft porn, under various pen-names. From a Quaker family, he converted to Catholicism in 1910, and joined the Ancient Order of Hibernians and United Irish League, whose views he promoted in a series of articles in the *Irish News* under the pseudonym A Newman, and later became a member of the Irish Volunteers. In 1914 he lost his insurance job after declaring himself a separatist.

On 10 July 1915, Pim – along with several other prominent republicans including Ernest Blythe, Liam Mellows, and Denis McCullough – was served with an expulsion order issued by Major-General LB Friend, head of the Irish Command, under the Defence of the Realm Act. Known as DORA for short, the regulations, passed in 1914, gave the authorities virtually unlimited powers – from forbidding citizens from talking about military or navy matters in public to using invisible ink, or speaking on a phone in a foreign language to buying binoculars – with further restrictions added as and when they were considered necessary. In this instance, Major-General Friend gave Pim a week, until 10.00 pm on 17 July, to leave the country and report his new address to the authorities.

Far from complying with the order, however, Pim went on the offensive, including addressing anti-British rallies during which he told his audience of how he had been ordered out of the country. Within days of the passing of his expulsion deadline, Pim was arrested at his home on the University

Road and deposited in the dock of a Belfast Custody Court that was full to overflowing, such was the interest in the case. In addition to having failed to leave Ireland as ordered, he was also accused of making "statements likely to cause disaffection to his Majesty, and statements likely to prejudice recruiting for his Majesty's forces". Pim wasn't allowed to even address the court and a Major Price, the military representative in the court, refused to give any information about the whys and wherefores of the notice despite being pressed by the defence. A suggestion by Pim's counsel, Mr Hanna, that it had been Pim's political opponents that had been behind the action being taken received loud applause and cheering in court, much to the annoyance of the magistrate, who ordered the room cleared. As police filed in to remove the spectators, Mr Hanna observed: "There are a lot of hefty young men there who are not in khaki." A short time later the spectators were allowed back in again for the sentencing – three months imprisonment, half the maximum term available to the court. Other republicans similarly ordered to leave Ireland also ended up before the courts for failing to comply.

On his release from jail Pim continued to write and promote republican views and in 1916 joined the Volunteer muster at Coalisland at Easter 1916, for which he was arrested again and sent to Reading Jail, being released in September that year and returning to his activities. With many of his republican associates still imprisoned, Pim became a leading figure and spokesman for the movement, though did the cause more harm than good as he was consequently bickering with friend and foe alike.

In 1918, however, he resigned from Sinn Féin, argued for the introduction of conscription to Ireland and began publicly backing the Ulster Unionists before leaving for London where he worked on the anti-republican and anti-Semitic paper *Plain English*. He later spent spells in France, taking French citizenship in order to get a divorce and marry his mistress, and in Italy before returning to Britain. He died on 12 May 1950.

A DEADLY ENCOUNTER IN NO-MAN'S-LAND:
Black Watch comrades-in-arms

On 10 July 1915, four men climbed over the parapet of their own trench and crawled out into No-Man's-Land on a patrol that they hoped would result in securing information about the enemy. Instead it ended in the deaths of two Belfastmen, reportedly the first from the city to die with the Black Watch, and a heroic bid by their friends and comrades to rescue them.

Prior to the First World War the 6th Black Watch, a territorial battalion, recruited heavily in Belfast and many men from the city went to war within the ranks of the Scottish regiment. By the summer of 1915 they were serving near Fleurbaix, in the Pas de Calais area of northern France. As the patrol neared the enemy lines it came across a German patrol, a dozen strong, and a fire fight ensued. Lance-Corporal Walter Newel and a second lance corporal, James Willis, were fatally wounded. Writing to HA Newel, Walter's father, at his home in Brookvale Avenue, Belfast, Major John Wylie, commanding the battalion, gave an account of the action:

"It was while engaged on an important and daring piece of work that Lance-Corporal Newel and his friend Lance-Corporal Willis were both mortally wounded. It is only men of special courage and resource that are chosen for the work in which they were engaged and your son had always proved particularly plucky and adept at it and had frequently been out and returned safely. His patrol was ambushed by a party of about a dozen Germans, and the two foremost were hit. The remaining two, Jenkins (also from Belfast) and Majury continued to fire at the enemy, and eventually crawled back for help."

Lance-Corporal Fraser, son of a builder from Willowbank Street in Belfast, and a close friend of both Newel and Willis, quickly organised a rescue party of volunteers, including Lance-Corporal Cronne, who had formerly played rugby for Collegians in the city, and Private Fred Deane, a Knock Rugby Club half-back, and led by Majury, they went out in search of the missing men. Major Wylie continued:

"They again encountered a hostile patrol, which they dispersed with rapid fire, and although they were under machine-gun fire for about an hour, they succeeded in locating their two friends – no easy matter amongst long corn and barbed wire – and had them carried into our lines, a very commendable piece of work. The doctor informs me that both were so badly hit that they must have been unconscious from the first, and it is some consolation to know that your son at least was spared suffering. Both were brought down to the dressing station about midnight, and your son was buried during the night by his comrades beside the graves of some other soldiers. I read a short service myself at the graveside, and the spot is being carefully marked with a cross. I can scarcely tell you how keenly this loss is felt both by officers and men who knew your son."

Lance-Corporal Newel was 26 and had completed his time with the territorial unit but when war was declared he volunteered again, joining his old regiment and giving up a job as a warehouseman in F Carlisle and Co, Howard Street, Belfast.

Lance Corporal James Denning Willis was 24 and a son of William Willis, a sanitary engineer. Major Wylie, who had headed the men's company before stepping up as battalion commander, wrote to his family at their home, Ashburton, Bangor:

"Our party encountered a patrol of ten or twelve Germans who were lying in ambush, and before our men could open fire lance corporals Newel and Willis fell mortally wounded. I believe your son was killed outright, and it is some little consolation to know that he had not any prolonged suffering. The other two men of the party fired on the Germans and dispersed them, and they returned for help. Your son was buried in a little graveyard, a short service being held at the graveside. His loss has been very keenly felt by both officers and men of his company, by whom he was regarded as a most capable and reliable NCO, with a very strong sense of duty. He has fallen in the execution of one of the most important and trying duties any man could be called on to do, and one which can only be carried out by men of special courage and ability, which your son displayed at all times."

The two men were initially buried in a little graveyard, close to the Wangerie Post at Laventie, between Rue-du-Bacquerot and Aubers. They were later reinterred in Rue-David Military Cemetery, Fleurbaix, some five kilometres south-west of Armentieres. Lance Corporal Newel had three brothers in the services, two of whom were also killed. Private David Lumsden Newel, 21, of the 20th Royal Fusiliers, was killed on 13 March 1916, being buried at Cambrin Churchyard Extension in France, and Company Quartermaster Sergeant George Frank Newel, 26, died with the 15th Royal Irish Rifles on 7 August 1917. A special memorial to him stands in Wieltje Farm Cemetery, Belgium. The family also erected a memorial to the three men in Belfast City Cemetery.

Lance Corporal Walter Newel, of the 6th Black Watch, sitting to the right, pictured with his three brothers, all of whom served during the Great War.
(From the Belfast Telegraph)

Lance Corporal James Denning Willis was killed in No-Man's-Land when his patrol came under fire.
(From the Belfast Telegraph)

BROTHER OFFICERS WHO DIED SIDE BY SIDE:
Melbourne and Kenneth Ross

George and Henrietta Ross were justly proud of their family's war service. Three of their sons, Melbourne, Kenneth and Harrison had left their home at Cultra, County Down, to join the 4th Royal Irish Rifles as second lieutenants in August 1914. Though Harrison later resigned due to ill-health, he re-enlisted in the North Irish Horse the following year and was again commissioned in the Royal Irish Rifles in October 1916. Though twice wounded, he survived the war.

The other brothers, Melbourne and Kenneth, were sent out together on 30 June 1915, to join the 2nd Royal Irish Rifles, and were subsequently killed side by side less than three months later, on 25 September, at Hooge, Belgium, in a subsidiary attack to keep German reinforcements away from the main offensive at Loos. Neither body was recovered and today they are commemorated on the Menin Gate, Ypres

Just two days before their deaths, Melbourne, who at 30 was the older brother, penned a letter that captured his fears and apprehension at what was to come:

"We know the worst now. Our battalion makes the attack for our brigade. Kenny's company and my one make the charge for our battalion, my platoon and another platoon lead off. So there you are! You can picture me charging over barbed wire, etc, and storming about 20 lines of German trenches, or else tripping over my own feet and falling back in to our own trench, which is more likely. This was to have been done a fortnight ago by another brigade, so it may be put off again; but when it does come the whole line for miles will be going at once, and it greatly depends whether we are in or out at the time, whether we take first or not... I don't know when it is coming off, but it is getting on everybody's nerves. I shall have a break down altogether. It is a case of 'I think of it by day and I dream of it by night, And I'm wearing my heart away with fright,' as the song says. I wish it was over, but am still in hopes of someone else doing it.

I am afraid my courage will ooze out before we get half going. You see we have to stand hours of shell fire first. (Now, shell fire puts me balmy.) Then, when that is over, rush at huge big Huns and stick them, then fight with bombs, and then start all over again, only they will do the (counter)

attacking. If one gets hit in the open it depends on one's self whether one gets back or not; if in a trench, one has to wait till dark unless the enemy retake the trench, when all one's troubles are over. Still we must trust in God and hope for the best. I hope that this work out here will count as part of our Purgatory. It ought to, as it is as near Hell as anything you could think of. You must excuse this doleful letter, but one ought to lead a good life for years and years before coming out here, then one could look on the future with a calm mind. My mind is centred on having another year's racing on Belfast Lough, with a short cruise on the West Coast, and I am afraid the Hun may spoil it and send me to an eternal Hooge, or a place nearly as hot."

Melly, as Kenneth referred to his brother, was always 'very cool and collected' while in the trenches whereas he was constantly concerned he might lose his composure. Writing to his father in July 1915, the 25-year-old Kenneth described a bombardment of the lines:

"We lay flat, I keeping my eyes in a small hole scooped in the ground as I dread losing them. It was a horrid experience. We had been warned that our shells were starting. Then they came very rapidly. They are timed to burst at first German trench. It is so close to us that, on bursting, parts fly into our trench. This is unavoidable. They whine as they come, and then burst with a tremendous bang that shakes the trench, then the little pieces scatter for a hundred yards in every direction, humming, as they go, like large gnats. Though terribly afraid, I could not but admire the accuracy of our gunners. 9-10th of the explosions must have gone into the German trenches and 1-10th into the space between and our trench; and when you think how close the trenches are, and how far off our gunners are, it is very good. However, some of it came into our trench, and then a message came that one of my men had been hit. The man next me, knowing it was my first experience of big gun fire, said he'd go and see about it. However, pulling myself together, I crawled along (you could scarcely imagine the inferno of a row). When I got there the man had been bandaged up more or less, so I crept along to get my brandy flask, till then untouched. I gave him a little. It revived him very much. In the night we got him away on a stretcher…"

UVF MAN INTERNED BY THE GERMANS:
David Perceval Doak

On 9 September 1914, Germany established an internment camp for British civilians at the racecourse at Ruhleben, on the outskirts of Berlin. It issued an ultimatum on 31 October, giving the UK five days to release all German citizens from British camps. The day after the deadline expired, they began the mass arrest of British civilians on German soil. The stables, haylofts, tea house and even the grandstand of the racecourse was used to house the new arrivals, with work starting later that year to build proper accommodation.

Among those detained were cousins David Perceval Doak, from a well-to-do County Down family, and the Rev James Somerville Wilson, of Ballyshannon. The pair had been in Leipzig to improve their German when war was declared. Wilson, as he was clergyman, was soon released and allowed to return home. Doak, however, though only a teenager, was moved from one place of confinement to another until, on 10 December, he arrived at the Ruhleben Camp.

In January Doak – who had been a sub-company commander in the Dromore Ulster Volunteer Force company – was summoned to appear before the camp commander who asked him what, as an Irishman, he would say of his time in German captivity should he be released. The teenager told him that he didn't consider it good treatment to have confined him in the first place, initially in a jail, then a workhouse and finally in an internment camp. His German host was understandably less than reassured and dismissed him with a curt "Good morning". Camp rumour had it that several other Irishmen who had been released earlier had been allowed home on terms agreed with Sir Roger Casement, who was in Germany attempting to raise an Irish Brigade from prisoners-of-war.

Life in the camp was considerably tougher for those without means of their own. Without money to buy their own supplies, internees had to survive on the fare supplied by the Germans supplemented by five shillings a week provided by the British relief societies. That, in the opinion of Doak, was insufficient to keep a man healthy. On the other hand, among the thousands of prisoners were many famous names of the day with which to rub shoulders. These, according to the teenager, included England international footballer Steve Bloomer, still fondly remembered today by Derby County fans, who had been coaching a German side, Britannia Berlin 92, in 1914; Scottish international

John Cameron; New Zealand rower and sculling champion Tom Sullivan, who had been coaching at the Berlin Rowing Club when war was declared; top violinist Godfrey Ludlow and the cellist Carl Fuch, who though German born had taken British citizenship.

Escape from the camp was possible, though getting out of the country was a much more formidable problem. Doak knew of two escapes that ended with recapture and solitary confinement on a bread and water diet for the prisoners involved. In time the Germans doubled the guard – which initially had been composed of new recruits – with convalescing soldiers wounded at the front, and issued orders to shoot on sight anyone making an attempt to flee.

Doak, whose father James, from Percy Lodge, Dromore, County Down, was a director of the firm Murphy & Stevenson, was released from Ruhleben in October 1915. Under military escort he was taken to the Dutch border, from where he made his way to England. He left behind at the camp a former school friend from his days at the Royal Academical Institution, Belfast, named Norman Carrothers, who would have witnessed the camp develop. It continued to operate until November 1918, with a total of 5,500 British men kept at Ruhleben over the four years of the war.

The German guards rarely entered the camp after September 1915, being content to patrol the outside to prevent escapes. As a result, a self-governing community developed with each barrack nominating a representative to a so-called Captains' Committee, which oversaw discipline in the camp, with the aid of the barrack police, and looked after the finances of the range of shops and services operated by the internees. With many of those interned being young, sport figured prominently. Two soccer pitches were created with barracks establishing teams to compete; a five-hole golf course was constructed; and seven tennis courts laid out. A range of other sports, including field and track, rugby, cricket, hockey and even baseball were also played.

VC HERO ON RECRUITING DRIVE:
Sergeant James Somers

After the initial rush of volunteers, the number of recruits coming forward to join the army dropped significantly. In consequence, recruitment drives were organised to inspire young men to follow in the footsteps of war heroes such as Victoria Cross winner Sergeant James Somers. On 18 October 1915, a Saturday afternoon, he was the star attraction at a soccer match at Grosvenor Park in Belfast between Distillery and Glentoran in the Belfast and District League. The *News Letter* reported:

"Doubtless many of the spectators had been attracted by the announcement that Sergeant James Somers, VC, of the 1st Royal Inniskilling Fusiliers, who hails from Belturbet, would be present, and certainly everyone in attendance was eager to catch a glimpse of and acclaim the Ulster hero, who had so gallantly and courageously upheld the glorious traditions of the province."

Just two days previously Sergeant Somers had been presented with his medal, won at Gallipoli earlier that year. Shortly before 3.00 pm, accompanied by a group that included UVF commander General Sir George Richardson, Colonel John Day, Officer Commanding the Belfast Defences, Lieutenant-Colonel TVP McCammon and John Ferguson, the organising secretary of the Ulster Recruiting Council, the sergeant arrived in the grounds to the "hearty cheering of the crowds which had gathered in the vicinity of the entrance". The paper continued:

"The cheering was quickly taken up in all parts of the grounds as the hero, walking between General Sir George Richardson and Mr Blacker Quin, made his way to a reserved space in the centre of the stand on the far side of the field. Many of the spectators eagerly pressed forward and shook hands heartily with the hero, while an elderly woman in particular, carried away by emotion, nearly hugged him, as she rained blessings on his head. Sergeant Somers was conducted around the playing pitch by Mr A McCaughey and Mr John Ferguson and was enthusiastically cheered by the spectators. He afterwards shook hands with the referee (Mr G Maginnis) and the captains of the respective elevens

(Mr J Kirkpatrick, Distillery, and Mr J Scraggs, Glentoran), and having, amid a fresh outburst of cheering, opened the game with a modest kick off, he returned to his seat in the stand, where he followed the game with much interest. There was more than a sprinkling of khaki in the crowd, and recruiting sergeants and collectors for Red Cross and other funds were numerous, while at one end of the stand there was accommodated a large party of wounded soldiers, who had been motored to the ground from the city hospitals, and who were entertained to afternoon tea by the Distillery Football Club, the arrangements at the ground being in the capable hands of the club secretary, Mr Walter Scott.

In addition to the customary band, the band of the 5th Battalion Royal Irish Rifles, under Mr HT Whiting, was in attendance, and gave a programme of inspiriting music prior to the match and at the interval. When the teams left the pitch for a breather at half time the distinguished visitors took the field, and recruiting meetings were quickly in progress in three different parts of the field, each having an audience numbering well over a thousand. Sergeant Somers proceeded directly across the ground in company with Mr WH Webb, who presided over one meeting. General Sir George Richardson, Lieutenant-Colonel McCammon, and others held a second meeting, which was addressed in vigorous and inspiring style by the General. At another corner of the pitch Mr Stewart Blacker Quin, who was accompanied by Sir William Maxwell, delivered a brief but forceful speech.

Sergeant Somers visited each 'platform' in turn, and was greeted with enthusiastic ovations, his quiet, unassuming manner and the sincerity of his few remarks winning for him the quick sympathy and admiration of his hearers. Sergeant Somers said it had afforded him great pleasure to visit Belfast and also to attend the match between Distillery and Glentoran. There were doubtless many young men in that crowd who were not engaged on munition work, and he thought it was a duty they owed to their country to get into khaki without any delay. If they could but realise the position of affairs that existed at the Front they would not hesitate a single moment, but would come forward at once and volunteer to fight for their country. He had been to London and had seen the destruction of property that had been caused by the last Zeppelin raid, and he could not help thinking that if the people of Belfast could but have seen the damage that had been done by the Germans they would enlist without delay. The brave soldiers at the Front were looking for men to back them up. If he could get a sufficient number to form a battalion he would go out again and head them. (Cheers)"

The appearance of Victoria Cross winner Sergeant James Somers at Grosvenor Park, Belfast, days after being awarded his VC by the King, was guaranteed to produce a full house.
(Courtesy of the Inniskillings Museum)

RETREATING WITH THE SERBIAN ARMY:
Beatrice Kerr

From hospital wards to harems, and from marching alongside a retreating army to sleeping in a monastery, Beatrice Kerr experienced more of an adventure than she could have ever imagined when she had signed up to join the Stobart Medical Mission to Serbia. The mission's founder, Anne Mabel St Clair Stobart, had previous experience of such work, having organised a medical mission during the First Balkan War of 1912. She had established the Women's Imperial Service League in 1914, sailing for Antwerp at the invitation of the Belgian Croix Rouge in September. The group had to be evacuated to France, however, as the Germans overran Belgium, with the mission relocating to Serbia in April 1915 under the auspices of the Serbian Relief Fund.

Miss Kerr, from Cookstown, County Tyrone, was the mission's honorary sanitary adviser, and had been based in a temporary hospital at Kragujevac, the headquarters of the Serbian army, some 50 miles south of Salonika, since the mission's arrival. She suddenly found herself in charge of the facility, however, after Mrs Stobart decided to head off to the front, accompanied by many of her staff, following Bulgaria's invasion of Serbia from the east. With the Austro-German attack from the north being pressed home, the Serbians had no alternative but to give ground and Belgrade fell on 9 October. With the Serbian army now in full retreat, the order was given on the 26th of the month to evacuate Kragujevac, with the only avenue of escape available to the medical mission being by way of Montenegro and Albania to the Adriatic.

Miss Kerr and four colleagues first headed to an ancient monastery hidden high in the mountains, where they had hoped they could continue their hospital work. Arriving there on 30 October, they were welcomed by the monks but soon realised their days there were numbered. Kragujevac fell to the enemy on 1 November and days later the first members of the Serbian army, being pursued into the mountains, began arriving in the vicinity of the monastery. On 10 November, the women left their sanctuary on foot. At Raska, Miss Kerr and her group, now numbering twenty-two and accompanied by a Serbian minister, was the last allowed across the bridge before it was blown up to slow down the Bulgarians.

The mission group finally met up with a hospital unit of American and English women and together they scaled the increasingly difficult mountain passes in torrential rain, which turned to snow the higher they climbed.

Provisions became scarce and at night they were forced to sleep in the open and by day marched alongside the retreating Serbian soldiers. One evening accommodation was found in the harem of a Turkish man, the British women sharing it with his wives. The following night they had planned to sleep in the open but were forced to march through the night after discovering they were virtually on the ever-moving front line, with the guns firing around them. The following day, as the women traversed the Montenegro Alps in a snow blizzard, Miss Kerr became separated from the rest of the party. Holding on to the horses and light artillery guns being pulled along the icy roads she attempted to keep going. An officer, spotting her plight, ordered that room be made for her on a bullock waggon and then sent a rider forward to halt the party of women until the column, and Miss Kerr, caught them up.

After a night of refuge in the Russian Ministry at Djakova, the group headed to Ipek, along roads that were sheets of ice, where they again slept in a harem. After twenty-four hours rest, the women set out to scale the narrow mountain pass, with some of the pack ponies used to carry the baggage plummeting to their deaths as the road narrowed to virtually a ledge cut out of the rock. That night and the one following were spent sleeping alongside camp fires, lit as much to keep away the wolves as for heat. By the third day they were reduced to trekking along steps cut out of the snow until they reached the summit then, in the face of a terrible gale, they set out to cross the mountains, reaching Podgoritza, close to the Albanian border, on 13 December.

Selling what they could to buy food and water, the group made for the coast, arriving at Skutari, Albania, on 16 December, from where they were carried in Italian ships to safety. Making her own way through Italy and France, Miss Kerr reached London on 23 December and, after a few days rest, Cookstown on 29 December.

SHELLED BY A GERMAN SUBMARINE:
William Crawford

For civilians living or working abroad, travel to and from Ireland became a dangerous and anxious experience following the German decision to wage indiscriminate war at sea, as William Crawford, of the Indian Civil Service, could testify. On his way back to the sub-continent from Belfast, where his father, Sir William Crawford, was a director of the York Street Flax Spinning Mill, he had been passing through the Mediterranean on 23 November 1915, when the vessel he was traveling on came under attack.

After a hearty breakfast he had just settled himself down on a deck chair when he heard a 'whish' and then a splash in the water close by. "My first thought was that something had slipped along the boat deck above our heads and dropped into the sea," he said.

"There was soon a second splash and then the native crew came running up to their boat stations. Just then it was clear we were being attacked. All the passengers moved to the saloon entrance and staircase, and it wasn't long before we all had on lifebelts and waistcoats. These waistcoats had been sewn up in white muslin covers so as not to be too conspicuous. It is really wonderful, but there was not the least sign of panic either amongst the passengers or native crew. Some of the children cried, and many of the ladies had damp eyes, but everyone was very quiet and calm. My little son was inclined to be frightened when I was putting on his waistcoat, but I told him he must be a little Britisher and put on a smiling face, and he did it at once.

Meanwhile there was a number of shots from the submarine, but gathered where we were under cover it was impossible to get a clear idea of what was going on. Most of the passengers were in the dining saloon and a number (including ourselves) in the lounge at the top of the companion way. There were several clergymen on board, and they at once led in prayer, and there were a number of hymns in which we all, of course, joined – *Jesus, Lover of My Soul* and *O God, Our Help in Ages Past*. After what seemed a long time word was brought down by the captain that he thought we had dropped the submarine behind, and then we all sang the Doxology and *God Save the King*, and gave three cheers for the captain and crew.

There was a great feeling of relief, as you may imagine, though we were advised to keep our lifebelts on. We kept them on a good part of the afternoon. While our boat was being fired upon the boats were slung out and brought down to the promenade deck level, and the stewards brought up tins of biscuits and other supplies in the quietest and most orderly manner. Another thing that cheered us while the firing was going on was that we had hoisted the Red Ensign."

Mr Crawford, who estimated that up to 10 shots had been fired by the submarine, said no-one had been injured with the only damage caused being from shrapnel shells that burst above the ship in front of the captain's bridge and over the stern. "Of the former a large piece – the whole cap that screws into the base of the shell – struck one of the wooden bars that are put to carry an awning just in front of the bridge, and from there fell on to the promenade deck immediately below," he recalled.

"The bar shows a deep dint and splintering where the piece of shrapnel struck, and there is a circular mark, too, on the deck. The piece has its threaded edge and is practically intact, and, further, bears a crown and H and a number. It is 3 inches in diameter, and the captain says it must belong to a 5-inch shell. He intends to hand it over to the naval authorities at Port Said, and it may be a most valuable piece of evidence as to the nationality of the submarine, for the bounders never showed any flag or number.

The captain's seamanship was splendid and our engines were put to their biggest speed, touching a speed they had never done before. We saw the submarine before it fired. It was on our left side three and a half miles away, and we at once turned to starboard (ie, to the right) so as to show the submarine our stern, making us a more difficult mark. While the firing was going on wireless signals for help were sent out, and we were informed that three Italian stations had replied that ships were being sent out. The captain says the submarine was shining like silver in the sunlight, and was probably of aluminium. He thinks, too, it fired two shots at one time, and would therefore have two guns (disappearing guns) on its deck. It would probably be one of their newest."

DRIVEN OFF ROCKY PEAK:
Sergeant J Robinson

Following the entry of Bulgaria into the war, and its invasion of Serbia, a considerable number of troops, including the remnants of the 10th (Irish) Division that had suffered severely at Gallipoli, were sent to Salonika from September 1915 to rebalance the situation in Macedonia. The 5th Royal Irish Fusiliers had arrived in the region with a strength of just 160 men and four officers, including Sergeant J Robinson, of B Company.

On the evening of 3 December the battalion had taken over trenches at Rocky Peak, north of Salonika, from the 5th Royal Inniskilling Fusiliers after many of its soldiers had fallen victim to frost bite. Its task was to stabilise the line and make contact with the retreating Serbians. "Two companies of ours lost about 60 men with frost before they were up for their forty-eight hours, as each company only did forty-eight hours. The weather was very severe at the time," Sergeant Robinson wrote in a letter to a friend back home in Belfast.

"The snow was almost knee deep, and our clothing at the time was not so good, but we stuck to it and kept ourselves very busy working at trench work, but the Bulgarians were lying very low for some time. On the morning of the 5th B Company relieved D Company, and everything was very quiet except at times our artillery would keep a hot fire on their trenches, and then the enemy would send over a couple of light shells, for he was waiting for some heavy guns."

At daybreak on 6 December the Bulgarians unleashed a heavy bombardment of the British lines that continued for almost eight hours. A lull followed, during which an enemy sniper troubled the men, with one round narrowly missing the sergeant, until he was silenced. The bombardment began again at 4.30 pm, principally targeting the Allied heavy guns but also peppering the frontline positions for a spell before a further lull. Sergeant Robinson continued:

"We settled down for a sleep. Then we all stood to arms from daybreak, and I sent four men to the village for wood and water before they would start to pepper us again; but they lay low, and at about 3 o'clock we got seven prisoners and they gave us good information about the intended attack, and that the Germans were no good as they only gave them one cigarette."

The sergeant readied his men for the expected attack by a combined force of Germans and Bulgarians but it had still not been launched by the time his men were relieved by C Company. No sooner where they back in the support lines, however, when Sergeant Robinson was ordered to take a platoon forward again.

"We got up without any casualties, although the shells were falling very thickly when we were advancing, and we manned our trench. The Bulgarians were massing behind the ridge in front of us when I noticed one of their machine-guns and we opened fire on it and put it out of action. They were too much for us, and we sent for reinforcements. The other companies then came up, and we started to let them know who were in front of them but they were ten to one, and all we could do was to hold on till we could get more reinforcements sent up.

Lieutenant Cullen came to our relief in time with one of his guns, and as the Bulgarians advanced in mass formation he cut down every line of them, but still they came on till at last he ran short of ammunition, and had to get his gun away in safety. He sent his men away, and stood to his post, and still wrought havoc on the enemy with his revolver till he was wounded, and could do nothing more. It was one of the finest resistances done by any troops what both these companies stood with so many odds against them, officers and men alike, every one doing his bit."

For nine hours the Irishmen held off the enemy, despite being hugely outnumbered, occasionally counter-attacking with the bayonet. Forced to abandon their trenches, they fell back to the mouth of the Dedli Pass, were they stubbornly held on for a further three days, allowing their Allies to withdraw to a new defensive line. Supported by the Inniskillings, the battalion fought a rearguard action along the open land north of Lake Doiran in torrential rain until able to rejoin the main force again.

Second Lieutenant Ralph Cullen, of Regent's Park, London, was 30 years old when he died in the battle of Rocky Peak. His body was never recovered and he is commemorated on the Doiran Memorial, Greece. The sergeant said of him:

"Lieutenant Cullen is greatly missed, for he was a good soldier and faced death like all true Irishmen have done before. His name will forever live in our hearts…"

"War is abominable. I shall never volunteer again in any capacity, for I have seen enough of it. It is not so much personal fear that would deter men, as the awful sights and nerve-shaking ordeals of fire one had to go through. You have no idea what an awful thing shell fire is. I have seen strong men become gibbering idiots as the result of a shell bursting near them and tearing men to pieces. Yet they were untouched. It will shake the strongest nerves."

Fr John Fahey, Rosmore, County Tipperary
with the Anzacs at Gallipoli

GALLIPOLI

A DOOMED CAMPAIGN

The Dardanelles campaign, aimed at opening a better supply route to Russia and knocking Turkey out of the war by opening a path to its capital Constantinople, was initially envisaged as a purely naval affair, with the Royal Navy attempting to bombard the fortified banks of the Straits into submission. The Straits ran for 65 kms and were 7 kms wide for much of the way, though the well named Narrows beyond closed to just 1,600 metres. To the north-west was the Gallipoli peninsula, with the Asia Minor coast to the south. A combined British and French fleet began pounding the Turkish forts on 19 February, repeating the process a week later, with limited success on both occasions. On 18 March a renewed attack involving sixteen battleships accompanied by smaller vessels failed, with five Allied warships lost to mines.

Following the failure of the sea campaign, it was decided that land forces needed to be deployed. In early 1915, however, the Turks had attempted to take the Suez Canal with the aim of denying Britain the quickest route to its colonies. Attacking across the Sinai desert from Beersheba with 25,000 men, they were met by a force of Indian and Australian infantry on the banks of the canal on 2 February and rapidly pushed back. A British assault on Gaza followed, the first two attempts being defeated in March and April before a third attack under Sir Edmund Allenby succeeded.

Given the importance of the region to the British, it was heavily garrisoned to ward off further Turkish aggression – meaning fewer troops were available for Gallipoli than had been intended. Nonetheless, on 25 April landings took place at Helles and at Ari Burnu, subsequently known as Anzac Cove, on the Gallipoli peninsula. The British forces – including the 1st Royal Dublin Fusiliers, 1st Royal Munster Fusiliers and 1st Royal Inniskilling Fusiliers – despite outnumbering the enemy, were pinned down by heavy machine-gun fire though they did succeed in securing the landing zone. The men of the Dublin Fusiliers were massacred as they attempted to exit the *River Clyde*, an old ship that had been converted into a landing craft of sorts, with only

Opposite: Despite the differences in the landscape, the techniques followed at Gallipoli, including mad dashes across No-Man's-Land, were much the same as on the Western Front. (*A Popular History of the Great War, published 1933*)

one officer and less than a third of its 987 other ranks making it ashore. The Australians, on the other hand, were initially unopposed and advanced to take the nearby high ground only to be pushed back to the beaches by a makeshift Turkish force. A stalemate quickly evolved, with both sides digging in, often with the opposing trenches only yards apart. Subsequent attempts by the British to break out of the encirclement and take the high ground came to little and on 1 May and 3 May the Turks launched major counter-attacks on the Helles beachhead, followed by renewed Allied attacks on 6 May and 8 May, with both sides incurring heavy casualties. The Turks similarly launched an attack on Anzac Cove on 19 May, suffering some 10,000 casualties in just six hours while the Australians and New Zealanders sustained only 160 fatalities. The British again tried to advance from Helles on 4 June, prompting Turkish counter-attacks. A series of such engagements continued throughout June and July.

The Greek island of Lemnos, and particularly the port of Mudros, became a major staging post for troops on the way to or from Gallipoli, just some 50 km away. Second Lieutenant David Campbell, of the 6th Royal Irish Rifles, was one such soldier destined to pass through it on the way to the Dardanelles. He had been studying at Trinity College, Dublin, with the intention of becoming a Church of Ireland clergyman, and had applied to join the university's Officer Training Corps. On 4 August 1914 – the day war was declared – he received a letter inviting him to apply to become an officer. He eventually rose to the rank of captain. His battalion, after finishing training in England, had sailed for Malta, then on to Alexandria before finally arriving at Mudros on the morning of 21 July 1915, being accommodated in tents. This was a whole new world for the Irish boys as he recorded in his diary:

"I associate many unpleasant things with our stay on this island off Mudros. The flies were an infernal nuisance. They began to become numerous on the fourth day of our stay and thereafter they gave us no peace, they punished us eternally. At meal time they swarmed around us and their buzz was well-nigh intolerable. We kept our food as well covered as we could with cloths, handkerchiefs, etc. This was a manner of eating; you raised a corner of the cloth that covered your plate, secured a morsel of food on your fork or spoon and conveyed it to your mouth as fast as possible at the same time lowering the cloth to its original position on the plate. If you were successful you neither swallowed a fly nor allowed one under your plate cover. Partial failure was the general rule, usually a fly or two succeeded in alighting on your mouthful before it reached your mouth and while you endeavoured to blow it off you probably allowed several underneath your plate cover. Many a fly was swallowed and our mealtime conversation was varied with remarks such as 'Damn that fly' or 'Good Lord I've swallowed another,' etc. The only meal we enjoyed was a dinner which we postponed till after sundown. Not only during mealtimes did the flies pester us, a few generally managed to get inside our nets and made peaceful rest during the day rather difficult. The flies had strong allies in the ants, small black ones. They invaded our valises, they penetrated the food baskets and got mixed with the bread and raw meat. They were particularly partial to bully-beef and simply wallowed in Nestles Condensed Milk if they got the chance and they often did…"

A further landing of five fresh divisions – including Second Lieutenant Campbell's 10th (Irish) Division – took place on 6 August at Suvla Bay, with the aim of linking up with the Australians at Anzac Cove, who launched an attempt to break out from the beach that day with the Sair Bair Ridge as their objective. At the same time the troops at Helles launched an attack of their own to tie down as many Turkish soldiers as possible. The plan went wrong from the outset, with the British consolidating their position at Suvla Bay instead of pressing on against a much inferior enemy. When they did eventually advance, the following evening, they encountered a much strengthened defence that inflicted heavy casualties on the British infantry. By 9 August, as the newly arrived troops set off to occupy the Tekke Tepe Ridge, the Turks were digging themselves in on its heights. Despite repeated attempts to break out, the Suvla Bay landing was now encircled as well. At Helles, meanwhile, the offensive had petered out after just days, and the Anzacs, though coming close to success, had failed to take the Sari Bair Ridge though made a name for themselves in the brutal hand-to-hand fighting at Lone Pine, for which seven Victoria Crosses were awarded.

The British made a further attempt to link the beaches at Suvla and Anzac, just five kilometres apart, on 21 August, launching attacks on both Hill 60 and Scimitar Hill. The former stalled immediately but, when renewed on 27 August, the Anzacs took the Turks' forward trenches only to discover a second, previously unknown, line blocking their path and resulting in the attack being called off. At Scimitar Hill the 29th Division succeeded in capturing its objective in dense fog but was subsequently forced to give it up due to the intensity of the Turkish fire.

The British attempt to take Gallipoli and secure the Straits had run its course. Despite appeals for further reinforcements, the decision was taken to evacuate. Ironically, it proved the most successful operation of the campaign and from 10–19 December some 105,000 men and 300 guns were taken off the beaches at Anzac and Suvla Bay, with another 35,000 taken off Helles from late December to 9 January 1916.

Men of the Royal Irish Fusiliers take cover in the trenches at Gallipoli.
(From The Great War magazine, published 1915-1919)

LANDING ON 'V' BEACH:
Captain D French

In the opinion of Vice-Admiral John de Robeck, commanding the fleet operations at Gallipoli, the landing at 'V' Beach on the morning of 25 April 1915, was likely to be the most difficult. It was flanked by an old castle and the village of Seddul Bahr on the east and perpendicular cliffs on the west, with the whole foreshore covered with barbed wire entanglements which extended in places under the sea. In addition to landing men by boats, the *River Clyde*, a specially adapted old collier, was run aground. Large holes had been cut in her sides and gangways constructed to allow the men to make their way along a 'bridge' of lighters to the beach.

Captain D French, of the 1st Royal Dublin Fusiliers, clambered into a small naval cutter with his men, one of four such vessels to be towed to the beach by the naval steam piquet-boat, and at about 5.00 am they headed to the shore amid a tremendous naval bombardment of the coastal defences. He recorded:

"About 6.30 am we were quite close to the beach in a little bay. The *R Clyde* had grounded before it was intended and a hot rifle fire was poured into her from the Turkish trenches. As soon as the 'tows' got into shallow water the piquet-boats, which had taken charge of us again, cast off and the bluejackets commenced to row. You can imagine how slowly we progressed – 6 men pulling a heavy boat with about 30 soldiers – each carrying over 60 lbs kit and ammunition on his body!!"

The Turkish forces waited until the boats neared the shore then opened fire with machine-gun, rifles and pom-pom accompanied by shrapnel shells fired from concealed howitzers.

"I was in the last boat of my tow and did not realise they had started at my boat until one of the men closer to me fell back dead – shot. I realised immediately that having practically wiped out those in the other three boats ahead they were now concentrating their fire on us. I jumped out at once into the sea (up to my chest) yelling to the men to make a rush for it and to follow me. But the poor devils – packed like sardines in a tin and carrying this damnable weight on their backs – could scarcely clamber over the sides of the boat and only two reached the shore un-hit while the boat just ahead of mine suffered as much – the same number escaping from it. The only other officer in my boat never even got ashore being hit by five bullets."

While the piquet boat turned back to rejoin the warships off the coast, taking with it the landing craft full of the dead and wounded, Captain French made for the shore. He continued:

"I had to run about 100–150 yds in the water and being the first away from the cutter escaped the fire a bit to start with. But as soon as a few followed me the water around seemed to be alive – the bullets striking the sea all round us. Heaven alone knows how I got through – a perfect hail of bullets. The breach sloped very gradually – fortunately. When I was about 50 yds from the water's edge I felt one bullet go through the pack on my back and then thought I had got through safely when they put one through my left arm. The fellows in the regt. had told me I was getting too fat to run but those who saw me go through that bit of water changed their opinions later."

Once ashore he found what cover he could and had his wound bandaged before rounding up the men in the immediate vicinity.

"I could find only 30 or 40 men intact and we commenced to dig ourselves into the low cliff. Why the Turks with their vast preparations did not level this bank of earth down I cannot imagine. Had they done so not one of us would have escaped. While the tows were being pulled into the shore the Munsters began to disembark from the *R Clyde* and they, too, suffered terribly. I was about 50 yds from where she grounded and as the men ran ashore they were 'mown' down. I counted 42 killed in one platoon, not a single man escaping. And still they came down the gangways. It was an awful sight but they were a real brave lot. After but a few minutes it became even harder for them to get ashore. After passing down the gangways and across lighters under a heavy fire they had to run along about 25 yds of jagged rocks, each side of the ridge now being covered with bodies. Well, we lay there all day and at night the remainder of the troops dis-embarked from the *R Clyde* which originally brought along with her 2,000 troops. Never shall I forget that night. Heavy rifle fire incessantly. Drizzling with rain. Wounded groaning on all sides, and surrounded by dead, I admit I thought it was all up."

LIVING A CHARMED LIFE:
Fr John Fahey

At dawn on 25 April 1915, the first companies of the 11th battalion of the Australian Imperial Forces began landing at Anzac Cove in the face of a determined Turkish defence. Among the first ashore, having ignored instructions to travel on a hospital ship in preference to staying with the men, was Fr John Fahey, who would emerge from the war as the longest serving chaplain of the conflict.

Under heavy machine-gun and rifle fire the battalion stormed the cliffs, digging in along the ridges. Fr Fahey, in a letter written to his Archbishop, described his landing:

"It was 4.30 am and there was a faint glimmer of dawn. Suddenly inferno broke loose from the shore. Such a fearful hail of bullets from rifle, machine-gun and shrapnel as passes all imagination. It was appalling. We were packed so closely together that one bullet would wound or kill three men and we could not hit back for the enemy was invisible. The order was given for us to man the boats and we tumbled in as fast as possible and pushed for the shore. It was only 300 yards away but it seemed miles.

There was dreadful slaughter in the boats. First the cox was shot, then an oarsman fell dead across my feet; then a bullet came through the boat and grazed the puttee on my leg; then another of the men collapsed without a sound and we knew he was dead, and so on. It was horrible. I got to the beach exhausted and had to lie down among the falling bullets to get my breath. I picked up a flat shone and held it in front of my head and it was fortunate I did so, because the bullet that would have brained me glanced harmlessly off it. The lad on my left, not feeling safe, began to dig with his entrenching tool. He was shot through the heart. The beach was strewn with dead and wounded. Two boats landed about 50 yards from where I was. They held 50 soldiers each, but only 20 came ashore altogether.

So far only a few minutes had elapsed from the time we left the destroyer and as there was a good number of men ashore the order was given, 'Fix bayonets and charge'. I could hear the click of the bayonets fitting on the rifles and then in the semi-darkness our men gave a wild

Australian cheer and rushed up the hill. Poor fellows, had they seen it in broad daylight they would never had attempted it."

John Fahey had been born on a farm at Rosmore, County Tipperary, on 3 October 1883. Ordained in 1907, aged 24, he left shortly afterwards for Australia. A talented linguist, scholar and sportsman, he was reputedly a crack shot with a rifle. Fr Fahey joined the Australian army on 8 September 1914, and was assigned as Chaplain 4th Class, with the rank of captain, to the 11th Battalion, 3rd Brigade, 1st Australian Division, raised in Western Australia. On Gallipoli he lived a charmed life: his haversack was riddled with shrapnel, shots went through his overcoat, a book was shot out of his hand, and a jam tin he was eating from, a tobacco tin and his waterproof sheet were all struck with bullets without him coming to any harm.

His near misses, however, did not deter him from getting into the thick of the action. Fr Fahey, who was awarded the DSO for his bravery, ended up in hospital in July 1915 as a result of illness. He returned to Gallipoli in August but was evacuated again to receive more medical treatment and took the opportunity to visit relatives in Ireland only to discover that reports had circulated that he had been killed! The chaplain rejoined his battalion on the Suez Canal in February 1916 and the following month accompanied it to France. Fr Fahey returned to Australia, and a hero's welcome, in March 1918. He died in 1959.

Born the same year as Fr Fahey, and ordained as an Anglican clergyman a year after the former became a priest, Everard Digges Le Touche had a very different war. He applied to be a chaplain with the Australian forces but, when turned down, immediately enlisted as a private soldier. Later commissioned, he arrived at Gallipoli on 5 August with the 2nd Australian Infantry and took part in the attack on Lone Pine the following day. He was wounded just minutes after the battle commenced and later died of his wounds. His brother-in-law, Sergeant William Ernest King, from County Galway, was killed in the same battle, with both laid to rest in Lone Pine Cemetery, Gallipoli. Everard's 30-year-old brother, Lieutenant Averell Digges Le Touche, was killed the following month at Loos, while serving with the 2nd Royal Irish Rifles. The brothers were born at Burrendale, Newcastle, County Down, and are named on the town's war memorial. Lieutenant Digges Le Touche's widow, Eva, the daughter of a Church of Ireland canon, returned to Ireland to live with her parents at The Rectory, Milltown, County Kerry.

BREACHING THE NARROWS:
Lieutenant Commander Dacre Stoker

Lieutenant Commander Henry Hugh Gordon 'Dacre' Stoker created a tale of daring and courage that his more famous cousin, Bram Stoker, would have been justly proud. In 1915, as the landings were taking place at Gallipoli, the captain of Australian submarine AE2 slipped by the Turkish defences to cause havoc in the Dardanelles.

Born in Dublin in 1885, the son of a doctor, he had joined the Royal Navy as a 14-year-old cadet in 1900, undergoing training on HMS *Britannia*, near Dartmouth. Emerging as a midshipman, he was briefly posted to the Channel Fleet battleship HMS *Jupiter*, then to the HMS *Implacable* in the Mediterranean. Promoted to sub-lieutenant in 1904, he spent a year on HMS *Drake* in the western Atlantic before transferring to the relatively new submarine service, undergoing his training at HMS *Thames* at Portsmouth. He was given his first command at the age of 23 and was posted to Gibraltar to set up the Royal Navy's first submarine base outside of Britain. In 1913 the Australian navy was seeking volunteers to bring 'home' from Barrow-in-Furness its new submarines, AE1 and AE2, with Stoker appointed "on loan". He arrived in Sydney harbour, after completing the longest submarine journey undertaken at the time, just months before the declaration of war. Both submarines were ordered out into the Pacific to hunt for German shipping and were involved in the taking of German New Guinea in September 1914. On the 14th of that month, AE1 was lost, apparently unable to resurface after diving. In early 1915, Stoker arrived in the Mediterranean theatre of war, having provided protection for a transport convoy carrying Anzac troops from Melbourne.

Stoker, who had repeatedly requested permission to attempt to breach the Dardanelles, was finally summoned by Commodore Roger Keyes and given the go-ahead. Admiral Sir John De Robeck, Vice-Admiral of the Mediterranean Fleet, had no doubt of the importance of the mission, telling him: "If you succeed there is no calculating the result it will cause, and it may well be that you have done more to finish the war than any other act accomplished."

In the early hours of 25 April 1915, the AE2 set sail for the 35-mile long Dardanelles. Spotted at Kephez and fired upon, Stoker dived and, still submerged, he negotiated the Turkish minefields, only coming up to periscope depth twice to check he was on course, the restraining wires of the mines scrapping against the submarine's hull. At one point, as he attempted to avoid

Turkish destroyers that were attempting to ram him, he ran aground under the land guns, but, as these couldn't be lowered sufficiently to fire on the beached submarine, it was able to be re-floated and escape. Stoker, who had torpedoed a Turkish gunboat and successfully avoided others sent to hunt for him, decided to wait on an underwater bank until dark and for 16 hours the crew sat in silence submerged at 80 feet. When he resurfaced he was able to make it into the Sea of Marmara, the first submarine to do so despite earlier attempts.

His achievement inspired others, with Royal Navy submarines subsequently penetrating the Turks defences in Stoker's wake. This led to AE2's downfall, however. On 30 April, as Stoker attempted to rendezvous with one of the Royal Navy submarines, he was caught on the surface by Turkish gunboats and his hull damaged by shellfire. Stoker ran up the white flag, or rather a white tablecloth, as an indication that he was willing to surrender so as to buy enough time to scuttle his ship and save the crew.

Although he had attacked a number of ships without success, Stoker had made his presence felt with the result that the Turks had abandoned plans to reinforce Gallipoli by sea. His actions won him the Distinguished Service Order (though Victoria Crosses were awarded to the commanders of the British submarines who had followed him through the Narrows). After the war he returned to the Royal Navy briefly before deciding on a change of career – turning to the theatre as an actor, writer and director. He regularly appeared on the West End stage, on radio, and had parts in eight movies. During the Second World War he served on the training ship HMS *Caroline* in Belfast, worked in public relations and was involved in the planning for the D-Day landings. Henry Stoker died in London on 2 February 1966, his 81st birthday.

PICKING UP THE DEAD AND DYING:
The Rev Robert Spence

Former soldier turned clergyman Robert Spence accompanied the Royal Munster Fusiliers ashore at Suvla Bay. From Maralin, County Down, he had fought in the Boer War with the Imperial Yeomanry at the turn of the century and was serving as junior minister of Lisburn Methodist Church in November 1914, when he volunteered to be a chaplain. Attached to the 10th (Irish) Division, his ship arrived off the peninsula before dawn, where he found the Royal Navy bombarding the Turkish emplacements in preparation for the coming assault. He wrote home:

"The division had been scattered for some reason, so I elected to accompany the stretcher-bearers who went with the first landing party. In a veritable shower of shrapnel we set off from the troop ship, tightly packed in a landing barge, to commence the work to which we had been looking forward for months. The day had at last come, and an ever-memorable one it must be, for every moment of it bristled with danger, and, but for the protecting care of the great All Father I would not now be writing to you. Our barge unfortunately ran aground too soon, and this gave the enemy an advantage he was not slow to take. He soon got the range, making it necessary for us to disperse by jumping into the water and swimming for it. One was not allowed to carry much pack, and the little we had was soon discarded as the necessity arose for helpers. What an experience it was! Shoulder deep in shell-swept waters, struggling to help wounded men to keep their heads above water, and get them ashore, expecting all the time a bursting shell to finish off both helpers and helped! It is impossible to say how long one was thus engaged – it might have been hours – perhaps only a few minutes."

He went on:

"As the men landed, they formed up hurriedly on the beach, and immediately began the assault on the enemy's position. What an ordeal was theirs! As soon as they emerged from their cover on the beach, landmines began to explode. These were quite unexpected, and might very well have had a demoralising effect on young and fresh troops; but braver men never fixed bayonets, and literally with the limbs and bodies of their comrades, who had been blown into the air, falling heavily upon them, they went forward, nervous and white – small wonder – but with steadiness, dash, and determination that merited the success that was achieved."

The Rev Spence stayed on the beach to help attend to the wounded and to give the dead a decent, if swift, burial, before following on, in pouring rain, behind the attacking troops. Darkness forced the stretcher parties to call a halt to their activities though sleep was almost impossible.

"Our clothes were wet, no kit was allowed to be carried, and so there were no blankets. The two days' rations had been soaked in sea-water and blood – so tired, cold, and hungry we lay down behind stones and rocks. But there was no sleep! The work and sights of the day just past, the rip of rifle fire, thunder of guns, and groans of wounded, made that impossible, and one welcomed the hour for rising."

Just before dawn, Spence was asked to take charge of a squad of stretcher bearers going up to the frontline to collect those who had been wounded during the night. He recalled:

"We left the beach at 3.00 am in a march that was weird in the extreme, a long line of men in single file winding their way silently through brushwood and over rock, presenting a serpent-like appearance as the darkness was lit up by the flashes from the guns of the fleet. Frequently we were challenged by an outpost, and frequently hailed by wounded men unable to make their way to the dressing-station. Sometimes we stumbled over the lifeless form of a brave fellow who had given his life for his country. One such incident brought home to me with tremendous force the gigantic tragedy of war. We were nearing the firing life and somewhat apprehensive, when, close by, in the gathering light of the early dawn, I saw a man lying face downwards, motionless, lifeless. There had been all too many such incidents earlier, but the forms could not be recognised. On looking closely at the features, I found it was my good friend Lieutenant Lee, a young fellow whose successful college career promised a future of rare brilliance. He had laid all on his country's altar.

Twenty-four hours before we were laughing and chatting together on the troopship, where he was so full of life and spirit. Now I was looking through tears on his lifeless body. A grave having been dug on our return from the firing-line later, we laid his broken body in its last resting-place, on a rocky slope overlooking the Aegean Sea."

The young officer was possibly Lieutenant Joseph Bagnall Lee, of the 6th Royal Munster Fusiliers, who was aged 27 and from Blackrock, County Dublin, and a newly-qualified barrister. His grave was subsequently lost and today he is remembered on the Helles Memorial.

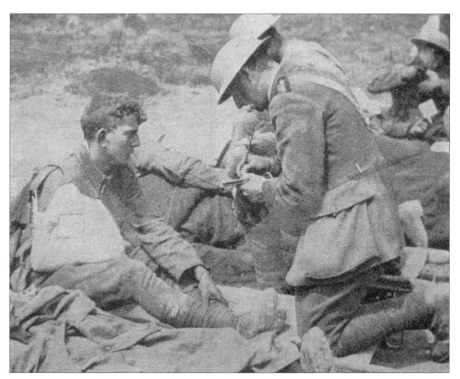

Army chaplains comforted the wounded, prayed over the dead and attempted to console in the man-made hell of the battlefield. Here a padre is writing a field postcard for a wounded man so his family will know he is still alive.
(From the Times History of the War 1914, published 1915)

LANDING AT ANZAC COVE:
Private P Murray

On the morning of 6 August 1915, the men of the 5th Connaught Rangers, attached to the Anzac Corps, began landing at Anzac Cove in a fleet of launches. After taking shelter under the cliffs, they began making their way along "Deadly Shrapnel Gully," according to Private P Murray. The Galway man recalled:

"All was peace and quietness, until the Australians started to advance, when there commenced one of the most terrific bombardments and rifle and machine-gun firing that ever was witnessed on the Peninsula before, and then our casualties started but they were very slight. Every shell passed over us where we were lying, but thanks to Colonel Jourdain's judgment we were in a place of comparative safety. For about eight hours or more the bombardment lasted, and it was about the most terrific ever was seen in the war. There were about 18 or more battleships playing on it along with our land artillery. About midnight on the next night we were served out with white armlets for identification purposes, and in a few hours word came for us to move up to the firing line, and then we began to see some sights of our comrades, hundreds of them passed us wounded, some of the awfulist wounds one could see. But that was not all; there were about twice as many killed, and every time we would look around you could see nothing but dying or dead. However, it had not much effect on the Connaughts for they were as jolly as if they were in camp in England, and mind you we had lost a few men ourselves."

Murray's battalion, part of the 29th Brigade of the 10th (Irish) Division, had formally been established on 19 August 1914. Raised by Lieutenant Colonel Henry Francis Newdigate Jourdain, it was initially based in Galway before moving to Dublin. Four days after the Connaught's arrival, they were thrown into the thick of the fighting. Murray went on:

"All went well with us till about the 10th August, when we marched the night before away from where we were, and word came that the rest of our Division, RIR, Leinsters and 10th Hants, were after making an advance on our left wing and that they were being driven back, so our regiment was sent for and after a few hours' march we arrived at the scene of action and just in the nick of time, when we arrived there, it knocked us out to see all the casualties among our Division; two-thirds of it was cut up. While we were resting, Captain RB Cooper, A Company, stood up and told us that there was a breastwork near the enemy's line, that some of our comrades were up there holding out and that there was no chance for them, so he told us that he promised the General that we (A Company) would get to the breastwork and hold it till not a man remained.

At our Colonel's word we advanced away from the hill and up towards the breastwork. Considering the size of the action we had very few casualties. There were a lot wounded but none killed, and all the time we were very short of water. A and B Companies advanced together and D and C Companies remained behind for supports. I was acting as observer to Captain Cooper, and in company with a signaller, Private Gilligan, when about at the crest of the hill Gilligan was ordered to send a message back, and no sooner did he raise his hand than he received two gunshot wounds which knocked him out of action. A few minutes later I was ordered to take the range of where our enemy was lying, and I had just set to work in the open when I got knocked out myself, passing my instruments to the next man, Private Marples, who was killed shortly afterwards."

Private Vesey Marples died on 21 August 1915, one of 220 deaths suffered by his battalion. His body was never recovered and he is commemorated on the Helles Memorial. The 10th Division, including the 5th Connaughts, were withdrawn from Gallipoli at the end of September and transferred to the Macedonian front.

Private Murray was later transferred to the 1st Garrison Battalion of Royal Irish Fusiliers stationed at Colaba Barracks, Bombay, India.

SLAUGHTER ON 'CAVE HILL':
Sergeant RT Nolan

The 6th Royal Dublin Fusiliers, formed at Naas in August 1914, landed at Suvla Bay on 7 August 1915. Among its ranks was Sergeant RT Nolan, a former student of St Malachy's College and Queen's University, Belfast, from Whitehead, County Antrim. It was to prove a rude awakening for him, as he told his father, Richard, in a letter sent from his hospital bed in Malta. Describing his experiences as a "horrible nightmare," his ordeal had begun as the men, in a fleet of small boats, approached the shore.

"Ye gods, what a sight! The whole coast was ablaze with shells and rockets, and the noise was terrific. It reminded me of the 'Waterloo' night we had at home. Whilst we were gazing in wonder there came my first shell, which burst alongside the steamer without doing any damage. And then a few more dropped round us. Our ship cleared. Half an hour later the lighters came along. Whilst leaving the lighter we were shelled twice, and two of my platoon were hit. We then had to advance along the beach for about one and half miles under frightful artillery fire. At one dip in the beach we had to wait until a shell would burst, and then rush forward before the next had time to come. We were lucky, and got to a small hill under cover. Not so other regiments."

The next few days were spent on fatigues, carrying water and ammunition up to the front lines, and dodging the Turkish artillery shelling. The Dubs then advanced over a dry lake, believing they were going to relieve another battalion in the trenches only to discover they were in support of an advance intended to take Chocolate Hill, its slopes rich in gorse bushes and olive trees. "We were engaging in a proper soldiers' battle – no trenches at all, but just a case of who could blow the other first to the land of sweety mice," wrote Sergeant Nolan.

"Suppose Cave Hill to be the hill – it is about the same height – and imagine that at the back of the Cave Hill is a sheer wall of rock – twice as high again – extending all along the back. About 3.45 am we came into action about, say, Whitewell. Day is breaking. Ah, God, what a day! We move along the Antrim Road round towards Old Cavehill Road. The

Turks seem to know exactly where we are. Now, if I could describe vividly all the sights I saw and what happened on that awful Monday, I would not. And the memory of that awful day is locked up in my head for ever.

From, say, Cavehill Road we were ordered to take the hill. We went up through the bushes and gorse in an atmosphere of bursting shells, smoke, screams, curses, dying moans, and the crack of rifles. Half-way up the hill we came into rifle fire. The bullets were dropping like hail. You could hear and feel them whizzing past you. Officers and men were falling like skittles. The Turks then caught us between two cross fires, and someone gave the order to retire. At one time a portion of the hill on our left caught fire. We then moved round to the right – we have to leave our wounded there. Shortly after that, something told me that a sniper was trying to pick me. That something proved right, for I got hit on the outside of the big toe of the left foot. It didn't take me long to hop into the nearest bit of cover, leave down my rifle, take off my puttee, then my boot, then my stocking, and dress the wound."

Nolan managed to make his way down the hill to a field hospital, which he found to be under enemy shelling. He was loaded into a wagon and taken down to a beach hospital, from which he was evacuated to Malta via hospital ship. His wound, he told the family, would soon heal but "the reaction of the fight has made me very nervous. However, it won't take me long to pull round, when back I go. Of the five officers in my company, one was killed and three injured. The regiment, as far as I can gather, is washed out, after having maintained the reputation of the 'Old Dubs'. I must have had someone's prayers whilst on that hill, as it seemed next to an impossibility to escape being killed."

The men of 6th Royal Dublin Fusiliers were relieved on 12 August, remaining on the peninsula until early October when the battalion was moved to Salonika, later serving in Egypt and Palestine.

A NURSE AT THE DARDANELLES:
Henrietta Breakey

Even before reaching the beaches of Gallipoli, 23-year-old Henrietta Breakey had proved to herself and those around her what she was made of. The Red Cross nurse, a member of the First-Aid Volunteer Detachment Riding Corps, had only just completed her crash course in basic battlefield aid when she was dispatched to the front. As her troopship entered the Aegean Sea it came under fire from Turkish cruisers.

"The loud reports of the guns in quick succession, and the bursting of the shells so terrified my comrade sisters that they stood in groups, weeping and wailing, totally unfit to do their duty, and were sent into the 'captain's den'. Putting my trust in God, I somehow overcame my terror and with the help of our only doctor, went into the midst of that awful struggle, lifting, tending, and soothing those who were speedily passing into the Great Beyond, as they fell one after another. The battle lasted from three o'clock in the evening till after six. Our losses were heavy, but otherwise we fared well. The horror of seeing our brave men who died so nobly being lowered into the deep waters of the Aegean Sea was a sight I could not look at, so I turned away with the feeling that I wanted to see no more of the war…"

Her spirits lifted again, however, when on reaching land she was promoted to staff sister in consequences of her cool head onboard ship. Writing home to Drumskelt House, Ballybay, County Monaghan, from No 8 Truter Camp on 28 September 1915, she described life amid the rolling hills, bad tempered mules, extreme temperatures and menacing enemy.

"When the sun sinks it would absolutely freeze you, and we feel the cold, sharp air piercing through and through us in our wet and sweaty clothes, with no means of changing them, as we are in the thick of the fray and a long way from camp; so we just pick up a dead soldier's great coat off the battlefield, wrap ourselves up in it, and in this way manage to evade catching chills and colds. We have no bed to sleep on in camp, but are just rolled up in a sleeping kit with a veil overhead to keep off mosquitoes. We have to work night and day, and can only get rest when opportunity permits, or when we are about spent up, and unable to stand the heavy strain on our constitution any longer without some rest."

It was part of her job, with the help of specially trained St Bernard dogs, to search the battlefield for wounded, with both friend and foe alike receiving the same treatment. "Life in the trenches is very severe on our soldiers, as they are there for days at a time," she wrote.

"When I landed it was to the trenches I was first sent, to oversee and direct a band of sisters there. How shall I describe the horrible sights which met our gaze, no matter where we looked! Where a shell burst the dead bodies of our men were literally piled one on top of the other. We dressed the wounds of those who were living, and made them comfortable, the dead we lifted tenderly, and put outside the trench, so that they would not be trodden over. After nine days of heavy work in the trenches, I was sent to the field, and worked in the thick of that terrible hand-to-hand fight, the fiercest battle ever fought on the Gallipoli Peninsula. It lasted four days and nights. We could not get more than an hour's rest at a time, and a number of our sisters, unable to stand the heavy strain, had to give up.

I had to manage somehow with about half of our usual staff, and was so terribly overworked and worried over so many sisters getting knocked up, I simply didn't know what to do. Of course, I cabled home to headquarters to send nurses at once, but that would not help us much, as it takes such a time getting to the Dardanelles. So we had to just buck up again and again, and force ourselves on to help our men. By the time the battle was fought we were all wearied out with want of rest and proper food. For days after that I had stinging pains all through me and was very much frightened lest I had caught the fever. I did not lie down, but worked it off by helping others who were in agonies of pain, and put my own troubles entirely in the background."

In October 1915, Staff Nurse Breakey was sent back to England with a hospital ship and when returning to the front was injured when the train she was travelling in was shelled. Despite shrapnel wounds to the groin and hip, she attempted to treat others in her carriage. After surgery she was sent back to Britain to recuperate, returning to duty in the Spring of 1916. After the war she married before immigrating to the United States.

A LAST LETTER HOME:
Second Lieutenant James Ellis

Second Lieutenant James Graves St John Ellis was killed at Gallipoli on 11 October 1915 while serving with the Royal Engineers. The 28-year-old, with a wife in Belfast and his parents in Dublin, was buried in Hill 10 Cemetery. His last letter home was dated 30 September. It read:

"It is a beautiful sunny day as I write sitting in my dug-out, overlooking a beautiful vista, embracing many hills that are now famous. The flies are buzzing around, they make rest during the day impossible for our worn-out men, and are hated worse than the Turks. An occasional shell bursts overhead or travels down to the beach – there goes one now – they sound so lazy, just like somebody trying to whistle without actually succeeding. Then the air crack of the rifles and the noise of ricocheting bullets – like large buzzing bees – occasionally one travelling sideways gives out a musical note in transit – dash these flies, I'll have to light my pipe. That's better! Things are very quiet here – perhaps the lull before the storm… War is hell! We work out between the enemy's and our own lines every night. Occasionally one sees nasty sights, smells nasty smells (only this all the time), and sees men die like men doing some simple task that is necessary for the safety of the others. Out there where we have done some wiring lie some thirty unburied Territorials – probably killed in August last. One officer is staring at the sky, his mouth open, yet still grasping his rifle with fixed bayonet – in death symbolic of the brave spirit he possessed.

We of the auxiliary services try to do our little bit, but let no man rob the infantry of their laurels. They are too splendid for words – work day and night – fatigues, digging, cleaning up – endless work – yet they are cheerful, and go out often to death with joke and smile. Let nobody talk of Irish disloyalty – our troops out here are simply splendid. I have seen all, Scotch, English, and Irish, but to the latter I give the palm, not that the others are less brave or enduring, but for the smile in the Irish eye, the passing round of the joke, the religious subcurrent so strongly in evidence here; I heard an Irish soldier, a rough, country chap, reprove a Scotchman for swearing. One night we were out in the open digging, trying to throw up in rocky soil a parapet to protect us from the enemy's snipers. It was slow, slow, heart-breaking work, and cost us many men. The enemy became suddenly very active – fing, phat, ping, buzz-z-z, came the bullets, mostly over our heads. An Irish voice a short distance from me broke the noise, 'Now an' aren't they a quarrelsome crowd!'

We heard the good news of the advance in France yesterday – same day as it happened. We get telegraphic bulletins each evening. I enjoy the home-coming. But my heart aches for those whose dearest lie beneath crude wooden crosses everywhere around here. The living sleep beside the dead, and many, many unknown graves abound with 'In loving memory of a comrade,' written in indelible pencil on two pieces of a biscuit box, the orthodox memorial on each tomb. John Turk buries his dead in his parapets, drinks from springs which flow underneath, and yet survives disease and the smell."

James Ellis had been born in Dublin in 1887 and was 28 years old when killed. Today his remains lie buried at Hill 10 Cemetery, which was created after the war by bringing in dead from the temporary graveyards next to the dressing stations and on the beaches. The second lieutenant had been a pupil of the High School, Dublin, Andrew's College, St Stephen's Green, Dublin, and Trinity College in the city. An assistant engineer with the Canadian Pacific Railway before the war, he had married his wife, Florence Kennedy, on 1 August 1912, at Boston, United States. They appear to have lived at Rugby Terrace, Belfast, on his return to Ireland. His father, barrister-in-law William Edward Ellis, from County Kerry, was a Justice of the Peace who worked as a Local Government Auditor. His mother came from Jersey, in the Channel Islands.

TOURING THE FRONTLINE:
Second Lieutenant James Stokoe

Second Lieutenant James Clarke Stokoe couldn't wait to get into the action. When he finally got close in November 1915, shortly after being commissioned, the 22-year-old did the grand tour, soaking in the atmosphere at Gallipoli and lamenting he hadn't the time to visit the frontline trenches. Born at Newry, County Down, he later attended Manchester Grammar School before going on to Oxford University, where he had been a member of the Officer Training Corps. His excitement shines through in a letter written to his mother on 6 November. A member of the 14th Manchester Regiment, but attached to the 11th Battalion, he had been tasked with bringing in a detachment of reinforcements and had arrived off Anzac beach shortly after 9.00 pm the previous evening, just as it was getting dark. "It was quite a bright night, for the stars were out in full force," he wrote:

"The whole thing looked just like the shows we used to see at Bellevue. The harbour from the boat looked like the lake, and then straight up from the shore the hills rose almost perpendicularly. Rifle fire was going on all the time, along with heavier reports of bombing. A destroyer was anchored on our right, throwing a searchlight on the Turkish lines, which came right down to the sea at that spot, and which we could see quite plainly, and they, of course, could see us. Big flare lights were continually going up there, because they were expecting an attack on a trench there which we captured the night before. Just as we arrived in the bay a cruiser a mile or two out at sea opened fire over our heads on the Turkish lines at the top of the ridge. Every time she fired we saw a flash of light, then heard a continuous whistling sound in the air above us, and quite a good while after the shell had passed we heard the bang of the explosion. Then we could see where the shells burst, and later on hear the bang of that. Over the ridge a Turkish searchlight was sweeping the sky for our aeroplanes, and occasionally a stray bullet cleared the ridge and went whistling past. Yet it was what was called a quiet night."

Stokoe and his men were transferred to lighters from the ship and taken ashore. On the pier he handed over his detachment to their officers before going "for a stroll round" as he put it. "I had to return on the same boat, but it did not leave till seven o'clock the next morning, so I had lots of time to potter about," he told his mother.

"I hadn't time to go out to the firing trenches, but I wandered around the gun pits and howitzer batteries and saw all there was to be seen and learned how they worked the firing. Then I went along all the coast and got half way up the ridge to an officer's dug-out. I finished my inspection at about three o'clock in the morning, and then I found a corner out of the wind, curled up and slept till six o'clock. It is funny that the rifle shots and bomb explosions and big guns firing did not keep me awake, but I never noticed them at all. It might have been the most natural thing in the world to go to sleep in a row like that. I got on a small launch at 20 past 6 to go out to the boat. The sun was just rising, and that was the signal for both sides to start a bit more shelling. A British destroyer anchored just a little way out started it and fired a line of shells all along the Turkish trenches on the ridge. The Turkish 'Beachy Bill' then started and shelled the beach we had just left, and some of the shipping had narrow escapes, but we were too far out. The same boat though had been hit three times only four days before, though no real damage was done. We left soon after 7 o'clock and had a very good passage back. It was a fine experience and I enjoyed it very much. I heard from the commanding officer of the Australians when I got back that my trip had entitled me to an 'Anzac' bar of the Dardanelles medal, but whether I get it is another question."

James Stokoe was never to see his medal. Back on the Gallipoli peninsula the following month, he was killed on 12 December and today lies buried in Green Hill Cemetery, close to the Anzac–Suvla road.

"In June, in my seventeenth year, I had decided to see what this Great War was like. I cannot plead I went on the advice of John Redmond or any other politician, that if we fought for the British we would secure Home Rule for Ireland, nor can I say I understood what Home Rule meant. I was not influenced by the lurid appeal to fight to save Belgium or small nations. I knew nothing about nations, large or small. I went to the war for no other reason than that I wanted to see what war was like, to get a gun, to see new countries and to feel a grown man. Above all I went because I knew no Irish history and had no national consciousness."

Tom Barry, Killorglin, County Kerry
Royal Field Artillery and future Irish rebel

1916

BLEEDING FRANCE WHITE

After conducting what was effectively a holding war throughout the previous year, the Allies were in a much better position to go on the offensive in 1916. They had extracted themselves from the Gallipoli disaster, freeing up more reserves; the divisions of the New Army had arrived in France and were being made battle ready; and the shell crisis had been addressed, with more guns and ammunition than ever before available. Even before the year had begun the decision had been taken to launch a joint British-French offensive on the Western Front that summer. The enemy, however, was similarly determined to make a move and on 21 February launched a campaign that aimed, in the words of the German commander Falkenhayn, to "bleed France white". The Battle of Verdun was to rage until 18 December 1916, and cost approximately one million lives. The great Allied offensive planned that year for the Somme front was brought forward to help draw off German reserves from Verdun, with the British having to undertake the lion's share of the fighting, though the French were still able to take part though to a lesser degree than initially envisaged.

Elsewhere trench warfare continued as before, with death and injuries a daily occurrence. Sergeant John F McGuinn, of the 2nd Irish Guards, was one of those to lose his life. He was killed in February 1916, shortly after he had posted his will to his brother in Galway with the message "life is a bit precarious". He went on:

> "I have been watching the shells all day; they come in droves roaring through the sky; there is no house left standing in the village. I had an impression that I would be nervous under shell fire, but when we came up last night I had a buoyant feeling that I never had before. It is just providence and God's goodness and I don't even mind the shells. I would not miss the sensation for worlds."

Another letter on 4 February told of how even the dead were not allowed to rest in peace: "Last night I was startled by an unearthly roar like a peal of thunder, and a terrible whistling overhead. They were the shells from our own

Opposite: The Royal Inniskilling Fusiliers and the Royal Dublin Fusiliers in action south of Hulluch, in April, 1916. (From The Great War magazine, published 1915-1919)

guns, and the retaliation from the Germans picked up the roads by the yard. In the graves where our soldiers were buried we saw crosses being hurled into the air by the explosions."

Much closer to home, the Easter Rising of 1916 completely caught out the military authorities. On Easter Monday, members of the Irish Volunteers and Irish Citizen Army marched into the city and began taking over buildings, including the General Post Office – which served as the rebellion's headquarters and seat of the declared provisional government – the Four Courts, Jacob's Factory, Boland's Bakery, the South Dublin Union, St Stephen's Green and College of Surgeons. The British army, initially outnumbered by more than two-to-one in Dublin, went on the defensive, including mounting guards on strategic buildings, while it summoned up reinforcements. Soldiers and police caught out in the open became easy targets.

One of the first victims that day was Francis Henry Browning, a former Ireland international cricketer and the serving President of the Irish Rugby Football Union. The Dublin man, a barrister, had raised and commanded a unit of the Association of Volunteer Training Corps. On the morning of Easter Monday the men, who were a form of Home Guard, were returning to the city after a route march. Dressed in civilian clothes with arm-bands, they carried rifles but no ammunition. As they passed along Beggars Bush they came under fire, with four killed and three others wounded. Browning, who was aged 48, was wounded in Haddington Road and died two days later. As the week went on the street battles became ever more intense while the use of artillery reduced some of the rebel strongholds to ruins before they unconditionally surrendered. The subsequent executions of many of the rising's leaders caused public outrage in Ireland. News of events in Dublin rapidly reached the frontlines in France – where the Germans put up placards opposite trenches held by the 16th (Irish) Division telling them of the uprising.

The end of May 1916, also saw the biggest naval battle of the war. Due to the British being able, unbeknown to the Germans, to decipher the enemy's secret codes they were aware of a planned raid on the southern English coast. On 31 May, the entire High Seas Fleet clashed with the Royal Navy's Grand Fleet at the Battle of Jutland. The Germans lost eleven ships, including a battle cruiser, light cruisers and five destroyers with considerable damage to many of the surviving ships, while the British lost three battle cruisers, four armoured cruisers and eight destroyers. Though the battle was inconclusive, it increased the German reluctance to engage with the Royal Navy.

Although the main fighting was on the Somme and further south at Verdun, the war of attrition continued unabated on the British-held front. It was the deaths of two Irishmen a long way from the front line in the summer of 1916, however, that caused the greatest public outrage, leading to an official protest from the British Government to be lodged with Germany. Both men were prisoners-of-war and as such should have been under the protection of the enemy yet were shot by their guards in separate incidents that made headlines in the newspapers. The Under Secretary for Foreign Affairs, Lord Newton, who had special responsibly for prisoners of war, told the House of Lords:

"The American Embassy in Berlin notified the Government on 7 July that Patrick Moran, of the Connaught Rangers, had been shot by a guard at the working camp, near Limburg, on 28 May. The commandant of the camp told the American representative that Moran, while intoxicated, attacked a guard, who shot him dead in self-defence. On 10 July the American Embassy informed the Government that another Irish prisoner, William Devlin, Munster Fusiliers, had been shot at the Limburg working camp. When Ambassador Gerard visited the camp in connection with the death of Moran the shooting of Devlin was concealed. It is important to note that according to our information both soldiers had refused to join Roger Casement in his proposed expedition to Ireland."

The British Government had addressed a strongly worded protest to the Germans on 13 July, he said, adding:

"We demanded an immediate inquiry, in the presence of a member of the American Embassy, into the shooting of the two prisoners and the punishment of those found guilty. We pointed out that the proceedings would be all the more infamous if it were found to be connected with the men's refusal to join Casement. On the 20th we received a detailed report of the shooting of Moran, from which it appeared that the German authorities refused to allow Ambassador Gerard to talk to witnesses accept in the presence of a German officer."

The initial reports, while largely correct, were inaccurate in some crucial details. It was actually Private 'John' Moran, not 'Patrick', who had been killed, and William Devlin was a member of the 2nd Royal Dublin Fusiliers, not the Musters. Both men had been in captivity since falling into the enemy's hands during the early fighting of 1914. Moran, from Dungarvan, County Waterford, had been in a group of prisoners who had been working on a project outside Limburg Camp on 28 May 1916. On their way back to their accommodation in a local village their German escorts took them to an inn, where they were permitted to have a drink. Moran, it was claimed, demanded further alcohol, becoming more and more agitated and threatening and attacking a local civilian official and his guard, repeatedly hurling objects at him until shot. An investigation found that his escort had acted in self-defence though was found to have broken military regulations by allowing the prisoners to consume alcohol. Devlin, from Dublin, was an 'old soldier' who had returned to his regiment on the declaration of war. Details of his death at Limberg Camp are sketchy, though the German authorities claimed that he had ignored two warning shots before being wounded by a third on 2 July 1916, and dying of his injuries the following day. It was concluded that the German corporal who had opened fire had acted in self-defence and no further action was taken against him. Devlin, who was 38 at the time of his death, lies in Cologne Southern Cemetery, and Moran in Niederzwhren Cemetery, Hessen.

In the air it was the German ace Manfred Albrecht von Richthofen, known as the Red Baron, who was making his mark. Just five days before Christmas 1916 he claimed his first Irish victims. Second Lieutenant Lionel George D'Arcy was a 28-year-old from the Ballinamore Bridge area of County Galway. A former member of the Connaught Rangers, he was serving with the 18th Squadron of the Royal Flying Corps when he took off in his FE2b bi-wing plane on 20 December. His observer was Sub-Lieutenant Reginald Cuthbert Whiteside who, though English-born, was the son of a County Armagh man, the Rev WC Whiteside, and had been educated at Campbell College in Belfast.

In the skies over Moreuil, in the Picardie region of northern France, the two Irishmen encountered Richthofen in his Albatros DII. The dog fight was short and brutal. The Red Baron struck first, wounding Whiteside and putting a bullet through the engine of the British airplane. As the FE2b plunged towards the ground Richthofen followed, continuing to fire bursts of machine-gun fire into the doomed plane until it crashed, killing both men. They were the Red Baron's 14th 'kill' and the second of the day. Others were to follow, including Second Lieutenant James Smyth, from Belfast, shot down south of La Folie Wood, France, on 11 March 1917, and Australian-born Captain James Maitland, whose family hailed from County Antrim, who was killed near Vimy Ridge on 13 April 1917.

FIRST ULSTER DIVISION DEATHS:
Second Lieutenant Robert MacDermott

Second Lieutenant Robert Wilson MacDermott, also known as Robin, was the first officer of the 36th (Ulster) Division to be killed in action. The 25-year-old, the son of the high-profile Belfast clergyman the Rev Dr John MacDermott, of Belmont church, was supervising a group of men from the 8th Royal Irish Rifles on 8 January 1916, when a German shell fell in their midst. In addition to MacDermott, Rifleman George Parkinson Connor, 23, from Moira, County Down, and Corporal Henry Murphy, a 27-year-old married man from Belfast, were killed. All three were laid to rest in what today is Auchonvillers Military Cemetery on the Somme.

News Letter Editor William Geddes Anderson was among a group of newspaper men taken to the front in France in order for them to be able to prepare a series of articles aimed at promoting further recruitment. By chance he was returning to his accommodation after his tour of the trenches when he came across the burial party. He reported:

"On our return to billet quarters I noticed the badge of the Royal Irish Rifles on two squads of men standing at a farm yard entrance, and spoke to them. They were the ration party of a battalion of the Belfast Brigade of the Ulster Division; the battalion was in the trenches. I heard sad news from them. On the previous morning a shell from the enemy had landed in one of the trenches, and it killed Second Lieutenant MacDermott, son of the Rev Dr MacDermott, of Belmont, and a corporal and a private who were standing close to him. 'We buried them over there this morning,' said the corporal of the party, pointing to an orchard surrounding farm buildings on the opposite side of the road. The orchard had been converted into a little cemetery. All round its margin were ranged lines of neatly-made, white-painted wooden crosses, each bearing the name of the dead hero who slept his last sleep below.

I crossed the road, passed into the little 'God's Acre,' and spent a minute's solemn communion with the dead at the foot of my young friend's grave, for I had known him in his revered father's congregation. He was as fine a young man as ever came out of Ulster. When he joined to do his bit for King and country with the rest of his battalion of the Ulster Volunteers Lieut. MacDermott had all the prospects of a fine future before him. That future is gone, but his end was glorious – killed at the post of duty in the very front of the firing line. Such is war. The funeral took place in the early hours of this (Sunday) morning by candle light in the village hard by, under fire from machine-gun and artillery. So Second Lieutenant MacDermott had a soldier's burial in very truth.

Since I have returned home I have learnt that two privates of C Company of his battalion have cut and erected on Lieut MacDermott's grave a very handsome little gravestone cut out of a block of chalk. This touching tribute to their late officer's memory is but symptomatic of the relationship that I found everywhere I went existing between the men and their officers. A splendid bond of brotherhood permeates the whole of our armies in France and Flanders, and it has a wonderful effect in maintaining the moral and the spirits of the rank and file."

Second Lieutenant MacDermott had attended Campbell College and Queen's University, Belfast, and had intended to train as a barrister. He had been a section commander in the UVF's 6th East Belfast Regiment before the war. His father, the Very Rev Dr John MacDermott, served as Moderator of the Presbyterian Church in 1903. Another of his sons, John Clark MacDermott, later Baron MacDermott, won the Military Cross during the war and went on to enjoy a highly successful political and legal career, including being Lord Chief Justice of Northern Ireland.

The first soldier of the Ulster Division to be killed in action was Rifleman Samuel Hill, who died of wounds on 22 October 1915. A member of the 12th Royal Irish Rifles, the 23-year-old was the son of Samuel and Elizabeth Hill of Rushpark, Whitehouse, Belfast. Although born in Ayr, Scotland, he had lived at Dunloskin, Carrickfergus, and had worked for Barn Mills and played football for Barn Swifts football team before the war. His grave is in Doullens Communal Cemetery Extension No 1.

AN AGONISING DEATH AT HOME:
Private William Coulson

The huge military war machine had only one goal: final victory. This unflinching attitude made the authorities virtually oblivious, and at times callously indifferent, to the emotions and problems of the ordinary men and women who had sacrificed so much in volunteering to serve. Suicides and self-harm, both at the front and at home, were not uncommon, though few faced a more agonizing or prolonged death than Private William Coulson.

Although originally from Christchurch, Dublin, he had enlisted at Coleraine, County Londonderry, in November 1915 and had been in training with the 3rd Royal Inniskilling Fusiliers only a matter of weeks when he received word that his wife, who had been in poor health for some time, had gone missing from their home. Returning to Coleraine on 6 December on two days' leave, he frantically searched for her but without success. Private Coulson applied to have his leave extended so he could continue the search but his request was flatly turned down. That evening he attempted to end his own life by taking ammonia but only succeeded in badly burning his throat. He quickly regretted his actions and sought help from his next door neighbour, who assisted in having him admitted to the workhouse infirmary in the town.

He was subsequently arrested by Sergeant Henry Holmes and charged with attempted suicide. Brought from his hospital bed to stand in the dock of a court, the Recorder directed that he be sent back to the hospital until the doctors could certify that he was fit to travel. Unable to eat due to his throat injuries, Private Coulson was transferred to hospital in Londonderry on 24 January 1916, in a very weak condition. According to a Dr Cooke, who gave evidence at the Coroner's inquest, the soldier was badly emaciated and unable to swallow more than a few drops of nourishment. An attempt to give him sustenance through rectal feeding was given up on 29 January when a decision to operate on Coulson, despite his weak condition, was taken. An opening was made in his stomach to allow food to be passed directly and appeared successful initially with some improvement in his condition. On 3 February, however, he took a turn for the worse and passed away the following day from "exhaustion". Private Coulson was buried in Londonderry City Cemetery. At the time of the inquest into his death, on 8 February 1916, his wife was still missing and presumed dead.

Another soldier to meet a callous end was Rifleman Patrick Sullivan. After serving 12 years in the Royal Irish Fusiliers, he had left the army and returned to civilian life. However, with the outbreak of the First World War he was quick to return to the colours, serving with the Royal Irish Rifles and taking part in the early battles. Following a German gas attack, however, he developed "consumption" and was sent back to Ireland, finally being discharged as unfit for further active service. He was admitted to Whiteabbey Sanatorium on 10 November 1915, remaining there until 31 December, when he signed himself out. His plan was to travel to England to meet up with a brother who was in hospital there after being wounded serving with the Australian troops in the hope of accompanying him back to Oz. However, he discovered on his arrival in Weymouth that his brother had been part of a draft of Anzacs that had left for Australia four days previously.

Penniless, Sullivan was now stranded in the English coastal town. He found work in a cinema but his hacking cough and collapsing lungs soon contrived to make him too ill to work and he was admitted to the workhouse. After a lingering illness he passed away. His apparent last gasp plea to the doctors and the priest who attended to him was not to be laid to rest in a pauper's grave. His request was passed on to the army, but the reply came back that Sullivan was not entitled to a military funeral. As a consequence, the remains of the veteran soldier were buried in an unmarked grave in the burying ground attached to the workhouse.

The form of burial was raised at a meeting of the workhouse Guardians, who expressed their profound indignation that a soldier who had served his King and the Empire, and who had contacted the disease which had killed him, tuberculosis, on active duty should have come to such an end. They again made representations to the military authorities to remedy the situation. There were even questions asked in Parliament with independent nationalist MP Laurence Ginnell, who represented North Westmeath, raising the matter several times with the Under Secretary of State for War, the Scottish Liberal MP Harold John Tennant.

Rifleman Patrick Sullivan's grave, however, did not remain unmarked. The Commonwealth War Graves Commission, although it had no say in how or where he was buried initially as his death had taken place in the United Kingdom, was mandated to commemorate his passing. Today, the remains of Private Patrick Sullivan lie in Weymouth Cemetery, one of 62 burials there from the First World War marked by a standard CWGC headstone.

TEENAGE SURVIVOR OF THE *LUSITANIA*

The German sinking of the *Lusitania*, in which a number of American civilians were lost, did much to change the public's attitude towards the war in the United States. The sinking soon featured on recruitment posters.

DOING A MAN'S WORK

A special memorial to 23-year-old Lieutenant Albert Bourke, who died at the Battle of Aubers in May 1915, stands at Le Trou Aid Post Cemetery, Fleurbaix.
(Courtesy of the Commonwealth War Graves Commission)

ORDERED TO LEAVE IRELAND
Herbert Moore Pim, who regularly
changed his political direction,
was among the first men ordered
to leave Ireland under the Defence
of the Realm Act. Pim, using
the by-line 'A Newman', was a
regular contributor to the *Irish
News* following his conversion to
nationalism.
(Belfast Telegraph)

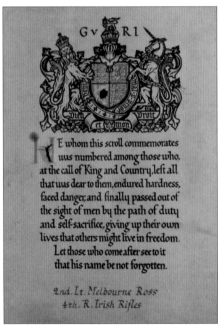

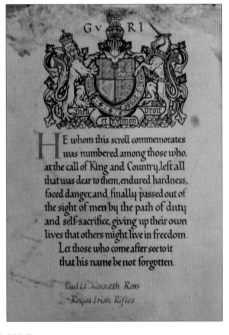

BROTHER OFFICERS WHO DIED SIDE BY SIDE
The death scrolls of brothers Second Lieutenant Melbourne Ross and Kenneth Ross,
who served and died together. *(Courtesy of the Royal Ulster Rifles Museum)*

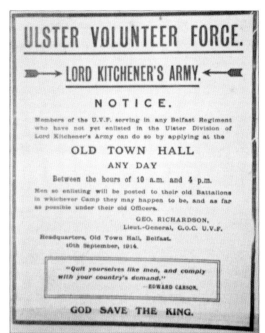

UVF MAN INTERNED BY THE GERMANS
While Ulster Volunteer Force members were being encouraged to enlist at home, David Doak was locked up in a former stable in Ruhleben Camp, Berlin. *(News Letter)*

UVF MAN INTERNED BY THE GERMANS
Conditions inside Ruhleben were cramped and food rations meagre, though the inmates had considerable freedom within the fences to organise their own entertainments. *(The Great War magazine, published 1915–1919)*

RETREATING WITH THE SERBIAN ARMY
After the entry of Bulgaria into the war, the Serbian army, with Beatrice Kerr and her fellow nurses in tow, was forced to retreat across snow-covered plains and into the mountains. She was forced to cling on to an artillery train after becoming separated from her party. (*The Times History of the War 1914, published 1915*)

RETREATING WITH THE SERBIAN ARMY
Medical units from throughout Britain were rapidly formed to travel to Serbia. Mrs St Clair Stobart led the field hospital, attending to both the wounded soldiers and refugees. She was later awarded the Serbian Order of St Sava and the Order of St John of Jerusalem. (*The Great War magazine, published 1915–1919*)

LANDING ON 'V' BEACH
The SS *River Clyde* beached at Cape Helles, Gallipoli. The ship was purposely run aground in order to facilitate rapid disembarkation of the soldiers through spacious doors cut in her side. *(The War Illustrated, published 1915)*

LANDING ON 'V' BEACH
The soldiers emerging from the converted steam collier the *River Clyde* were slaughtered as they attempted to make it ashore at 'V' beach.
(From A Popular History of the Great War, published 1933)

LIVING A CHARMED LIFE
Fr John Fahey landed with the
Australian troops at Anzac
Cove and was often to be found
in the frontline with the men.
*(Courtesy of the Archives of the
Catholic Archdiocese of Perth)*

BREACHING THE NARROWS
This sketch, drawn by a naval officer during the operations in the Dardanelles in
March 1915, shows how difficult it was for the Royal Navy to operate in such a
confined and heavily defended space.
(A Popular History of the Great War, published 1933)

LANDING AT ANZAC COVE
During the landings at Anzac Cove the 5th Connaught Rangers was attached to the
Anzac Corps. Gully Beach often came under artillery fire from the Turks after the
advances from the landing zone stalled.
(A Popular History of the Great War, published 1933)

A LAST LETTER HOME
After the landings all supplies came in by sea, along with the support troops such as
Second Lieutenant James Ellis serving with the Royal Engineers. Ultimately destined
to die at Gallipoli, he saw a beauty in the sacrifices being made every day.
(A Popular History of the Great War, published 1933)

TOURING THE FRONTLINE
The brutal reality of war was lost on Second Lieutenant James Stokoe on his first trip to Gallipoli as he went on his grand tour.
(A Popular History of the Great War, published 1933)

The Compulsory Service Act, passed by Parliament in January 1916, came into force on 2 March of that year but did not apply to Ireland.
(A Popular History of the Great War, published 1933)

1916: BLEEDING FRANCE WHITE
The French army was 'bled white' at Verdun, leading to it being unable to play as big a part in the Battle of Somme as had been previously planned. In this photograph a group of French soldiers are decorated for their bravery on the Verdun front.
(A Popular History of the Great War, published 1933)

FIRST ULSTER DIVISION DEATHS
Second Lieutenant Robert Wilson MacDermott, the first officer of the Ulster Division killed, was buried in what was then a makeshift cemetery in a little orchard. *(Author)*

MURDER AT PORTOBELLO BARRACKS
The fighting in Dublin during the Easter Rising resulted in many casualties and huge damage to the city. Here British troops take cover behind a makeshift barricade.
(A Popular History of the Great War, published 1933)

MURDER AT PORTOBELLO BARRACKS
Francis Sheehy Skeffington, pictured wearing a trilby hat, was an innocent victim of the uprising. He was murdered along with fellow journalists Thomas Dickson and Patrick McIntyre.
(The Great War magazine, published 1915–1919)

FUSILIERS SHOT AS SPIES

Men who became separated from their units behind enemy lines ran the risk of being viewed as spies and shot when eventually caught. A plaque on the wall marks the spot at Le Catelet where two Royal Irish Fusiliers soldiers were executed. *(Courtesy of Amanda Moreno, of the Royal Irish Regiment Museums Group)*

Royal Irish Fusiliers Donohoe and Martin, along with Englishman Private William Thorpe, lie side-by-side in Le Catelet Churchyard.
(Courtesy of Amanda Moreno, of the Royal Irish Regiment Museums Group)

THE BATTLE OF JUTLAND
An artist's impression of the British fleet coming into action at the Battle of Jutland.
(The Great War magazine, published 1915–1919)

THE BATTLE OF
JUTLAND
A mural on
the Kilcooley
estate, Bangor,
commemorating
the exploits of VC
hero Commander
Edward Barry
Bingham who
commanded
HMS *Nestor* at
Jutland. *(Author)*

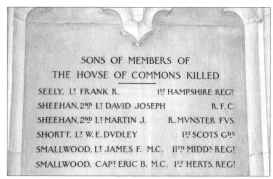

SONS OF MEMBERS OF
THE HOVSE OF COMMONS KILLED

SEELY, LT FRANK R.	1ST HAMPSHIRE REGT
SHEEHAN, 2ND LT DAVID JOSEPH	R.F.C.
SHEEHAN, 2ND LT MARTIN J.	R.MVNSTER FVS.
SHORTT, LT W.E.DVDLEY	1ST SCOTS GDS
SMALLWOOD, LT JAMES F. M.C.	11TH MIDDX REGT
SMALLWOOD, CAPT ERIC B. M.C.	1ST HERTS, REGT

WAR ON TWO FRONTS
The war took a terrible toll on some families, including that of Captain DD Sheehan, MP, of the Royal Munster Fusiliers, who lost two sons and a brother-in-law. He was invalided home in 1917 and is photographed here in Ballincollig Barracks, Cork, towards the end of that year. A commemorative panel in the House of Commons, London, is dedicated to 'Sons of Members of the House of Commons Killed'. *(Courtesy of Niall O'Siochain)*

WAR ON TWO FRONTS
Lieutenant Daniel Sheehan was killed in action on 10 May 1917 while flying a Sopwith Pup fighter biplane of 66 Squadron, Royal Flying Corps, based near Arras, France. *(Courtesy of Niall O'Siochain)*

LOST AT SEA

Earl Kitchener, an Irishman, was the Secretary of State for War and the face of defiance. He died two years into the war when HMS *Hampshire*, taking him to Russia for a secret meeting, sank after striking a mine off the coast of the Orkney Islands in Scotland. *(A Popular History of the Great War, published 1933)*

ULSTERMAN WHO SAVED 25,000 LIVES

25,000 Armenian refugees were saved from Turkish forces by Captain George Gracey, who armed some of them so that they could defend the convoy as it fled. They marched some 30 miles a day for five days under the watchful eyes of their protectors. *(The Great War magazine, published 1915-1919)*

LORD OF THE ARTILLERY SHELLS
Making munitions, which became a major industry during the war, was primarily undertaken by women. *(The Times History of the War 1914, published 1915)*

MOVED BY PLIGHT OF DISPLACED CIVILIANS
The Rev Samuel Chambers served at First Holywood Presbyterian Church from 1907–16 before following many of the young men from his congregation to France as a chaplain.
(Courtesy of First Holywood Presbyterian Church)

THE UNSINKABLE VIOLET JESSOP
Violet Jessop lived a charmed life, even though the ships she sailed on didn't. Violet was stewardess aboard the *Titanic* when it struck an iceberg and was on board Her Majesty's Hospital Ship *Britannic,* serving as a Red Cross nurse, when it hit a mine near the Greek coast.

THE UNSINKABLE VIOLET JESSOP
The White Star liners, including the *Britannic* on which Violet served, are remembered along Donegall Place in Belfast city centre. *(Author)*

SOMME: THE WALK OF DEATH
The sunken road at Thiepval, pictured in 1927, where many of the injured and dying sought cover on 1 July 1916, was later dubbed Bloody Road as it was covered in Irish blood.
(Courtesy of the Somme Museum)

DEFENDING DUBLIN CASTLE:
John Carrothers

John Samuel Carrothers joined the army in 1915, being accepted on to an officers' training course that December. Based in London in April 1916, he was making his way home to Farnaght, Tamlaght, County Fermanagh, when he was caught up in the Easter Rising. Arriving in Dublin on the Monday evening, just hours after the start of hostilities, he made his way to the nearest military barracks at Shipquay Street, where he was to remain throughout most of the week. In letters home to his mother he recorded some of the happenings going on around him, including living almost entirely on bully beef and biscuits. On the Wednesday he noted:

"We have done a good deal of sniping out of the windows with very good result. The 'Sinn Féiners' are rotten shots, they only hit this barrack once. A chap was standing in the open street and they fired a volley at him but never hit him. There have been some narrow escapes. A chap had his bayonet blown off his rifle, and another fellow had the back of his coat cut by a bullet. There must be an enormous number of people killed because it is a fearful thing to fire even a rifle in the city, let alone machine-guns or artillery."

The following day he had a lucky escape himself, making him seriously wonder about what lay ahead of him in France:

"There have been a large number of soldiers shot last night (Thursday). I was on a grave digging party, but as soon as we started work we were sniped at from a house. Some chaps got into the graves but I saw that we were taken at a disadvantage and you would not have seen me for the dust I kicked up running away. Two snipers appeared at a chimney quite close and we opened rapid fire on them, the chimney fell and also both the snipers. One was only wounded and he was brought in as a prisoner. His coat was covered with the blood and brains of the other sniper. A night like this soon puts the notion of war out of one's head."

On Saturday a sergeant standing close to him was shot through the head, though the end of the uprising now appeared to be in sight:

"Last night and to-day the artillery were going constantly. They have nearly levelled Kingstown and have blown up dozens of very important places in the city all because there was no other way of getting the Sinn Féiners out of them. There is a great cheering now, we have just been told that the Sinn Féiners have tendered an unconditional surrender, I suppose the 18 pounder artillery put the fear of God in their hearts."

Throughout the Sunday there was much coming and going as the soldiers moved in to make arrests. Carrothers noted:

"Prisoners are being brought in in hundreds. It is said that the SFs in Jacobs have refused to surrender. They have hoisted the flag of the Irish Republic. The streets appear to be safe enough today but there is still an occasional shot. The Russian Countess who led this rebellion was brought in here as a prisoner today. It was Connolly the leader who surrendered. He was brought in here on a stretcher by six SF Officers. I suppose the papers are full of his 'heroic' surrender. These barracks are part of Dublin Castle and it is the headquarters of the whole campaign. I was through the Castle today. It shows the traces of hand to hand fighting. The great marble staircases are torn with bullets and pools of clotted blood are at almost every door. Important papers are being tramped over and office accoutrements are scattered everywhere. Sackville Street is half demolished by artillery. It is a great pity that it suffered so much as it is one of the finest streets in the world. The GPO is a thing of the past. In a little green square in the Castle we have buried about 40 soldiers and 3 or 4 officers and there are still a big number to be buried here. There is a big hospital attached to these barracks and it is full of wounded."

The 'Countess' referred to was Constance Georgine Markievicz, who had been second in command of the St Stephen's Green rebels. Taken from Dublin Castle to Kilmainham Gaol, she was sentenced to death at her court-martial, later commuted to life in prison. The Countess was released the following year under a general amnesty.

James Connolly, wounded on Thursday 27 April, remained at the General Post Office until the Saturday, when he was carried to the Red Cross hospital at Dublin Castle. Too ill to stand, he was strapped to a chair to be shot by firing squad at Kilmainham Gaol on 12 May.

John Carrothers was later appointed a second lieutenant and posted to the 8th Royal Inniskilling Fusiliers. On 16 August, he took part in the Battle of Langernarck, part of the Third Battle of Ypres, being wounded in the knee. After initial treatment he was being carried further back on a stretcher when he was killed by artillery fire. His body was never recovered and he is remembered on the Tyne Cot Memorial. He was just 19 years old.

Liberty Hall, in Beresford Place, Dublin, one of the insurgents' strongholds, was badly damaged during the fighting.
(From A Popular History of the Great War, published 1933)

MURDER AT PORTOBELLO BARRACKS:
Captain John Bowen-Colthurst

Captain John Colthurst Bowen-Colthurst was, at best, a damaged man, his mind ruined by war, and at worst a zealot who believed those disloyal to the Crown did not deserve to live. From Dripsey, County Cork, and standing almost 6ft 4ins tall, he had been commissioned into the 1st Royal Irish Rifles in 1899. After service during the Boer War, followed by seven years in India, he was promoted to captain in 1907. However, the Home Rule crisis and his pro-unionist views brought him into conflict with his commanding officer Colonel, later Major-General, Sir Wilkinson Dent Bird. At Le Cateau, during the retreat from Mons in 1914, Bowen-Colthurst ignored orders to retire, turned his company about, and advanced towards the Germans, telling his commanding officer that he was tired of retreating and preferred to fight and die if necessary. Bird immediately relieved him of his command but he was reinstated a few days later. On 16 September at Aisne, two companies were sent forward by the colonel to gauge the strength of the enemy's forces. Captain Bowen-Colthurst led the reconnaissance force and was badly injured, with bullet wounds to the chest and an arm, while half his men were killed or wounded.

While he physically recovered, his reputation could not. A report prepared by Colonel Bird, who was also badly injured at the same battle, losing a leg, recommended that Bowen-Colthurst not be further promoted or be sent back to the BEF. Bowen-Colthurst, whose only brother, 31-year-old Captain Robert MacGregor Bowen-Colthurst, of the 1st Leinster Regiment, was killed in March 1915, was instead given a recruiting role in Dublin, being attached to the 3rd Royal Irish Rifles at Portobello Barracks.

On 25 April, the day after the beginning of the Easter Rising, Bowen-Colthurst took it upon himself to take the war to the rebels. Accompanied by about 40 men, and using Francis Sheehy Skeffington, a well-known journalist in the city with political links though not himself involved in the violence, as a hostage, he made his way to a tobacconists shop at the corner of Upper Camden Street and Harcourt Road, owned by nationalist councillor James Kelly. On the way Bowen-Colthurst, who believed the declaration of martial law had given the military the right to make summary decisions, encountered teenager JJ Coade. After a brief interrogation, he allegedly struck him with his rifle butt then, as he walked away, shot the boy in the back. At Kelly's shop the soldiers detained two other men, both journalists. Thomas Dickson was editor of a paper called the *Eye Opener*, while Patrick McIntyre edited the *Searchlight*. Along with Sheehy Skeffington, the men were marched back to Portobello Barracks and placed in the guardroom. The next morning Bowen-Colthurst returned, took the three men into a yard to the rear of the barracks, and had them shot. An attempt to cover up the killings was undone when a young officer, Major Sir Francis Vane, who had attempted to have the authorities in Dublin take action without success, reported the matter directly to Secretary of State for War Lord Kitchener, who ordered Bowen-Colthurst's arrest.

On 6 June 1916, Bowen-Colthurst's general court-martial opened in the gymnasium at Richmond Barracks, Dublin, with Major-General Lord Cheylesmore as president. He was charged with three counts of murder and three alternative charges of manslaughter. Lieutenant William Dobbin, son of a former soldier and governor of the borstal at Clonmel, County Tipperary, had been in charge of the guard. He told the court martial that Bowen-Colthurst had told him: "I am taking these men out of the guardroom, and I am going to shoot them, as I think it is the right thing to do." His reasoning, the court was told, was that there was a possibly that the barracks might be stormed by the rebels and he wanted to prevent the men's escape or rescue. Another witness told of how Bowen-Colthurst had ordered the men to remove their hats and say their prayers before he himself announced: "O Lord God, if it should please Thee to take away the life of this man forgive him for Our Lord Jesus Christ's sake." After the shootings, Dobbin went out into the yard behind the guardroom and saw that Sheehy Skeffington was still alive and was ordered by Bowen-Colthurst to shoot him again, which he did.

The medical evidence pointed squarely to an unsound mind. Captain Lawless, medical superintendent of Armagh District Asylum, said Bowen-Colthurst's "state was one of mental instability"; Major Purser described him as a man who acted upon impulse without regarding the wisdom or otherwise of his actions; and Major Goodman, who had known Bowen-Colthurst for many years, said he was capable of doing very eccentric things when in a state of high tension. The court found the captain guilty of all three murders, but ruled he was insane at the time. He was committed to Broadmore Asylum for the Criminally Insane, and later transferred to a private asylum. By 1921 he had been released and given permission to move to Canada where he lived for the rest of his life. Bowen-Colthurst died in December 1965, almost 50 years after the Portobello shootings.

PRAYERS FOR A LOST SON AND TROUBLED COUNTRY:
The Rev James Berry

On Sunday 14 May, just two days after the execution of James Connolly, the last of the Easter Rising leaders to face the firing squad, the Rev James Fleetwood Berry took to the pulpit of St Nicholas's Parish Church, Galway. It was the first time he had faced his congregation since word of the death of his only son, Edward, in Mesopotamia had reached the rectory. There was hardly a dry eye in church as he began his sermon. Galway, he said, had sent many of her sons to war, but there was work to do by those left behind.

"And part of our work at home is to bear our burden cheerfully. Oh the tension and the strain and the anxiety of it all. Waiting and watching – day after day and month after month – for news that never comes. Oh, the longing for news of some great victory, some advance. Oh, the cruel disappointment again and again, when we had hoped we were on the eve of hearing of some success, to hear of some disaster, aggravated by the consciousness that it was due to some colossal mistake of those in high places of authority. Mistakes in Gallipoli, mistakes in Mesopotamia, mistakes in Ireland. And for all these weary weeks to go on bearing up in the prolonged anxiety – while all the time (like Joseph) we would weep in secret and wash our face and come forth to appear cheerful before men.

And then, as if all the sorrow and suffering in the world was not sufficient, as if the river of human blood that goes on flowing like water was not deep enough; there comes this rebellion in our own land with all the loss of life it entailed – lost and wasted – and all the ruin and destruction. Poor Dublin! And Galway, too. We tremble as we think what might have been, what almost did happen. What surely would have happened only for the mercy of God, only for our grand Navy, only for our gallant troops, only for our splendid Constabulary that we are so proud of and so grateful to.

As I stand here today and look around these venerable walls and see the congregation worshiping God in peace and quietness and think of what might have been in the name of this congregation I thank our gallant forces."

Captain Edward Fleetwood Berry was 27 years old when killed in action on 17 April 1916. He had been born in Sligo in May, 1888, and after attending Abingdon School, Oxfordshire, passed out of the Royal Military College, Sandhurst, in 1906. He was commissioned into the Wiltshire Regiment, being posted to Jhansi, India. In 1909 he joined the 2/9th Gurkha Rifles stationed at Dehra Dun, and was appointed ADC to Lord Carmichael, Governor of Bengal, in 1913. Home on leave in Wexford when war broke out, he helped train recruits for three months before being transferred to the 9th King's Royal Rifles. Berry joined his own regiment in Flanders in October 1914, when it arrived from India, and was awarded the Military Cross for "brilliant dash and leadership" at Neuve Chapelle on 10 March 1915. In December 1915 the battalion had been transferred to Mesopotamia. Captain Berry was fatally wounded on the night of 17–18 April 1916 and buried in a trench along with Royal Field Artillery officer Captain David Rutherfoord by the Rev AE Knott, chaplain of the 7th British Field Ambulance. No marker was put in place at the time but a cross bearing their names was later added and the ground, about 200 yards from the banks of the Tigris, below Kut, was consecrated by Berry's uncle, the Bishop of Nagpur, when he visited the site several months later. After the war, however, when the area was searched for bodies, the graves could not be found and today both men are commemorated on the Basra Memorial.

The Collegiate Church of St Nicholas, built in the 12th century, is the largest medieval parish church in Ireland. A Great War Memorial in the form of a Celtic cross at the church records the names of those from the parish who died. On the south-east face of the base it records: "Edward Fleetwood Berry, MC, Captain & Adjutant, the 8th Gurkha Rifles, only child of the Rector of this parish, killed at Bait Aiesa, Mesopotamia, 17th April, 1916, aged 27 years."

Captain Berry's father was later made Archdeacon of Tuam and passed away in 1925; his mother, Mary Emily, nee Chatterton, who was from Monkstown, County Cork, remained in Galway until her death in January, 1956.

FUSILIERS SHOT AS SPIES:
Privates David Martin and Thomas Donohoe

In the confusion of war men could become separated from their units. Most were picked up by the enemy within hours, days or at best weeks. But some managed to remain at large over the coming months and even years, though the longer they retained their freedom the more hard-line the German attitude towards them became. In 1916 a deadline of 30 April was set for those on the run to hand themselves in and still be regarded prisoners-of-war. After that date, they were warned, they faced the possibility of being viewed as spies and shot. William O'Sullivan, from Barrackton, County Cork, took the opportunity of turning himself in. With days to spare he left the village of Villeret, north of St Quentin, where he had been part of a group of British soldiers sheltered by the French residents. He had been on the road only a matter of hours when he was detained. Others from the group, which at one time had numbered nine men, attempted to leave the village to make good their escape but, finding the area full of Germans, returned after a couple of days. Little more than two weeks later, at dawn on 16 May, the Germans raided Villeret. In a hayloft they captured three soldiers, two of them Irish, while a fourth man escaped into the nearby woods. The three prisoners – Private David Martin, a 28-year-old married former cook who had been living in the Castlereagh area, on the outskirts of Belfast, before the war; Private Thomas Donohoe, 32, a farmer's son from Killybandrick, County Cavan, and Englishman Private William Thorpe – were marched five miles to Le Catelet, the German administrative headquarters in the area.

Martin and Donohoe, both with the 1st Royal Irish Fusiliers, had become separated from their battalion following fighting at Haucourt on 27 August 1914. After hiding out together they came across Thorpe then later still Robert Digby, another Englishman. Within days more men had joined them, including O'Sullivan. The trapped men hid in a quarry for a while, then a fishing hut, with the landowner insuring they were well fed, before the villagers of Villeret decided to take them in, where they posed as natives, working in the fields and carrying false papers

Following their arrest, Martin, Donohoe and Thorpe were tried in the chateau and sentenced to death by firing squad. On 27 May they were taken to the place of execution by open cart along deserted streets. After shaking hands with each other, they were bound to posts and shot by firing squad.

Digby, who had escaped the initial German raid on the village, later handed himself in and was shot several days later. All four men were buried in Le Catelet Churchyard. A special memorial to another Irish soldier, 31-year-old P Russell, of the 2nd Royal Munster Fusiliers, from Kilkee, County Clare, killed on 4 October 1918, stands in the same cemetery.

Another Irishman, Trooper Patrick Fowler, from Dublin, was hiding in the nearby village of Bertry at this time. A member of the 11th Hussars, he had become separated at the Battle of Le Cateau on 26 August 1914, when his horse had been shot from under him and had spent the next five months surviving alone in woods. A local man discovered him on 15 January 1915, and took him to the home of his widowed mother-in-law, who lived with her 20-year-old daughter. Fowler said: "After the good people had fed me, the problem was to find a hiding-place. Suddenly the widow's daughter had a brainwave – the cupboard." The wardrobe measured less than 6ft tall and 20ins deep. The right half was shelved and filled with household items, with the door always left slightly open to avert suspicion and allow in more air to Fowler, who sat with his knees tucked up. With the farmhouse often used to billet Germans, he had to remain perfectly still and silent throughout the day, only able to come out in the evenings to stretch his legs and eat. When the farmhouse was requisitioned, and the family moved to a small cottage, Trooper Fowler and the wardrobe came too. On 10 October 1918, the British finally entered Bertry and a ragged and malnourished Fowler spilled out on to the street to be promptly arrested as a deserter. "By an amazing coincidence I was taken before the very same officer who had commanded me at Le Cateau. He immediately recognised me, and I was set free," he remembered.

Private Fowler, after being granted an extended leave, rejoined his unit. He survived the war, and settled in Scotland afterwards, where he died in 1964 at the age of 90. Madame Belmont-Gobert and her daughter were lauded both at home and in Britain, being awarded the OBE for their actions, receiving money from the War Office to cover the Irishman's messing costs, and presented with £3,400 donated by readers of the *Daily Telegraph*. The wardrobe was purchased from them and moved to the 11th Hussars regimental museum in Winchester.

THE BATTLE OF JUTLAND:
Commander Barry Bingham

The Battle of Jutland was the greatest navel battle of the First World War. On 31 May 1916, the British High Seas Fleet and Grand Fleet encountered the German High Seas Fleet, with the action going back and forth. Ultimately the Germans lost a battle cruiser, a pre-Dreadnought, four light cruisers and five destroyers as well as sustaining substantial damage to many of its surviving ships; the British lost three battle cruisers, four armoured cruisers and eight destroyers.

Turning north to meet a German torpedo attack, the British ships, including HMS *Nestor* commanded by the Honorable Edward Barry Stewart Bingham, who had been born in Bangor Castle, County Down, opened fire at 10,000 yards. "I promptly manoeuvred to close this range. At 4.45 the *Nomad*, my immediate follower, was hit in the boiler-room and hauled out of line disabled. We in the *Nestor* got the range very quickly, and pumped in three or four salvoes from our 4-in guns," he wrote in an account of the battle.

"Two German destroyers disappeared beneath the surface, and though it is unreasonable definitely to claim the credit of sinking a given ship where many are concerned, my control officer is still prepared to affirm that the *Nestor*'s guns accounted for one of them. At 4.50 the enemy's destroyers turned tail and fled. Pursued by the British they divided themselves into two portions, one half of which made for the head, while the other took cover under the tail, of the German battle-cruiser line."

While Bingham in the *Nestor*, along with the remaining ship HMS *Nicator*, gave chase to one group of the enemy, the other two divisions mounting the attack went after the others. Coming under sustained fire from the enemy's battle-cruisers, Bingham was forced to veer away though not before firing three torpedoes. About 5.00 pm a German light cruiser delivered direct hits on the *Nestor*, putting out two of its boilers.

"A huge cloud of steam was rising from the boiler-room, completely enshrouding the whole ship, and it was painfully apparent that our speed was dropping every second. Our speed died away gradually, until at 5.30 pm we came to a dead stop."

His guns were still working, however, and he was able to drive off a German destroyer that came too close. Soon, as the battle moved over the horizon, the *Nestor* found itself alone briefly before the main enemy fleet returned, retracing its steps.

"Their course necessarily led them first past the *Nomad*, and in another ten minutes the slaughter began. They literally smothered the destroyer with salvoes. Of my divisional mate nothing could be seen; great columns of spray and smoke alone gave an indication of her whereabouts. I shall never forget the sight, and mercifully it was a matter of a few minutes before the ship sank; at the time it seemed impossible that any one on board could have survived. Of what was in store for us there was now not the vestige of a doubt…

From a distance of about five miles, the Germans commenced with their secondary armament, and very soon we were enveloped in a deluge of shell fire. Any reply from our own guns was absolutely out of the question at a range beyond the possibilities of our light shells; to have answered any one of our numerous assailants would have been as effective as the use of a peashooter against a wall of steel. Just about this time we fired our last torpedo at the High Sea Fleet and it was seen to run well.

It was a matter of two or three minutes only before the *Nestor*, enwrapped in a cloud of smoke and spray, the centre of a whirlwind of shrieking shells, received not a few heavy and vital hits, and the ship began slowly to settle by the stern and then to take up a heavy list to starboard. Her decks now showed the first signs of havoc amongst life and limb. It was clear that the doomed *Nestor* was sinking rapidly, and at that moment I gave my last order as her commander, 'Abandon ship'."

Bingham, after waiting until the last moment, was forced to swim for it and was picked up by the ship's heavily laden motorboat. He went on:

"Looking now towards the *Nestor*, we saw the water lapping over the decks, and the forecastle high in the air, still the target of the German gun-layers, some of whose projectiles fell uncomfortably near us in the motor-boat and rafts. In about three minutes, the destroyer suddenly raised herself into an absolutely perpendicular position, and thus slid down, stern first, to the bottom of the North Sea, leaving a quantity of oil and wreckage to mark the spot where she had last rested. As she sank, her sharp stem and stockless anchors alone visible, we gave our gallant but cruelly short-lived *Nestor* three rousing cheers and sang *God Save the King.*"

After 15 minutes a German destroyer picked the British sailors up. Bingham was awarded the Victoria Cross for his actions at the Battle of Jutland. He retired from the Royal Navy in 1932 with the rank of Rear-Admiral, and died in London in September, 1939, just weeks after the beginning of the Second World War.

Commander Barry Bingham, VC winner and hero of the Battle of Jutland.
(From The Great War magazine, published 1915-1919)

WAR ON TWO FRONTS:
DD Sheehan

Daniel Desmond Sheehan, who preferred to be known as DD Sheehan, was a Westminster MP of 15 years standing by 1916, representing the Mid-Cork constituency. Following a split from John Redmond's Irish parliamentary party, he formed the All-For-Ireland League, which argued for the granting of Home Rule by political consent rather than it being imposed on the minority Protestant community. On the declaration of war he threw himself into encouraging recruitment in the Royal Munster Fusiliers, joining himself in November 1914 at the age of 41, and being commissioned to the 9th battalion.

Back at the Somme front after having returned to Ireland following the Easter Rising of April 1916, he wrote:

"France once again! The verdant woodlands and the waving cornfields, the glory of nature and the richness of cultivation everywhere as we speed north to where the grimness and the greatness of war await us. I leave behind a country where discontent and unsettlement are rife. I come out to where the sons of that same land – some gathered together from all the fair provinces – in loyalty and love and devotion to great ideals are rendering noble service and building up new monuments to the imperishable fame of Irish chivalry and valour. I left the trenches for other duty when the murkiness and greyness and biting cold of early spring tested the spirits and endurance of our troops. They were cheerful there – these Irishmen and Scotsmen, and London Territorials, whom I knew so well and whom it was my pride to be associated, in duty and danger, with. I never met a grumbler amongst the lot. They were all animated by the same high purpose. They had come out to strike a blow for liberty and the great causes of civilisation. They came from all ranks and grades of society, and from every quarter of our mighty Empire. Patriotism was a religion with them – sacrifice their daily bread, and for the rest they took life as it came, and if so be that the fortunes of war claimed it they generously and gladly gave it up that England may be throned in sea-grit security, and the Empire continued in its freedom."

Sheehan said he had returned to an army that was keener than ever for the coming battle on the Somme and where every man was either a hero in fact or in the making.

"Men are men out here, neither saints nor yet very great sinners, but men who are made strong in character and stout of heart by reason of the fact that risk and danger and death are ever in their pathway, and that the consciousness of a righteous cause sustains and elevates and strengthens. And so it is good to be here, for here one knows nothing of petty party strife, or the littleness of parochial politics, or the smallness of men's ways in a selfish and self-seeking world... No doubt I missed some of the brave comrades who had marched and manoeuvred with us in the old days in the South of Ireland but I had the gratification of knowing that those who had fallen had done their duty nobly and well by their native land. It was from the best impulse of patriotism they had joined Kitchener's Army. Many of them were my own recruits in the sense that they had come along in response to my personal appeals and had enlisted in the same regiment with me. I can vouch for it that they were as good Irishmen as ever did honour or brought glory to their country. They were patriots in the best and truest sense. May God receive those who fell so nobly into His tender keeping. We who are left behind will carry on the cause our departed brothers have sanctified a thousandfold by their sacrifices. And this I would also say, that our fellow-countrymen at home have their duty to the memory of these fallen heroes. Their places have got to be filled, and not by Englishmen or Scotsmen or Welshmen. It is Irishmen and Irishmen alone who can fill the gaps in the Irish divisions and regiments."

The war took a terrible toll on DD Sheehan and his family. He was invalided home in 1917 suffering from deafness caused by shellfire and later that year left the army due to ill-health. Two of his sons were killed, Daniel Joseph Sheehan, flying with the 66th Squadron of the Royal Flying Corps, died on 10 May 1917, and is buried at Cabaret-Rouge British Cemetery, Souchez, and Martin Joseph Sheehan, of the 13th Squadron Royal Air Force, killed on 1 October 1918, and buried at Anneux British Cemetery. Sheehan also lost a brother-in-law, Sergeant Robert O'Connor, of the 2nd Leinster Regiment, who was killed at Passchendaele on 31 July 1917, and is commemorated on the Menin Gate, Ypres, Belgium.

Sheehan stood down from Parliament in 1918 and in the face of republican intimidation moved to England for a spell. On his return he continued fighting on behalf of the poor and ex-servicemen while working as a journalist and Labour activist. He died in 1948.

LOST AT SEA:
Secretary of War Lord Kitchener

The loss of Lord Kitchener, the Secretary of State for War, shocked a nation already two years into the greatest conflict the world had ever seen. This old soldier was quite literally the face of defiance, staring out from the famous recruitment posters stern and unmoving – the rock on which, surely, the Hun aggressor would perish. It was a German mine, however, that ended the life of this Irish-born bulldog. On 5 June 1916, he and close to 650 others died when the HMS *Hampshire*, taking Kitchener to Russia for a secret meeting, sank within minutes off the coast of the Orkney Islands in Scotland. The ship had set sail from the Orkneys at 4.45 pm, picking up its destroyer escorts an hour later. However, the weather rapidly deteriorated and the two supporting vessels were sent back to port. At 7.45 pm the *Hampshire* struck a mine and rapidly sank with only 12 survivors making it ashore. The Secretary of State was last seen, apparently unperturbed, talking with members of his staff on the ship's bridge.

Kitchener, however, was not the only Irishman on board. Two others were part of his 13-strong party, while at least another two were among the Hampshire's crew. Perhaps the most overlooked of these was a man whose job entailed him blending into the background. Matthew McLoughlin was 37 years old and from Kilcommon, County Tipperary, but had lived much of his adult life in London. Like many young Irishmen, he had found work on the building sites of the English capital when he first arrived in 1900, though he had his eyes set on higher things. He applied for, and was accepted, into the Metropolitan Police, rising to detective sergeant and transferring, in 1909, to Special Branch. His superiors recognised in him a man who could conduct himself with decorum while being an alert and enthusiastic officer and he was appointed to personal protection duties. Before the war Sergeant Detective McLoughlin looked after the security of royalty, including both Edward VII and George V, and, as a fluent French speaker, had served Kitchener earlier in the war when he visited the Western Front. His selection to accompany him to Russia was, of course, to be his last mission. It is assumed he remained with Lord Kitchener to the end and, as the Secretary of War had refused an invitation to climb into one of the lifeboats, his fate had been sealed. The body of Detective Sergeant McLoughlin, a married man and father of one, like that of his charge, was never found.

Another member of the Kitchener party was diplomat Hugh James O'Beirne. The 49-year-old from Jamestown, County Leitrim, had joined the Diplomatic Service in 1892 with Petrograd, where Secretary of War's meeting was to take place, being his first posting. In 1906, following placements in America, Turkey and France, he returned to Russia, where he was to serve another nine years under two Ambassadors and earning himself the rank of Foreign Office Minister. As a sign of his seniority, he was sent to Bulgaria in 1915 as the Charge d'Affaires though his negations in Sofia were unsuccessful as the Bulgarians eventually joined the Axis powers and invaded Serbia. Mr O'Beirne returned to London, serving in the Foreign Office and, for a spell, heading up the War Department. In March 1916 he was among the British representatives at a conference in Paris. With so much relevant experience, Mr O'Beirne was a natural choice to accompany the Secretary of War on his mission.

The two Irish members of the HMS *Hampshire* crew to perish were Surgeon Hugh Francis McNally and Sub-Lieutenant Humphrey F Vernon. Doctor McNally, aged just 24, was the son of a school principal and had attended St Malachy's College in Belfast, after which he served an apprenticeship as a chemist in the city. He attended Queen's University, studying medicine and training with its Officer Training Corps, and shortly after graduating in 1915 applied for a commission in the Royal Navy, being appointed to the *Hampshire*. Dr McNally had also been an officer in the Irish National Volunteers in Belfast. Sub-Lieutenant Vernon, aged 22, from Belturbet, County Cavan, had six years service in the Royal Navy and had previously served on HMS *Shannon*. His father, Fane Vernon, was chairman of the Great Northern Railway Company of Ireland and he had two brothers serving in the army. Neither of the men's bodies was recovered and they are commemorated on the Portsmouth Naval Memorial.

RUSSIAN SOLDIER AND BRITISH SPY:
Charles Bryson

Charles Bryson was a man of words. Educated in his native Belfast, Dublin and Paris, he had been working as a professor of modern languages for the Imperial Russian Education Department in Vilna when war was declared. He immediately applied to join the British army but, because of poor eyesight, was rejected for active service though he was recruited by the intelligence services. However, determined not to be denied getting into the action, he joined the Imperial Russian Horse Artillery, serving as an officer.

Writing to a friend at home in 1916, the 29-year-old outlined one of his 'adventures' – a raid in force behind the German lines.

"I, of course, volunteered, as well as several artillerymen (whom it was necessary to teach in about ten minutes how to load a rifle, as they had never handled one in their lives). In all there was a pretty bloodthirsty company of 140 men, consisting of dragoons. Uhlans, and artillerymen, with three officers. A peasant (and a pretty old fellow, too) offered to guide us through the enemy's lines. At about 5.00 pm we started off on foot, without greatcoats, every man with about 10 or 12 bombs. The village in question is distant from our lines not more than eight versts (six miles), but we took a roundabout way, and at 12 o'clock at night were further away from it than ever; at half-past three we entered the village without firing a shot. At both ends of it were posted parties of 20 men. I was put in charge of one such post, whose duties were to prevent the Germans from getting out. The main party then quietly patrolled the village once, and then, with a noise like all the devils in hell let loose, began work. Every window was smashed with the butts of rifles, and bombs thrown into every house. The Germans, taken by surprise, ran out into the streets, some in their shirts, all only half-dressed. Our fellows up to this had not fired a shot. Now began the most horrible hand-to-hand fight I ever hope to see. The yells of the slayers and the groans of the wounded made the most terrible sound I ever heard. Up to this I and my party had nothing to do but to look on. The village began to burn from the bursting of the bombs, and we could see everything without being seen. After some time a German came running up the village, but we soon stopped him by the question 'Kto tam?' (Who's there?). The poor beggar found nothing better to do than answer 'Svoye' (It's I). As we had a parole we knew it was a German and gave him a bullet. Others came along and met the same fate. All this time the fight in the village continued. The Germans in the trenches beyond the village opened fire on the village, but killed and wounded more of their own than ours."

With dawn breaking, the Russian bugle was sounded to withdraw but Bryson and his men, despite being reinforced with a dozen soldiers from the main raiding party, were pinned down. One man had been seriously wounded, taking an 'explosive bullet' in the thigh, with similar rounds cracking and whistling around them from all directions. He goes on:

"I took out my compass and resolved to take the risk and make a rush for it at the point of the bayonet straight for the east. This we did with success only to find that we were surrounded by another party from the outposts. For eight long mortal hours we sat in a marsh up to the waist in icy water, firing only when we were sure of hitting. About five o'clock in the evening one fellow volunteered to creep out and send for help. He got as far as our Cossack outpost, who as soon as it was dark came to our assistance and gave us cartridges. Out of our thirty-two, twenty were already wounded. An explosive bullet hit my rifle and made it useless for further firing – another smashed the bayonet, and at the final rush I was obliged to use the butt. At last we got out of the marsh to the Cossacks' positions. They fed us and we lay down and slept till morning, when we learnt that some other small parties had come through. We telephoned 'home' for our horses and rode back the twenty miles along our front to our village. During two days our fellows came filtering through, and in the end nearly all reached us. A few days afterwards a German prisoner told us that their losses were over 400, for in the village we attacked was quartered a battalion and a half."

Bryson, who was to have many more 'adventures' during the Russian Revolution, served in the Intelligence Corps during the Second World War. By then he was already a successful writer. Under the pseudonym Charles Barry, he had twenty-six detective novels published and worked for the BBC European Service. He died in 1963.

ULSTERMAN WHO SAVED 25,000 LIVES:
Captain George Gracey

Of the estimated two million Armenians living in the Ottoman Empire before the First World War, it is thought that approximately three-quarters died during the Turkish genocide of 1915 and the years immediately following. Many were massacred, deported, or made to take part in death marches. Others were lost to starvation and disease, while tens of thousands were forced to convert to Islam.

A witness to this human tragedy was George Frederick Handel Gracey. Born in 1878 in Belfast, the son of an organist whose veneration for a particular composer influenced the choice of Christian names, he had worked as a carpenter in the city's shipbuilding industry before turning to the church. By 1914 he had been an 'industrial missionary' for ten years on behalf of the American Near East Relief Committee which ran an industrial institute at Urfa. While apparently speaking English with a broad Belfast accent, he was fluent in Turkish, reasonably good in Armenian and had passable Kurdish and Russian. He was also familiar with northern Mesopotamia and much of Armenia, making him a natural recruit for the British Military Mission at Tiflis. Made a captain, he served as an intelligence officer.

In August 1916, Captain Gracey was the only European in the region of Lake Van when the war arrived in earnest. According to newspaper reports, on word that nearby Mush had been retaken by the enemy, he organised a huge evacuation of some 25,000 Armenians so they wouldn't fall into the Turks' hands. "The only available line of retreat lay through the pass of Behri Kala, a lonely mountain outlet infested by Kurds and other marauders," reported the *Belfast Telegraph*.

"No Russian soldiers guarded this gateway to safety, and Mr Gracey began by hastily arming with rifles 250 volunteers. This improvised force seized the pass, dealt with the Kurds, and secured the retreat of a hundred times their number from interruption. In the guerrilla warfare there were a number of casualties and some deaths, but worse was avoided. The Russian troops at Van were, at Mr Gracey's request, drawn across the route in a cordon, through which only a thousand of the refugees were allowed to pass every two hours. By this device the column was distributed automatically over many miles of road, a halt of two hours being arranged every five hours. For five days the march continued. The average distance covered was thirty miles a day, and the twenty-five thousand refugees, with their six thousand cattle, took two days to pass any given point. Five babies are known to have been born en route, and all survived the experience."

As the war was drawing to an end, Gracey worked for the Foreign Office among the Kurdish tribes, attempting to curb Turkish propaganda. He was taken captive by the Bolsheviks in October 1918, spending the next nine months, along with other members of the Caucasus Military Mission, in Moscow until an exchange of prisoners was organised with Britain. He returned to his charitable work, serving as general secretary of Friends of Armenia. From 1929 he acted as the overseas delegate for the Save the Children Fund – a charity started in 1919 to help the starving children of the defeated nations – serving as general secretary from 1937 until his retirement in 1948.

George Gracey, who had been awarded the DSO in 1919 for his services, died on St Patrick's Day 1958. The following day *The Times* newspaper said:

"Both as overseas delegate from 1929 to 1937 and as general secretary from the latter year until his retirement in 1948, Gracey infused an almost evangelical fervour into the work of the Save the Children Fund. During the war he led the Fund in setting up residential and day-time nurseries in Great Britain and he was tireless in attending committee and other meetings in this cause. For it he won the support of the Save the Children Fund throughout the Commonwealth and of the Save the Children Federation in the United States, with the result that many of the Fund's war-time nurseries in this country bore Commonwealth or American names and from time to time were visited by delegates from those lands."

LIFE AMID LIONS, HYENAS AND CROCODILES:
Sapper RJ Kerr

German East Africa was the only enemy colony not to fall to the Allies within the first months of the war. The small German force held out until 1916 and even then continued the fight by mounting a guerilla campaign, including the use of native troops, until the end of the war. As a consequence, many British troops who could have served on the Western Front were tied up in Africa. Among these soldiers was Sapper RJ Kerr, of the Royal Engineers. He had landed at Mombasa, on the east coast of Kenya, the former capital of British East Africa, and travelled across to Bagamoyo, in modern day Tanzania. It had been the original capital of German East Africa and one of the most important trading ports along the east African coast. On 15 August 1916, the Allies overran the town in an operation that included air and naval attacks.

Sapper Kerr, formerly employed in the telegraphists' section of the General Post Office in Belfast, outlined his experiences to a friend in the city in November 1916:

"To describe the scenery and sights of this country after a two months' sojourn is no easy task. There has been so much variety that I've almost ceased to observe things. I think nothing could surprise me now unless to find myself suddenly at home. The coast itself, seen from the steamer, is very fine, it is usually flat or hilly – fine strands, lined with coconut palms and other trees unknown to me, some being very beautiful, especially one tall, slender tree not unlike the silver birch. Flowering shrubs of most glorious colours are everywhere, while through the trees glimpses of white houses with pillared verandahs and red roofs surmount all the higher land. These are the European houses, and in their setting of green, with a clear blue sky as a background, they are most picturesque. Few native huts can be seen on the shore; they are usually behind the town or hidden by the trees.

As we travel inland by rail we rise through different zones first. The appearance would remind one of the greenhouses in the Botanic Gardens at home – there is abundance of banana trees, limes, and palms, with a heavy undergrowth, and lots of wild flowers. Rising higher trees are not so common, and dotted here and there are native villages. The grass in places is brown. Below, the sea creeks appear like inland lakes; ahead tower lofty mountains. Soon the interior plateau is reached, covered with scrub and ant hills. Lions and hyenas prowl around, and their howling and 'laughing' break the stillness of the night. For miles there is no sign of human habitation.

Nearer the mountains native villages are more numerous and small trees are seen at intervals. But generally the plains are without variety – sandy wastes, from which the glare of the sun almost blinds one. Soon clothes, boots, hands, and face assume the colour of everything within sight – a bright chocolate red. One inwardly prays to be delivered from it all. Water is scarce and bad. Not a drop can be drunk without boiling. As for washing – well, a dry 'wipe' usually serves, and the thirst is maddening. About 5.30 the sun sinks, and before we are aware it is pitch dark night; but the stars shine bright, and distant camp fires cast a weird, dim glare. Mosquitoes buzz all round – going ping-ping at every opportunity. Beetles, bugs, caterpillars (4 or 5 inches long), hornets, crickets, and ants (by no means last) pervade everything and make sleep impossible, often even when worn out with fatigue."

Sapper Kerr found German East Africa very different, being more mountainous, better wooded and covered with lush green grass. He went on:

"Large rivers cross our path, with heavy undergrowth along their banks; while crocodiles wallow in the mud and the hippopotamus occasionally crashes through the trees. Then as we descend toward the coast again the scenery is enchanting. Behind we leave the lofty purple mountains, in some places tree-clad, as far as the eye can distinguish; around us narrow valleys covered with a profusion of flowering shrubs, trees, and plants. Here the coffee plant grows to perfection, for what beans can equal those produced on the slopes of Kilimanjaro? As we proceed rubber plantation and sisal (for which this country is famous) abound. Reaching the coastal slopes again we pass through continual palm and orange groves; the banana becomes common, and an indefinable 'tangerine' perfume pervades the atmosphere."

The German coastal towns were generally superior, he concluded, with stately buildings and tree-lined streets, with promenades, impressive gardens and bandstands crowned by a fine partially enclosed harbour. "The native village, quite untouched by civilisation, lies behind the town," he added.

"Well-to-do Indians were everywhere in fine dresses and with abundance of jewellery worn by the girls and women on ankles, arms, breast, as well as in the ears and nose. They, with the Portuguese, form the trading portion of the inhabitants, while the Suahelis are the hewers of wood and drawers of water."

'Sisal,' mentioned above, is a species of Agave and yields hemp that can be used to make rope, twine, paper, cloth, carpets and dartboards.

Dar-es-Salaam, the capital of the German colony in East Africa, was captured on 3 September 1916. (*The Great War magazine, published 1915–1919*)

LORD OF THE ARTILLERY SHELLS:
Viscount Charlemont

The first Caulfeild came to Ireland during the Elizabethan wars as a soldier of fortune, being rewarded for his service with the grant of lands in County Tyrone and a title. In 1913, the eighth Viscount Charlemont, James Caulfeild, inherited the title at the age of 33, taking up residence at the family seat at Drumcairne, near Stewartstown. On the outbreak of war he received a commission in the Coldstream Guards only to be found medically unfit for active service. Not to be beaten, however, he sought an alternative way to aid the war effort, finding himself a job making shells at the Woolwich arsenal in London. Describing himself as a "munition worker," he told a friend of his new found vocation:

"Woolwich is two miles or so away, and I have to be there at 8.00 every morning, and arrive back about 8.30 every night, so I have a good day's work. I don't work Sundays, as a rule, but they have a right to call on my services then, as at any other time. I was very lucky to get in there… It is quite impossible for anyone 'to get a job' in London unless he knows exactly what he wants, and whether there is a vacancy. All the Ministers are besieged with people 'willing to do anything'. They haven't time to look about for jobs for such people, and though I had the best of introductions to Sir E Carson, Balfour, Walter Long, the Military Secretary, Sir Percy Girouard, and so on, I consider myself very fortunate in holding the position of 'ordinary mechanic' in a Government factory at 25s a week, and any more piece work that I can add on. So far I have never sunk below £1 15s, and have risen to £3 10s – not at all bad when you come to think that I am really in status equal to the ordinary mill hand at Coalisland.

The shop I am in employs about 250 men by day, and the same by night, is about as big as Great Victoria Street Railway Station, has 200 machines in it, and a railway, several steam hammers and presses, and a forge; is fairly noisy, fairly hot, rather draughty, and very dirty. While I generally stick to one lathe, I have been on others, and also machines for boring out the insides of shells. I have some knowledge of metal turning already, and liking machinery in general, have fallen on my feet. I do not really count as 'unskilled labour,' and have been on the same 'bit of work' as a trades unionist without any comment being made. I expect I shall end by joining the tinplaters. All sorts and conditions of men work in the shop – Gents, labourers, tradesmen, chauffeurs, grooms, gardeners, and they turn out about double the quantity of stuff it was estimated they would. Average intelligence, backed by a desire to do one's best, after a bit of practice, have beaten the skilled labourer at his own game, and subsequently has upset his temper a bit. But this is really only collectively. I have never met any individual who was anything but most obliging and helpful."

Viscount Charlemont, who was evidently proud of both getting his hands dirty and earning a workman's wage, went on:

"You would think it very monotonous, as the machine does all the curving, and so on, but it really isn't as machines require watching, like humans, and the taking the shells out and putting them in quickly increases one's output immensely. In starting to do this, unfortunately, it comes hard on one's fingers, as they are heavy, sharp, and often nearly red hot. One gets bad cuts, burns, and crushed nails with truly dreadful frequency; but, like everything else, one gets used to it. The hot steel splinters have a trick, too, of getting into one's eyes, which is rather uncomfortable. The machine, as I said, always takes the same time; it is the manipulation before and after that counts. The first day I did 30 ten-pounder shells (and thought it jolly good), the second day 50, and I do now from 130 to 150 quite easily. They weigh (being unfilled) about 10 lb apiece. I have been on 60 pounders also. Nasty things these to tackle, weighing about 40lb apiece, and about 2ft 6in long. I can do about 50 or 60 of them a day, and each one pays me 2½d. The miserable 10-pounders are only 1d. I believe I am on boring this week. Boring is interesting but terribly hard work, as the machine is not strong enough to do the trick, and has to be assisted. Fifty to seventy 10-pounders is a good day's work on this."

Viscount Charlemont's time as a machinist was to be short-lived as he was later in 1916 made inspector of munitions, a position he held until 1918. He was elected to the Northern Ireland Senate in 1926 and served as Education Minister; was Vice-Lieutenant of County Tyrone, and District Commandant of the Cookstown B-Specials. He moved from Stewartstown to Newcastle, County Down, in 1936, and died at his home there in August 1949.

MOVED BY PLIGHT OF DISPLACED CIVILIANS:
The Rev Samuel Chambers

The Rev Samuel Waugh Chambers had been installed at First Holywood Presbyterian Church, County Down, in October 1907. Many of the young men of the congregation had enlisted early in the war and the cleric, with his congregation's permission, followed them to France as a chaplain, running a YMCA facility providing refreshments to the troops. In a letter written on 6 October 1915, and intended to be read at a Sunday service, he wrote:

"This is a land of tears and of sacrifice, with an undertone of strange job in it all. The newcomer is struck by the number of people in mourning for their dead – one woman in every ten or twelve draped in black. France is suffering terribly. Tens of thousands of people whose homes were in the district devastated by the German invaders had to abandon their earthly all and seek a shelter and a livelihood as best they could in other parts of the country. A man, for instance, who had been a prosperous builder and contractor in Soisson is now penniless, and is earning his bread as overseer of the workmen engaged in erecting a wooden hut for the YMCA – a hut that will take the place of the tent in which I am serving. He is one of the more fortunate. An elderly Belgian – a business man in other days – in the rush to escape the despoiler got separated from his wife and family, and although fourteen months have passed he has not heard of them since. He comes here daily to cook our middle meal, and is solely dependent on the francs we pay him. He knew nothing about cooking in his former life, but in these times, with the country in distress, people are ready to turn their hand to anything.

Women are largely employed at men's work, and, as at home, are suffering without complaint and doing their part most nobly. I saw some yesterday sweeping the streets in a neighbouring town. But so far as one can judge from what one sees and hears, all the suffering heaped upon them, far from breaking their spirit, is purifying it and bracing it to the utmost effort and sacrifice so as to win in this world struggle for freedom and right. France is finding her soul again. One cannot but feel that our people at home don't yet realise the tremendous seriousness of this conflict and the labour and pain and self-denial that it will exact before it ends. Our soldiers on the spot know what it means and are meeting the cost of it in a way that makes me proud of the Empire that has sent them forth. I have heard no bragging nor boasting. I have heard almost no grumbling, and it is very rare to meet with any feelings of personal animosity towards the individual men in the trenches opposite."

Mr Chambers found the soldiers more willing to listen to his Christian message at the Front than they would have been at home. "An average of from 2,000 to 3,000 soldiers visit the tent every day, the bulk of which are going up or coming down the lines," he added.

"Arriving, as they often do, cold and hungry, refreshments are provided at nominal cost. There are books and papers and writing materials, of which they make liberal use. Next to his rations the soldier is most particular about his correspondence, and when one sees men sitting in here or standing around absorbed in letters they have just received one can measure the strength and value of the home ties. If the news is good you see the cheer of it in their faces for days. In the evenings the musical ones organise a sing song or an impromptu concert, and before the closing hour I or one of my colleagues hold an informal service or a brief talk on some vital theme, prayer and a few hymns. I have also a Bible class one evening a week for the permanent men in the camp, who are chiefly army bakers.

One of the impressions made upon me is the cheerful and determined spirit of our men in the face of many discomforts and hardships. They need all the support and help that those at home can give them, and I trust that our womenfolk will be able to send out as many comforts this winter as they did last. I shall ever be grateful for the opportunity I have had of seeing something of the conditions of life here and of doing even a little for our brave soldiers. I owe this opportunity in large measure to your forbearance and generosity, and I hope that some benefit may accrue from it to you and to me."

In fact, the congregation got very little further service out of their minister. Moved by his experiences on the Western Front, Mr Chambers resigned from the church soon after his return from the war and took up a business career. He died on 6 December 1951.

THE UNSINKABLE VIOLET JESSOP:
The loss of the *Britannic*

Just after 8.00 am on 21 November 1916, a huge explosion ripped open the hull of Her Majesty's Hospital Ship *Britannic*. The blast, caused by a mine, was extensive with the sea rushing into five of the sealed compartments. A fault with the waterproof doorways resulted in a sixth taking in water, dooming the ship to a watery grave.

Completed by the Harland and Wolff shipyard at the end of 1915, a sister ship of the ill-fated *Titanic*, the *Britannic* had immediately been requisitioned for war service. By November the following year she was on her sixth mercy mission. Making her way to Mudros from Naples to pick up further war casualties, she was sailing the Aegean Sea, off the Greek coast, some forty miles south of Athens, and close to the island of Kea, when disaster struck. Initially the captain had hoped to beach the ship at Kea, but she was taking in water rapidly and listing to one side. The crew, anticipating the abandon ship order that came some twenty-three minutes after the explosion, had already begun preparing the lifeboats. Two of the craft, however, were dropped into the sea while the *Britannic* was still attempting to make for the island and were smashed to pieces.

On board one of these was the remarkable Violet Constance Jessop, who was serving as a Red Cross nurse but who already had considerable experience at sea. Seeing the danger, she leapt from the lifeboat into the water as it approached the propellers and was sucked under, banging her head on the keel when she resurfaced. Many years later, when being examined for regular headaches, it was discovered that she had fractured her skull but it had gone undiagnosed at the time. Fellow survivors pulled her to safety and she got to witness the *Britannic* sinking:

"She dipped her head a little, then a little lower and still lower. All the deck machinery fell into the sea like a child's toys. Then she took a fearful plunge, her stern rearing hundreds of feet into the air until with a final roar, she disappeared into the depths, the noise of her going resounding through the water with undreamt of violence…"

Violet, who reportedly spoke with a slight Irish accent, had been born in Argentina to emigrants William Jessop and Katherine Kelly, both from

Dublin. The family had returned when her father had died. Her mother found work as a stewardess for the Royal Mail Line and Violet followed suit in 1908. After two years she switched to the White Star Line to work on passenger liners, sailing on the *Majestic*, *Adriatic* and *Oceanic*. In 1911 she joined the *Olympic*, being onboard when it was in collision with HMS *Hawke* off the Isle of Wight. The following year she signed on to serve on the *Titanic*, and was in her bunk when it struck the iceberg. Ordered up on deck, she was placed in a lifeboat and given a baby to care for. She was later picked up by the *Carpathia* and found the child's mother was already onboard. Violet rejoined *Olympic* where she remained until leaving to train as a voluntary nurse and ultimately her appointment to the *Britannic*.

The *Olympic* was also requisitioned for war service, being fitted out to carry up to 8,000 troops at a time to the Gallipoli campaign, and to and from Canada and America. It holds the distinction of being the only passenger vessel to sink a submarine – the U-103. On 12 May 1918, the U-boat was sighted on the surface and engaged by the ship's gunners. The *Olympic*, on its way to France with American troops on board, turned to ram the submarine, which in turn crash dived. The *Olympic*'s propeller, however, sliced through the hull, forcing the crew to scuttle the submarine.

Violet, who went on to serve on a number of other ships, retired from her life at sea in 1950, aged 63, and lived a quiet life in Suffolk until her death in 1971. Two other survivors of the *Titanic* were also onboard the *Britannic* – stoker John Priest and lookout Archie Jewell.

"From 2 o'clock pm, the Germans rained shells of every description on the ground they had lost, and also on Thiepval Wood and our communication trenches – whizz-bangs, high explosives, five-nines, tear shells and stink shells of all kinds. The stretcher-bearers were working in shirt and trousers, tunics being discarded. The smell of the stink shells was nauseous, and as one of our men said 'The Germans were throwing over everything but shite'."

Sergeant Robert McKay
109th Field Ambulance, 36th (Ulster) Division

SOMME

THE WALK OF DEATH

The opening day of the Battle of the Somme is seared into the collective consciousness. The main Allied attack of the year, and six months in the planning, it was meant to be a walkover for the British and French troops. The greatest artillery barrage ever delivered up to that date, involving around 3,000 guns, had pounded the German lines for a week, from 24 June, and was further extended after the inclement weather led to a postponement of the infantry attack. At 7.30 am on 1 July, 10 minutes after the detonation of the Hawthorn mine under the German lines, one of 17 such explosions, the whistles were blown and along a 30 kilometre front men lumbered out into No-Man's-Land, formed up in lines, and began walking slowly towards the enemy front trenches. As the creeping barrage lifted from the front line, the Germans, who had been largely immune from physical harm in their underground shelters, emerged to man their machine-gun posts and line the parapets to inflict a terrible toll. The British army suffered 58,000 casualties, a third of who were killed – a macabre record for losses suffered in one day that still stands a century on. Virtually along the entire line the British were driven back to their starting trenches with limited successes only achieved in a handful of places with some of these, such as with the Ulster Division's gains at Thiepval, being largely lost again for want of reinforcements and the failure of units on their flanks. Among the troops who took part on the opening day of the battle were both 1st and 2nd Royal Dublin Fusiliers, the 1st Royal Irish Rifles, 1st Royal Irish Fusiliers, 2nd Royal Irish Regiment, the 1st and 2nd Royal Inniskilling Fusiliers and all four Tyneside Irish battalions of the Northumberland Fusiliers.

At least 11 sets of Irish brothers died on 1 July 1916, with two families losing three boys. Of these 24 men, 19 have no known grave and are commemorated on the Thiepval Memorial. Three black edged telegraphs arrived at the home of Mary Donaldson at Ballyloughan, near Comber, County Down. Her three boys, John, 26, James, 23, and 21-year-old Samuel had been serving together

Opposite: An artist's impression of the storming of the Schwaben Redoubt, a German strongpoint briefly taken by the men of the 36th (Ulster) Division on 1 July 1916, the opening day of the Battle of the Somme. *(From The Great War magazine, published 1915–1919)*

in B Company of the 13th Royal Irish Rifles when killed. The extent of the tragedy was equally devastating in the Hobbs household in Armagh. Sergeant Robert Hobbs, 38, and privates David and Andrew were all members of the 9th Royal Irish Fusiliers.

Three sons of James and Jeannie Hewitt, of Altamont, Mornington Park, Bangor, County Down, died during the war, two of them on 1 July 1916. Lieutenant Holt Montgomery Hewitt, born on 11 June 1887, had joined the 13th Royal Irish Rifles, and was later commissioned into the 9th Royal Inniskilling Fusiliers, then transferred to the 109th Machine Gun Company in early 1916. As he led his gun teams across No-Man's-Land they were swallowed up in the artillery and machine-gun fire. The 29-year-old's remains were buried at Mill Road Cemetery, close to the Ulster Tower, Thiepval. William Arthur Hewitt was the youngest of the brothers , aged just 23 when killed with the 9th Royal Inniskilling Fusiliers. EW Crawford, Adjutant of the 9th Royal Inniskilling Fusiliers, told his parents: "Willie led his platoon fearlessly over the top. One of his men told me that he was wounded but still carried on, but had to stop – from loss of blood. He was a grand boy, one of the finest characters I have seen." The third son, Ernest Henry, was killed in June 1915 at Festubert and is commemorated on the Le Touret Memorial, Pas de Calais, France.

The Hollywood brothers were killed with different regiments. Arthur Carson Hollywood was 24 and a lieutenant with the 9th Royal Irish Fusiliers. He was fatally wounded by machine-gun fire as he attempted to make it to the second line of enemy trenches. His younger brother James, 23, had been commissioned from quartermaster sergeant in the reserve 18th battalion of the Royal Irish Rifles into the 12th Rifles. The telegrams telling of the brothers' deaths arrived at the family home, Bayswater, Princetown Road, Bangor, a day apart.

The Burke brothers, John, 20, and Joseph, died with the 9th Royal Irish Fusiliers. They were the sons of John and Annie Burke of Guardhill, Newbliss, Clones, County Monaghan, and are buried at the AIF Burial Ground, Flers, and Puchevillers British Cemetery respectively. William and George Larmour, of Fitzroy Avenue, Belfast, were both serving in the Royal Irish Rifles, one in the 9th battalion and the other in the 14th battalion. Teenagers John and James McGowan, sons of Jane McGowan, of King Street, Ballymena, County Antrim, were both serving in the 12th Royal Irish Rifles. The Philbins, 35-year-old William and John, 32, were from Cloonaghboy, Swinford, County Mayo. The older man was a private in the Tyneside Irish battalion of the Northumberland Fusiliers, while John was serving with the 1st Royal Inniskilling Fusiliers.

Donegal men Andrew and Ezekiel Smyth, aged 25 and 23 respectively, were the sons of Thomas and Mary Smyth of Convoy, County Donegal, and were serving with the 11th Royal Inniskilling Fusiliers. Samuel and William Watson were not only in the same battalion as the Smyths but had also been neighbours. Samuel, 28, a married man, was buried in Connaught Cemetery, Thiepval. Gilbert Wedgwood, 22, was serving in the 109th Machine Gun Corps and his brother Philip in the 16th Royal Irish Rifles. Their father, the Rev George Wedgwood, of North Road, east Belfast, was a well known figure in the city. Philip was buried at Mill Road Cemetery.

The British persisted with their attacks over the coming days and finally succeeded in taking most of the enemy's front lines by 11 July. By that stage the Germans had begun moving troops from Verdun to reinforce the lines at the Somme, further reducing the chances of success. Mametz Wood was taken on 12 July and a push made towards High Wood. A new offensive, the Battle of Bazentin Ridge, opened at dawn on 14 July and ran for three days, with the villages of Bazentin-le-Grand, Bazentin-le-Petit and Longueval secured. A bid to take Martinpuich, however, proved a disaster as the Germans still held much of High Wood. The bloody battle to take Delville Wood, marked by hand-to-hand fighting, began on 15 July and ran until 3 September with the South African Brigade suffering heavily. A subsidiary attack by the Australians and British to take the high ground of Pozieres Ridge, begun on 23 July, finally succeeded after two weeks of hard fighting, though the heavily defended Mouquet and Thiepval remained in German hands.

The 16th (Irish) Division was heavily involved in the Battle of Guillemont, which opened on 3 September, with the village and Leuze Wood beyond falling to the British, and the taking of Ginchy less than two weeks later, sustaining more than 4,300 casualties over the period. The Battle of Flers-Courcelette, opened on 15 September, saw the first use of tanks, with only 15 of the 49 notoriously unreliable machines available making it to the front line. Martinpuich, Flers and Courcelette, along with High Wood, all fell to the Allies. Heavy rains in October turned the battleground into a muddy quagmire and while the fighting continued little ground was gained and the battle finally came to an official end in mid-November, when the 10th Royal Dublin Fusiliers helped capture Beaumont-Hamel, which had been one of the first day objectives. British casualties at the Battle of the Somme were estimated at 420,000, the French lost 195,000 and the Germans some 650,000.

WITNESS TO SLAUGHTER:
Fred Percy Crozier

Fred Percy Crozier, from an Anglo-Irish family, commanded the West Belfast UVF battalion before the war. Appointed as second-in-command of many of those same men when they became the nucleus of the 9th Royal Irish Rifles, he later took over the battalion's reins when the original CO returned home ill. On 1 July his Shankill boys were in the last wave of troops to cross No-Man's-Land. By then the attacks of the 29th and 32nd divisions on either side had failed, leaving the Ulstermen vulnerable to fire from their flanks. Crozier defied divisional orders to lead his men through Thiepval Wood and on to the battlefield before returning to his dug-out directly behind what today is Connaught Cemetery.

In his book, *A Brass Hat in No Man's Land*, he describes the scene:

"Suddenly the air is rent with deafening thunder; never has such man-made noise been heard before! The hour has struck! 7.30 am has arrived. The first wave goes over, 'carrying the creeping barrage on its back.' We wait. Instantly the enemy replies, putting down a counter-barrage which misses us by inches. Thanks to the steep slope of Speyside we are immune. That half hour is the worst on record, for thoughts and forebodings; so we sing, but it is difficult to keep in tune or rhythm on account of the noise. At last our minute, our own minute arrives. I get up from the ground and whistle. The others rise. We move off, with steady pace. As we pass Gordon Castle we pick up coils of wire and iron posts. I feel sure in my innermost thoughts these things will never be carried all the way to the final objective; however, even if they get half way it will be a help. Then I glance to the right through a gap in the trees. I see the 10th Rifles plodding on and then my eyes are riveted on a sight I shall never see again. It is the 32nd division at its best. I see rows upon rows of British soldiers lying dead, dying or wounded, in no man's land. Here and there I see an officer urging on his followers. Occasionally I can see the hands thrown up and then a body flops to the ground. The bursting shells and smoke make visibility poor, but I see enough to convince me Thiepval village is still held, for it is now 8.00 am and by 7.45 am it should have fallen to allow of our passage forward on its flank."

Arriving at the frontline, Crozier gave his officers some last minute instructions as they passed him and out into No-Man's-Land. He goes on:

"I blow shrill whistle calls and signal the advance. They go on their last journey… And what of the dead and wounded? This spirited dash across no man's land, carried out as if on parade, has cost us some fifty dead and seventy disabled. The dead no longer count. War has no use for dead men. With luck they will be buried later; the wounded try to crawl back to our lines. Some are hit again in so doing, but the majority lie out all day, sun-baked, parched, uncared for, often delirious and at any rate in great pain. My immediate duty is to look after the situation and not bother about wounded men. I send a message to brigade and move to my battle headquarters in the wood. It is a deep dug-out which has been allocated to me for my use. It needs to be deep to keep out heavy stuff. The telephone lines are all cut by shell fire… A wrong thing has been done. I find the place full of dead and wounded men. It has been used as a refuge. None of the wounded can walk. There are no stretchers. Most are in agony. They have seen no doctor. Some have been there for days. They have simply been pushed down the steep thirty feet deep entrance out of further harm's way and left – perhaps forgotten. As I enter the dugout I am greeted with the most awful cries from these dreadfully wounded men. Their removal is a Herculean task, for it was never intended that the dying and the helpless should have to use the deep stairway. After a time, the last sufferer and the last corpse are removed. Meanwhile I mount the parapet to observe. The attack on the right has come to a standstill; the last detailed man has sacrificed himself on the German wire to the God of War. Thiepval village is masked with a wall of corpses."

Crozier, who later rose to the rank of brigadier-general, finished the war with the 40th Division. He later commanded the Auxiliaries, made up of former officers, in Ireland but resigned early in 1921 in disgust after running into official opposition as he tried to discipline his men for a spate of unauthorised actions. He died on 31 August 1937.

MP CARTED FROM THE BATTLEFIELD:
Captain Charles Craig

The son of a millionaire whiskey distiller, Charles Curtis Craig had served as the Member of Parliament for South Antrim since 1903. In 1914, he joined the 11th Royal Irish Rifles, largely made up of Ulster Volunteer Force members from his constituency. At the Battle of the Somme he had led his men across No-Man's-Land and deep into the German lines until wounded and falling into the enemy's hands. Writing to his wife from his hospital bed at Gutersloh, in the Westphalia region of Germany, he described how he had been directing his men as they attempted to turn a stretch of trench in the enemy's C-line into a defensive position when, about 10.00 am, he was struck by a piece of shrapnel in the back of his leg below the knee. After having his injury bandaged, and sending off a runner to find another officer to take over from him, he crawled into a nearby shell hole where he lay much of the day. He wrote: "During this six hours the shelling and machine-gun fire was very heavy, but my shell-hole protected me so well that I was not hit again, except for a very small piece of shrapnel on the arm, which only made a small cut."

At about 4.00 pm the enemy launched a counter attack, during which Captain Craig was found and taken prisoner. He described his treatment:

"I had to hobble into a trench close at hand, where I stayed till ten o'clock, till two Germans took me to another line of trenches about 400 or 500 yards further back. This was the worst experience I had, as my leg was stiff and painful. The space between the lines was being heavily shelled by our guns, and my two supporters were naturally anxious to get over the ground as quickly as possible, and did not give me much rest, so I was very glad when, after what seemed an age, though it was not more than fifteen minutes or so, we got to the trench. I was put in a deep dug-out, where there were a lot of officers and men, and they were all very kind to me and gave me food and water, and here I spent the night. My leg was by now much swollen, but not painful except when I tried to walk. There were no stretchers, so in the morning I had to hobble as best I could out of the trenches till we came to a wood. Soon after I passed a dug-out where some artillery officers lived, and the captain seeing my condition refused to allow me to go any further on foot, and took me in and gave me food and wine, and set his men to make a kind of sling to carry me in. This proved a failure; as I was so heavy, I nearly broke the men's shoulders. He then got a wheelbarrow, and in this I was wheeled a mile or more to a dressing station, where my wound was dressed, and I was inoculated for tetanus. That night I was taken to a village, and had a comfortable bed and a good sleep."

The officer who took over from Craig in the trenches, Lieutenant Reginald Henry Neill, was also initially reported to have been captured on 1 July but later confirmed killed. The 21-year-old from Craigavad, County Down, is commemorated on the Thiepval Memorial.

Captain Craig, whose brother Sir James Craig was to become the first Prime Minister of Northern Ireland, returned to politics after the war, being elected to the Antrim constituency in 1922 following the abolishment of the South Antrim seat. He retired from Westminster in 1929 to take up a post with the Royal Mint and passed away in January 1960.

Captain Charles Craig was already 45 years old when he joined the Royal Irish Rifles in 1914. After the war he returned to his role as MP for South Antrim and is seen here delivering a speech at the opening of a hockey pavilion near Lisburn in 1925. *(Irish Linen Centre & Lisburn Museum Collection)*

BEASTS WHO KILLED OUR BOYS:
Lieutenant Fred Barker

The 14th Royal Irish Rifles was in the reserve trenches on 1 July, destined to follow the first wave of the attack across No-Man's-Land. The men, many of them members of the Young Citizen Volunteers of Ireland, which had formed the core of the battalion's volunteers, had been waiting for hours for the order to go. Along with the 11th Royal Inniskilling Fusiliers, they were to consolidate the first two German lines, turning round the defences to ward off any enemy counter-attack, while pushing forward patrols to keep in contact with the first wave as it pressed on.

Lieutenant Fred Barker had only recently been commissioned. From Fitzwilliam Street in Belfast, he had joined the Black Watch in November, 1914, quickly rising to the rank of sergeant. In 1916 he was at the 7th Cadet Battalion at the Curragh for officer training and was sent to Dublin during the Easter Rising. Now he was about to lead the men of the 14th Rifles into their first major battle. "Dawn broke, cold-grey, and cheerless and found us crowded uncomfortably in a narrow communication trench just behind the front line," he was later to write while confined to a hospital bed recovering from wounds.

"For three long hours we had stood there, listening to the hum of our shells spreading and waiting for the moment when the whistles would blow and we would go 'over the top'. Daylight brought its own new misery. Yesterday morning we had assembled in a cosy camp far behind the lines. How clearly we had learnt the plan of today's attack! How jovially we had sat down to lunch; how smartly we marched away over the clear white road – for it was summer – and how we sang!

Now as we froze in our narrow trench, yesterday was buried in a world that we had left a long time ago. The dull burst of each shell echoed through the brain like the clang of a hammer. To each of us, I think, came that feeling of utter weariness that only a soldier knows. What was the use of it all? With a sudden crash, a shell exploded some yards away and still trying to keep a cool head I made my way to the spot, for the shell had burst among my platoon. Four men were dead and a corporal lay at the bottom of the trench with both legs gone and a great hole in his side. As I bent over him his eyes opened and looked in mine. Their mute appeal of unfairness, their patient wonder haunt me still. Tears rolled down his cheeks slowly and then with the sigh of a tired child he was gone.

I glanced at my watch; only a few more minutes now and the artillery barrage would lift, the first wave of men would 'go over'. Even now the firing seemed to die away as the gunners altered their fuses. For the fraction of a second there seemed to be quietness and in that space of time my senses and reasoning powers returned. The whistles blew, the first wave climbed out of the trenches and with the swish of the shells there rushed through my mind a thousand and one things – thoughts of home and all that was dear to me – a feeling of fear, especially fear of showing that I felt it. It was the greatest moment in the greatest war of all time. Thoughts crowded in and filled my mind – thoughts that are more deadly than the venomous guns spitting their fire a few hundred yards away. Quickly we took our places. Machine-guns from the enemy opened fire and the heavy shells plumped around us. 'Nearly time isn't it, sir?' yelled my sergeant. I looked at my watch. I yelled back and put my whistle to my mouth. One blast and we climbed the trench, but that blast blew from me all thoughts, except the memory of my dead corporal and before my eyes there was only the inferno opposite, where we were slowly making our way and where I would find the beasts who had killed the boys – our boys."

Lieutenant Barker had been an original member of the Young Citizen Volunteers as well as a member of the South Belfast Regiment of the Ulster Volunteer Force and Windsor and Stranmillis Unionist Clubs. He was wounded twice more in October 1916 and again at the Battle of Messines on 7 June 1917.

TAKING THIRTY PRISONERS:
Samuel Turner

Samuel James Turner was clearly a man of strong beliefs. In 1912 he had left his home at Pembrooke Cottages, Dundrum, County Dublin, to travel to Belfast, where he had family ties, in order that he could sign the Ulster Covenant at Crumlin Road Lecture Hall. Aged 42 in 1914, the father of five young children again uprooted himself, this time to join the 36th (Ulster) Division, serving in the 9th Royal Irish Fusiliers. Turner, however, a deeply religious man, was not a hot head and during the Battle of the Somme performed an act of bravery that most certainly saved the lives of many enemy troops and possibly of some of his comrades. Writing to a cousin after the battle he told of how he had got to his knees and asked God for His protection, after which "I walked in fearlessly". He went on:

"We marched on to the first line of trenches, which we captured by storm. Bullets were whistling about our ears everywhere. Sometimes I walked on with my rifle slung. I saw some of our men marching on to the second line of trenches. I doubled up and overtook them, and helped to capture it. We got prisoners in both trenches. Then we marched on to the third line, and captured it, and took more prisoners there. We marched again to the fourth line of trenches and attacked it. I had gone on a trench too far, as my place was at the third line. I went back. On my way back I entered a dugout, and sat on the bottom steps to have a rest, as I was pretty tired.

At the entrance of the dugout there was a table on its end, as if for a barricade. I mentioned to a comrade that it looked as if the Germans had made a barricade, asking 'how did they get out without knocking down the table?' I found some candles and lit one. Then I entered in cautiously. I was standing in the middle of the floor, with the candle in my hand all alone, as none of the lads would venture in with me. While standing there I heard a voice saying 'Kamarade'. I looked up the steps, and thought that some of our lads were trying to frighten me. I asked them did they speak, and they said not. Then I heard the same voice saying 'Kamarade'. I looked down far in the dugout and shouted 'Kamarades'. An answer came back 'Kamarades'. I repeated it. Then the same voice shouted 'Prisoners'. I answered back. I then handed up my rifle and bayonet, so that I would be unarmed to encourage the prisoners. I ordered the prisoners to come up unarmed, and sent up word to some of our men to prepare to receive some captives. All the lads cleared up the steps to leave room for the prisoners to get up. I was there alone in the dugout and unarmed. The first to come up to me and put up his hands in token of surrender was a captain of the Prussian Guards. He stood and said 'Prisoners'. I said 'Yes, sir, walk up the stairs; there's an escort up there.' He seemed quite relieved, shook me by the hand, and said something in German which sounded as if he said I was brave, and walked up the stairs. After him came about fifteen officers and men in single file. Each stood as he came to me, put up his hands and surrendered, saying 'Prisoners'. Some of them shook me by the hand, tapped me on the shoulder, stepped in front of me, and had a good look at me, shook their head, and said 'Brave English'. One lieutenant seemed shaken with fear. He almost hid behind another officer. When he saw that I was unarmed he stepped up to me and put his hand in mine, and, one arm leaning on my shoulder, said, 'Brave man'. He shook hands again, and walked up. Then two others came helping a wounded comrade. I ordered one of them up, and said I would help the wounded man up with his comrade. I asked them if all were up. They said all were. We brought up the wounded man to the top of the steps, where all were marched off except the wounded soldier. I lost count of the prisoners as they came up to me and surrendered. Some of the lads said there were thirty, not a bad batch for one man to get, and he unarmed."

Private Turner searched the dugout, turning up some letters, maps and paperwork, which he gathered up with the intention of finding an officer to hand them over to. "While there the sergeant ordered me to throw them down, and get up and man the parapet as the Germans were counter-attacking us. We held what we had secured until we were relieved. I looked then for the letters, but they were gone. But I believe they reached the right hands."

HOW THE COLONEL CAME BACK:
Lieutenant Colonel Fitzroy Curzon

Lieutenant Colonel Fitzroy Curzon, of the 6th Royal Irish Regiment, was killed at the taking of Ginchy on Saturday, 9 September 1916, when, in the face of ferocious German opposition, the 47th and 48th Brigades of the 16th (Irish) Division had succeeded where others had failed. Major William Redmond, MP, brother of the Irish parliamentary party leader John, related the affect the death of the 57-year-old colonel had on the battalion he had raised and trained:

"The position to be assaulted had already, in the course of the long draw-out battle, been assaulted six times, but without success. For two years the Germans had been entrenched there, and they had, as well they know how, made the position very strong. Barbed wire entanglements of the most intricate kinds; machine-gun emplacements where the guns, by cunningly contrived lifts, could disappear during bombardment and reappear at once afterwards. Everything that could be contrived to ward off attacks had been contrived, and quite openly the enemy boasted that the place was impregnable. Now, however, the joyful news came that in the seventh attack the 'old Irish Division' had won through.

The following day the victorious battalions worked hard 'consolidating' the ground won and digging themselves in to resist counter-attacks. When night came they would be relieved by fresh troops; and so when night did come, and it came loweringly, with angry, black clouds sweeping across the moon, the field kitchens were sent up the long dark road down which the men would march from the battlefield. Midway along the road some of the battalions would bivouac for the night at each side. So the transport officers hurried off the field kitchens to meet them and to prepare hot soup, tea and everything possible for the weary soldiers who for two days and two nights had been fighting and advancing with only such food as they might carry in their haversacks. This long, dark road was intermittently shelled; but had it been shelled on every yard of it the transport men would willingly have gone up it to meet their battle-worn comrades.

The great majority of the wounded had been picked up and dealt with; but after an action, wounded men are encountered singly and in little groups – men who have been sheltering in shell-holes and unable for the time to reach assistance or make their plight known. From these returning sufferers much information is gleaned by the men of the transport as they pass along. Comrades are inquired for and officers asked after. Sometimes the answer is 'Dead,' sometimes 'Wounded,' and sometimes it is hard to get definite news. On the night to which the writer refers the transport men of a certain battalion asked many questions of the men they met coming down from the front. Nearly all the questions included inquiries as to the colonel. 'How is the old CO? Is he all right? Particularly anxiously did the colonel's groom ask this question. At last there is the steady noise of marching feet. The battalion has arrived, and all is stir about the kitchens.

The colonel's servant meets a man of his own company, very tired, very muddy, and very careworn-looking. 'Hullo, Pat! Glad to see you, old man! Is the CO come?' 'The CO? Yes, ah, yes! The CO has come!' And heartily rejoiced at the news, the colonel's servant hurries off to the cook sergeant for the hot tea he has arranged to be ready for his master. Even the most weary and worn-out soldiers let their tongues wag when they come to the field kitchens and know that some hot food is at hand. It is strange to-night, though, how silent the men are. They sink to the ground slowly, they seem even indifferent to the greetings of the transport men – they even ignore the kitchens!

The colonel's servant comes hurrying along with a steaming cup in his hand. He stops near the shelter he had put up for his master behind the wagon. There is an officer standing close by. 'Very glad to see you safe, captain! Is the colonel here, sir.' The officer looks up, his face haggard. Pointing to the shelter, he replies to the servant in a low voice. 'Yes, oh, yes, the colonel is here.' Very eagerly the servant goes towards the rude shelter, saying, 'Colonel, indeed I am glad you are back. I have your tea, sir; or perhaps you would like a little soup; or else may –' The officer interrupts him, and, laying his hand upon his shoulder, says 'Don't you understand, man? – the colonel – '. The two men stare at each other. In a flash the servant now understands!

Very tenderly they raise the covering from the body, and by the light of an electric torch they look at the calm, dead face. Yes, the colonel is here. He might, indeed, be sleeping, so peaceful he seems, his hands clasped across his breast, over the mud-stained and blood-stained uniform. A long, cruel gash spreads over one cheek – not disfiguring but rather, indeed, ennobling the more the face which the men had always thought looked noble. When the morning dawned they carried him, mourning and with respect, to the graveyard in the little ruined town nearby. And thus it was the colonel came back with his battalion."

Lieutenant Colonel Curzon's grave lies in Carnoy Cemetery, next but one to another battalion commander, Lieutenant Colonel John Lenox-Conyngham, of the 6th Connaught Rangers, from Moneymore, County Londonderry, who had been killed six days earlier on 3 September 1916, aged 54. *(Courtesy of the Commonwealth War Graves Commission)*

FOR THE SAKE OF IRELAND:
Lieutenant Tom Kettle

Tom Kettle was already in Belgium when the German army invaded in 1914 – attempting to buy arms for the Irish Volunteers and going on to cover the early fighting as a journalist. From a staunchly nationalist farming family, he had been born in north County Dublin in 1880. A year after being called to the bar he was elected MP for East Tyrone, at the age of 26, but resigned his seat after four years following his appointment to a professorship of national economics at University College Dublin. Kettle had been a vocal opponent of the war in South Africa but, passionate in his support for the liberation of Belgium, actively encouraged nationalist recruitment into the army, admitting: "It is a confession to make and I make it. I care for liberty more than I care for Ireland."

Commissioned into the Royal Dublin Fusiliers, he remained on home duties initially because of his heavy drinking. However, in July 1916, following the Dublin Rising – during which his brother-in-law, Frank Sheehy Skeffington was murdered at Portobello Barracks – he was sent to France to join his unit. Even then, with his health failing due to the harsh trench conditions, he had the chance to escape frontline soldiering, but insisted on staying with his men. Together with a fellow lieutenant, James Emmet Dalton, Kettle moved his men into position for the coming battle at Ginchy on the evening of 8 September. "I was with Tom when he advanced to the position that night, and the stench of the dead that covered our road was so awful that we both used some foot-powder on our faces," recalled Dalton.

"When we reached our objective we dug ourselves in, and then, at five o'clock pm on the 9th, we attacked Ginchy. I was just behind Tom when we went over the top. He was in a bent position, and a bullet got over a steel waistcoat that he wore and entered his heart. Well, he only lasted about one minute, and he had my crucifix in his hands. Then Boyd took all the papers and things out of Tom's pockets in order to keep them for Mrs Kettle, but poor Boyd was blown to atoms in a few minutes. The Welsh Guards buried Mr Kettle's remains. Tom's death has been a big blow to the regiment, and I am afraid that I could not put in words my feelings on the subject."

All told, the fighting around Guillemont and Ginchy in early September had resulted in the 16th (Irish) Division sustaining more than 4,300 casualties, of which close to 1,200 were fatal.

Lieutenant Kettle had prepared a letter to be sent to his wife in the event of his death. In it he says:

"Had I lived I had meant to call my next book on the relations of Ireland and England *The Two Fools; A Tragedy of Errors.* It has needed all the folly of England and all the folly of Ireland to produce the situation in which our unhappy country is now involved. I have mixed much with Englishmen and with Protestant Ulstermen, and I know that there is no real or abiding reason for the gulfs, saltier than the sea, that now dismember the natural alliance of both of them with us Irish Nationalists. It needs only a Fiat Lux of a kind very easily compassed to replace the unnatural by the natural. In the name, and by the seal, of the blood given in the last two years I ask for Colonial Home Rule for Ireland, a thing essential in itself, and essential as a prologue to the reconstruction of the Empire. Ulster will agree. And I ask for the immediate withdrawal of martial law in Ireland, and an amnesty for all Sinn Féin prisoners. If this war has taught us anything it is that great things can be done only in a great way."

Lieutenant Dalton, who was awarded the Military Cross for his courage at Ginchy, survived the war and went on to play a major part in the turmoil that shook Ireland in the years following. Born in the United States, he was raised in Dublin, had joined the Irish Volunteers in 1913 and the British army in 1915. On his return from the war he took up arms for Michael Collins, rising to the rank of Major-General. He was in charge of the artillery that bombarded the Four Courts and was alongside Collins when he was fatally wounded. Dalton stepped down from his post in 1922 to briefly become Secretary to the Senate and later moved into the movie business. He died, aged 80, in 1978.

THE FINAL FIGHTING:
Lance Corporal Smith

The Battle of the Somme officially came to an end on 13 November 1916. On that day the Highland Division launched an attack at Beaumont-Hamel, which had been an objective on the first day of the battle. For the 6th Seaforth Highlanders, following up the lead battalions, this was its first full-scale attack. The men left their trenches at 5.45 am, just as the huge Hawthorn mine was detonated, moving forward as the fifth and sixth waves. The attack had originally been planned for 24 October but had repeatedly been postponed due to bad weather, and the ground was still a sodden mass. A thick fog covered the battlefield and, with no preliminary bombardment, the Germans were taken by surprise. The enemy frontline fell quickly and the 6th Seaforths pressed on to the second line. Going forward with his detachment was Lance Corporal Smith, son of the superintendent of the agricultural station at Athenry, Galway.

"From the German second and third lines star shells began to go up, and then crack, crack, went the rifles, machine-guns opened fire, and a perfect hail of lead began to fly round us in all directions," he recorded.

"I was keeping close to the corporal of my section and although I was excited for the first second or two, I soon steadied down and began to take a view of our general surroundings – men were falling on every side, and the roar of the artillery was so deafening that you could not hear your pal speak even although only a foot away. Our artillery was simply magnificent, in fact it always is, and outclassed the German artillery. We encountered little opposition in the first two German lines, but in the third there was determined fighting for a time with bayonet and bomb, but eventually our boys got the upper hand and on we went to our final objective, the sixth German line, which is a ridge."

Lance Corporal Smith spotted a German "poking his nose out of a dug-out" and with a few men went to investigate.

"When I reached the entrance to the dug-out I saw there were two Germans, and shouted at them to come out; they were evidently very scared and would not come out, but instead called that I should go down to them. Well, I had often heard of German treachery and I would not go down, but pulled out a 'Mills' hand grenade with the intention of throwing it amongst them if they did not come out. When they saw the bomb they began to shout and came up the stairs – out of the dug-out 53 of them came altogether and we marched them down the communication trench to our lines."

German snipers constantly harassed the group, killing as many German prisoners as British troops in the communication trench. Lance Corporal Smith had a very narrow escape, a bullet striking the rim of his helmet and tearing through an ear. He went on:

"The Germans seemed very glad to be taken prisoners, evidently they understood how Britain treats her captives. One German prisoner said to me 'You, boys, don't know what a bombardment is, we have been in hell for the past two or three days.' Another pointed to my knees which were badly cut with barbed wire and said, 'The kilt is very bad for the trenches.' Some of the prisoners appeared to be nice intelligent young chaps, while others have a cut-throat look about them that nobody could admire. They fired at our wounded while being carried on stretchers, and in some cases bayoneted our wounded when they got the opportunity. My impression of the German is – that he is a good soldier, good at trench warfare, his artillery is good, but he seems to be short of munitions, and we outclass him now, but at hand-to-hand fighting he is an absolute coward, whether he be Prussian Guards, Bavarian, or anything else – whenever the British come to close quarters it is a cry of 'Mercy, mercy, kamerade'."

Lance Corporal Smith finally made his way back down the line to have his wounded ear bandaged. Feeling in good spirits, he bumped into a senior officer at the dressing station who asked how he was. "He asked me where I was from, and on telling him the West of Ireland, he said 'Why are you in kilts?' 'Well,' I said, 'because they frighten the Germans, sir, and I think anyone will tell you the same'."

A granite cross, bearing the Irish inscription 'Do Cum Glóire Dé Agus Onóra Na hÉireann', or 'To the Glory of God and Honour of Ireland', was erected at Guillemont, on the Somme front, in memory of the men of the 16th (Irish) Division. *(Author)*

"I am sure you have been rather uneasy for the past few days for by this time you will have seen that the Ulster Division has been in action again. Well we have made another name for ourselves and have been in another big battle and I am thankful to say I am one of the very few who have come through it… Most of the officers with me are getting home but they are all very badly wounded and two have died beside me so that I am glad I am stopping here instead of being badly wounded."

William Moore, Belfast, 12th Royal Irish Rifles writing from No 20 General Hospital, France

1917

WAR OF ATTRITION

The Germans were on the move early in 1917. Beginning in February, they carried out a strategic withdrawal, destroying everything in their wake including flattening villages, cutting down trees, planting booby-traps, destroying roads and poisoning water supplies. Together with the devastated battlegrounds of 1916, the Allies now inherited a wasteland that ran for several miles before halting at the Hindenburg Line, a series of linked strong points that gave the enemy all the geographical and military advantages while the British had to begin digging in afresh.

Further north, however, an old obstacle was finally about to give way. Vimy Ridge, which dominated the plains of Artois below and overlooked the Allied-held city of Arras, had been attacked time and again by French and British troops, its ground churned up with countless shells. Beginning on 9 April, Easter Monday of that year, the Canadians finally succeeded in pushing the Germans from the high ground they had held since September 1914.

While the British were celebrating the French were in disarray. The disastrous Second Battle of the Aisne in April had sparked a widespread mutiny in the army. A new military commander, Henri-Philippe Petain, re-established order but had to withdraw from offensive operations for a time. It was an additional burden for the British but one they seemed well equipped to handle. After weeks of an artillery bombardment by more than 2,500 guns and heavy mortars, and the detonation of 19 mines under the German lines at 3.10 am on 7 June, the British swept across the enemy positions at Messines. The men of the 16th (Irish) Division and 36th (Ulster) Divisions fought side by side in the battle, with members of the latter bringing in the most famous casualty, William Redmond, MP, and brother of John Redmond, leader of the Irish parliamentary party. All the initial gains hoped for were in Allied hands within three hours and the final objectives by mid-afternoon.

The Rev B Fisher, a Church of England chaplain with roots in Ireland, administered to some of the wounded and dying at No 7 General Hospital,

Opposite: The Russian army, soon to withdraw from the war, seen manning a line during the fighting in Poland. *(The Great War magazine, published 1915-1919)*

based at St Omer in northern France. One of those he attended to was Corporal John Kane, a 26-year-old serving with the 15th Royal Irish Rifles, one of the Belfast battalions of the 36th (Ulster) Division. On 12 June 1917, he wrote to his widow:

> "I want to send you a line of deepest sympathy on the sad loss of your brave husband Corpl. JA Kane 19/209 which took place in this hospital at 1.00 am on 9.6.17. He was admitted here on 7.6.17 and in that short time I saw a lot of him because poor fellow he was so bad and the first of my countrymen to come in from the great push. He was quite ready for the call and quite clear in his mind to the last. He said to me don't go and I answered 'no my son, I will not leave you', and I did not until I had closed the dear boy's eyes with a prayer for you. I was sorry to lose him. He had every care, but the brave fellow had shrapnel wounds in arms and legs. He was thinking of you up to the last. I buried him in the Souvenir Cemetery at 2.00 pm on 9.6.17. The grave will be properly marked and all his things have been sent off to you. May God bless you and give you grace to bear your loss. We can ill afford to lose such fine brave men."

Messines was a precursor to the much more ambitious Third Battle of Ypres, better known as Passchendaele and launched on 31 July. However, hopes of a breakthrough in Flanders rapidly petered out in the mud and torrential rain though the fighting continued until 6 November. More than four million shells were fired in the preliminary bombardment, which began on 18 July. Within days of the infantry going forward, it began to rain, turning the ground into a quagmire that sucked men to their deaths. The Battle of Langemarck, launched on 16 August, resulted in minor gains and heavy casualties, with the 16th and 36th Divisions again fighting side-by-side. A series of small-scale battles followed, achieving limited gains, with the fighting concluding with the capture of the village of Passchendaele. In total, Third Ypres cost some 360,000 British casualties. One of the biggest Irish losses was not a fighting man at all. Father Willie Doyle, from Dalkey, was a Jesuit priest serving as a chaplain with the 16th (Irish Division). On 16 August he is said to have run "all day hither and thither over the battlefield like an angel of mercy" as he administered to the wounded and dying. A holder of the Military Cross, he had been with the division throughout the Somme and Messines but was to lose his life that day at Passchendaele.

Tanks, unable to play any useful part at Passchendaele due to the ground conditions, came into their own at the Battle of Cambrai when they were used in large numbers for the first time. At dawn on 20 November, some 476 tanks, supported by six infantry divisions and two of cavalry, advanced without a preliminary bombardment. Taken by surprise, the German Hindenburg Line was breached for the first time as the enemy fell back some 6 km within hours. Within a week, however, German counter-attacks had won back virtually all the lost ground.

In the Middle East, the British had recaptured Kut-al-Amara in February 1917, and marched on Baghdad, which the Turks began to evacuate on 10 March, allowing the British to enter the city the following day without difficulty. In Gaza, Turkish forces were attacked on 26 March as a prelude to an assault to take Palestine, but the outcome was inconclusive. A renewed attempt on 17 April proved similarly fruitless. However, following the appointment of the Anglo-Irish general Sir Edmund Allenby, the British at last began making headway. On 31 October, shortly after the arrival of the 10th (Irish) Division in Egypt, he launched the Third Battle of Gaza by attacking a flank and using his cavalry to capture the local water supplies. The Turks retired on Jerusalem, only for the city to fall to the British two weeks before Christmas 1917.

Two events that were to contribute hugely to the course of the war the following year began in 1917. One was the withdrawal of Russia from the conflict. Tsar Nicholas II had abdicated on 15 March, with the Bolsheviks overthrowing the new Russian government on 7 November. Little more than a month later they had signed an armistice with the Central Powers (followed on 3 March by the Treaty of Brest Litovsk peace agreement) that allowed the Germans to withdraw vast numbers of reserves from the Eastern Front to the Western. The enemy's advantage in numerical strength was threatened by the other major event of 1917, the United States' declaration of war in April on the side of the Allies which, in time, would see millions of American soldiers becoming available on the Western Front. The first batch of 14,000 'Doughboys' was landed at Saint Nazaire in France on 26 June 1917. It wasn't until October that year, however, that US troops were considered sufficiently battle ready to take over a section of line alongside the French in the Luneville sector, near Nancy. The first American soldiers to die in the war were killed on 3 November 1917 in a German raid on their trenches. They included Thomas Francis Enright, a 30-year-old from Pittsburgh, Pennsylvania, and the son of Irish immigrants.

SICKENED BY AUTHORITIES' ATTITUDE:
Doctor Tom Collins

On 20 January 1917, Lieutenant Thomas Francis Collins sat down to write a letter that he had been fuming over for the best part of three weeks. Just after Christmas he had received a notice from the Clifden Board of Guardians, Galway, demanding that he pack his bags and return to his post as medical officer of the Clifden Union or face dismissal. Obviously peeved, and having already had his solicitor contact the guardians on his behalf, the lieutenant wrote directly to them himself from "somewhere in India":

"Do you understand that I am somewhere in India doing my duty as a medical officer in a war hospital for British troops, where your gallant sick and wounded lie, and remember also you granted me permission to join the Royal Army Medical Corps; and again allow me to inform you that when I joined I had to sign a contract with the British Government, and that contract cannot be broken."

Reminding the guardians that he had obtained all the necessary permissions from the authority and the Local Government Board, including agreeing the terms and conditions of his leave, he went on:

"I ask you as rational beings can you expect me to comply with your request? Don't imagine I am an aeroplane and that I can fly to you in a moment. I intend to forward a copy of your order to the War Office, local and daily papers, and Boards of Guardians all over Ireland for their remarks and criticisms, and also to ask the Irish and British Medical Associations to work in conjunction with my solicitor and to spare no cost in this matter, should you interfere in any way with either my house or dispensary district."

Lieutenant Collins finished by posing a number of questions to the guardians:

"Did you recall your other officer who is serving his King and Country? Did you grant him full pay or half-pay? Did you promise him his position on his return? Do you intend to keep your word, as men ought to do, with him? Did I not propose a man of non-military age to do duty for me in my absence and you would not accept him? Did you then elect a Medical Officer of military age? Did you afterwards appoint him to another position, and why? Did you then elect another Medical Officer of military age to the position he left, and when this officer resigned, did you not appoint the first officer to both districts? Are you now dissatisfied with your doings and trying to avenge it on me? Where is the man of non-military age I proposed now? Is he not to be got, if the officer you chose is unable to do both districts? Do you remember my words in the Board Room, when I said I did not want full pay, half pay, or anything else, but that I would insist on getting my house and dispensary district back on my return as I left it? Did you then cheer and grant me leave? What did you mean by putting on your agenda 'A consideration of an application to purchase the Guardians' interest in the Doctor's residence at Roundstone?' Was this question not fully argued previously and settled by me? Are you still getting the offer from a stranger, backed up by an MP, for my residence? Did you think at the last time you put this house question again on the Agenda that I was 'somewhere in France'? In short, I ask you, do you defy the British Government with your order, or are you again bullied by an angry Guardian? Irishmen, Countrymen, I appeal to you. Is this fair treatment to a Medical Officer who is doing his bit in a tropical climate, where, not alone have I treated your sons who are sick and wounded here, but where I have to combat with the terrible scourges of tropical diseases, and where just a few miles away, hundreds, to say the least, die of plague alone every day. Imagine your own sons sick or wounded lying in the heat of a tropical climate without medical attendance? I say it is nothing but a down-right shame and a disgrace to you, the members of the Clifden Board of Guardians. Had I the option, France would be my selection, where I might distinguish myself and return to you with the honour of wearing the well-envied VC. But no such luck."

Lieutenant Collins, who told the guardians that he was waiting on his promotion to captain coming through, finished with what sounded like a veiled threat: "Gentlemen, remember some day I may return and deal with you in a prompt and proper manner which may involve you in very heavy costs."

FIVE DAYS ADRIFT AT SEA:
Loss of the *Bray Head*

The *Bray Head*, a steamer operated by the Ulster Steam Ship Company of G Heyn & Sons, Belfast, was making its way back to its home port from New Brunswick, Canada, on 14 March 1917, when it crossed the path of the German submarine U-44. Commander Kapitanleutnant Paul Wagenfuhr was not a man to waste his precious torpedoes on easy prey, so instead turned his guns on the 3,077 ton ship, sinking her some 375 miles off Fastnet. Of the predominantly Irish crew of 41, only 20 survivors were ultimately picked up by HMS *Adventure* after five days afloat on a lifeboat.

An account of their ordeal, marked "Passed by Censor," appeared in the Press:

"How the crew of the *Bray Head* survived one of the most awful ordeals to which mortals could be subjected is a psychological enigma of which even they themselves can furnish no adequate explanation, writes a special representative who had a pleasant chat with some of them on Monday. The vessel formed one of the fleet of the well-known 'Head' Line of Belfast. The survivors landed locally included the chief mate, Mr McCartney, Belfast; wireless operator, Mr WJ Woolley, Dublin; third mate, Mr Henderson, Belfast; second engineer, Mr McBride, Belfast... The Captain ordered the men to the boats. He himself took charge of No 1 lifeboat containing 18 men, and the chief mate took command of the other boat with a similar complement. The greatest difficulty was experienced in lowering the boats, for a very heavy sea was running and the Huns kept on firing all the time. In less time than it takes to chronicle the dreadful event, the boats were got safely out... Then came the worst struggle. It was blowing very hard and high seas were running, so the difficulty of navigating frail craft is quite apparent to anybody who is not a longshore-man.

The two boats, under 'lug' sail, managed to keep together (though the mate's craft was leaking) until... about midnight, when the line with which they were attached in the darkness broke, and they separated, never to reunite. As no details are thus to hand regarding the Captain's boat, we will confine the narrative to the other boat. The latter shipped a good deal of water, which rendered constant baling necessary, and with her nose for the West coast, she ploughed the seas with a determination and a staying power that bordered on the miraculous. The men 'dined' twice daily, morning and evening, on a sea biscuit and a glass of water each, but even this meagre fare had, naturally, to be taken under the greatest difficulties, and some of the men were quite unable to negotiate the biscuits.

Through some mishap, one of the kegs of water burst, so the supply became very limited. The cold was intense, and was accelerated by the fact that the men had not had time to don overcoats or the like before leaving the ship. On Thursday night, one of the men named William Keenan, a greaser from Belfast, died from the effects of those abnormal conditions. As Friday was ushered in amid a strong wind and heavy seas, the strain of the awful conditions was fast making its mark on the men. Sleep was impossible, and huddled together as they were with nothing but a two inch plank (leaking) between them and death, they were fast becoming victims of a morbidity and a numbness and indifference quite in keeping with the situation. One man above and beyond all was literally the guiding light of these helpless Irishmen – the Chief Mate, who did the best he could under the circumstances. Next night came on with the wind risen to half a gale and mountainous seas running, and so bad were the conditions that the mate found it necessary to heave-to and cast out the sheet anchor for the night, otherwise they would have been engulfed."

By now many of the men had become fatalistic about their chances and for others "their imagination was playing havoc with them, and they thought they were living under totally different circumstances," a situation made worst by the fact some had begun to drink the sea water. Crew members were also still dying, with 22-year-old Belfast man James McAree, who had served onboard as a cook, passing away just hours before the remaining survivors were rescued.

The *Bray Head* was one of twenty-two ships sunk by U-44, with another two damaged and three taken as prizes. However, on 12 August 1917, commander Wagenfuhr's luck ran out when his submarine was rammed by HMS *Oracle* off the coast of Norway, sinking with the loss of all 44 crew members.

FINDING AN ALLY AND LOSING AN ADMIRAL:
Major-General Charles Callwell

On 1 February 1917, the German navy resumed its unrestricted attacks on civilian shipping in defiance of a pledge given to the United States the previous year. Two days later the US severed diplomatic relations with Germany. Following the sinking of a number of American ships, and news breaking that the Germans had been attempting to bring Mexico into the war, the States finally voted in April 1917 to join the Allies. President Woodrow Wilson appointed General John J Pershing to lead the American Expeditionary Force and he arrived in England on 7 June. Among those on the quayside to meet him was Major-General Sir Charles Edward Callwell, who had been "dug-out" of retirement to serve as Director of Operations & Intelligence and later adviser to the Ministry of Munitions.

An established writer who had enjoyed a distinguished military career, the Anglo-Irish general recorded:

"General Pershing and his staff arrived in England just at this time, and I enjoyed the pleasure of meeting them and discussing many matters. The attitude of these distinguished soldiers, one and all, impressed us most agreeably. One had heard something about 'Yankee bounce' in the past, which exists no doubt amongst some of the citizens of the great Republic across the water. But here we found a body of officers who, while manifestly knowing uncommonly well what they were about, were bent on learning from us everything that they possibly could, and who from the outset proved themselves singularly ready to fall in with our methods of doing business even where those methods differed widely from what they had been accustomed to."

President Wilson's closest adviser, 'Colonel' Edward Mandell House followed and Callwell was again among the party to meet him. All, however, did not go to plan:

"Some weeks later (in the capacity of War Office representative) I accompanied Lord Jellicoe and Admiral Sims, together with Sir I Malcolm and Sir W Wiseman of the Foreign Office, to Devonport to meet a large party of high officials from the United States who were coming over to Europe to take general charge of things in connection with the American share in the war. It was headed by Colonel House, and included the Chiefs of the Naval and Military Staffs with their assistants, as well as financial and other delegates.

We arrived some time before the two cruisers conveying the party were due, so we proceeded to Admiralty House. While waiting there, one was afforded a most welcome opportunity of learning something about how the strings were being pulled over the great water-area which was under special charge of the local commander-in-chief. The whole thing was set out on a huge fixed map covering, I think, the billiard-table. On it were shown where the various convoys were at the moment, the minefields, the positions where German U-boats had recently been located, and numberless other important details…

Just about dusk the two cruisers were descried coming in past the breakwater, so it became a question of getting to the Keyham dockyard where they were to fetch up. Ever keen for exercise in any form, Lord Jellicoe decided to walk, and the commander-in-chief went with him. Knowing the distance and the somewhat unattractive approaches leading to the Keyham naval establishments, and as it, moreover, looked and felt uncommonly like rain, I preferred to wait and to proceed in due course by car, as did all the rest of our party. The flag-lieutenant and the naval officer who had come down with Lord Jellicoe from the Admiralty likewise thought that a motor was good enough for them. By the time that the automobile party reached the dockyard it was pitch dark and pouring rain, and the cruisers were already reported as practically alongside; but to our consternation there was no sign of the two flag-officers.

Now, a dog who has lost his master is an unperturbed, torpid, contented creature compared with a flag-lieutenant who has lost his admiral, and there was a terrible to-do. All the telephones were buzzing and ringing, the dockyard police were eagerly interrogated, and there was already talk of dispatching search-parties, when the two distinguished truants suddenly turned up, exceedingly hot, decidedly wet, and, if the truth must be told, looking a little muddy and bedraggled. However, there was no time to be lost, and we all rushed off into the night heading for where the vessels were to berth. How we did not break our necks tumbling into a dry-dock or find a watery grave tumbling into a wet one, I do not know. We certainly most of us barked our shins against anchors, chains, bollards, and every sort of pernicious litter such as the sister service loves to fondle, and the language would have been atrocious had we not been out of breath – the Foreign Office indeed contrived to be explosive even as it was. However, we managed to reach the jetty after all just as the two big warships had been warped alongside, winning by a nose. So all was well."

Callwell, though born in London, was the only son of Henry Callwell, from Ballycastle, County Antrim, and his wife Maud, from Ross, Connemara.

Major-General Sir Charles Edward Callwell, standing to the front with his hands in his pockets, during one of his visits to Russia in connection with munitions supply and Russian co-operation. *(From* Experiences of a Dug-Out, *published 1920)*

KILLED BY A GERMAN MINE:
Loughanebeg fishermen tragedy

Galway doctor WA Sandys was making his way home after calling with a sick patient when a huge explosion rocked his car. Looking towards the coast, he could see a huge mushroom of dense black smoke that quickly began obscuring his view of the sea. It was 5.30 pm on warm Friday evening in June 1917, and he had just witnessed the worse tragedy ever to strike the small hamlet of Loughanebeg, some 16 miles west of Galway town. The *Irish Times* correspondent reported:

> "When he got out the people were mad with excitement. He motored to Costello, and brought back the Coastguard officer. Within 400 yards of the beach he found part of a man's body; further on he found another portion of human remains, and about 60 yards further he found other portions, and here and there limbs and portions of the bodies were strewn about. He dressed the wounds of the survivor."

Earlier that day four fishermen working a short distance off the coast had come across a barrel-shaped object in the water with handles on both sides. In recent months the sea had given up a variety of 'treasure' in the form of barrels of petrol, tallow and various oils from torpedoed ships. Believing their luck to be in, they attached ropes to their find and towed it ashore not realising they had hooked a German mine. On the beach they were joined by half-a-dozen other fishermen, who helped roll it away from the shore. One of the group, Joseph Flaherty, was uneasy with the find and warned against tampering with it. However, when his words went unheeded he took cover behind a large rock. As one of the young men began unscrewing the head of the barrel, it detonated, the explosion being heard at Spiddal, some four miles away.

The nine men gathered around the mine died instantly. The oldest was a 55-year-old father of six, Edward MacDermott, two were in their thirties with another six children between them, while of the remainder all were in their 20s apart from teenagers Peter Folan, the youngest at 17, and 18-year-old Tim Keady. The distraught relatives were comforted by Fr Heany, the parish priest. The *Irish Times* reporter noted:

> "When I visited the scene in the evening the villagers were beside

themselves with grief. The crying of the women could be heard on all sides. Several men were still engaged in collecting the poor scattered remains of the dead; a sole of a boot here, portion of a flannel waistcoat there."

Among those who rushed to the beach to offer help was Baron Killanin, who had briefly represented Galway in the House of Commons and was to become the Lord Lieutenant for the county the following year. At the inquest held later that evening under the deputy coroner Louis E O'Dea, survivor Joe Flaherty, who had suffered a head wound, told of how the men had been fishing when they spotted what looked like a large pot floating in the water. "Some of them towed it in, and noticed that it had spikes sticking out, and a Maltese Cross was painted on it. The men were fiddling with it and witness told them to be careful. He suspected that it was dangerous, and he got behind a large rock. In a few moments he heard a terrific explosion, and remembered no more until he saw someone bending over him," it was reported. Flaherty described the mine as being wide at the top and narrowing towards the bottom. As they had rolled it up the beach the men had concluded that it was probably an empty oil tank. "He noticed one of the spikes opening, and something like a bicycle tube came out. It was then that they got afraid, and the witness ran away. Ned MacDermott advised them to bring it up the beach, and report the matter to the police," the *Irish Times* added.

The inquest jury, which had attempted to determine whether the mine had been British or German – if it had been the former it would have allowed the families to claim compensation for their loss – found death had been caused by a mine explosion. It added: "We strongly recommend the government to take into consideration the loss and suffering of the relatives of the deceased men, and we heartily sympathise with them in their deep sorrow and affliction."

A FAMOUS MESSINES CASUALTY:
Major William Redmond

William Hoey Kearney Redmond was one of the older soldiers serving on the Western Front. The brother of John Redmond, the leader of the Irish parliamentary party and himself an MP, he held a commission in the 6th Royal Irish Regiment. At the age of 56, the Wexford politician had implored his commanding officer to be allowed to take part in the Battle of Messines on 7 June 1917, only to be wounded shortly after leaving his trench. The Rev William John Redmond, Church of Ireland chaplain with the 36th (Ulster) Division, attended to his wounds and left an account of his encounter with one of the most famous Irish soldiers:

"It was impressive to see what a feeling of security before the battle the Ulster Division had regarding their left flank. They knew that if flesh and blood could get through to its objective the 16th Division would get through. And the same utter confidence in the Ulster Division was felt by the 16th Division. This feeling of goodwill and confidence between the two divisions had been growing for some time. I wish the entire North and South which they represent could participate in the same spirit. During the battle a dramatic, and what in its results will I hope make it a historic incident, took place. Major Wm. Redmond, MP, was forbidden by General Hickey to take part in the attack but he besought the general to allow him to do so as if he did not he could never lift his head in Ireland again. Finally, the general came to a compromise and agreed to allow him to take part in the fight for a couple of hours. Before the two hours expired a shell fell amongst his party and he was wounded in the arm in front of his elbow and in the leg below the knee. He made nothing of his wounds and his men pressed on.

The first to find him was a soldier of the 14th RIRs, who got him on his shoulders to carry him in but was soon wounded and could not proceed any further. The next to find him was two stretcher bearers of the Ulster Division who carried him into the advanced Aid Post where Dr Johnston of 9th R. Innisk and I were working. He was suffering much from shock though the wounds were not very severe. But he was a man of all but sixty years. When he was brought in he said he was going to die. He knew by my uniform that I was a Chaplain and I told him that I was C of I or more strictly speaking Church of Ireland. He said he was Catholic but that he had great respect for my religion and asked me if I thought that God would accept his sufferings for his sins. I told him that Another had suffered for his sins and that His sufferings would be accepted for him. In the course of conversation he said that he always wanted to be friends with Ulster. He also spoke of the good feeling existing between the Irish (16th) and the Ulster Divisions and of the confidence that the 16th Division had in Ulster Division on their right. He asked me to give his last message to his wife. He said 'Give her my love and thank her for all the help she has given me and tell her that if we do not meet again in this world I hope we shall meet in the next'. I helped the doctor to dress his wounds. He was given some refreshment and some morphine and allowed to rest awhile before we sent him to 108th Field Ambulance. When leaving he was feeling so much better that he said he now felt that he was going to recover. But alas! He died in the Field Ambulance next day. I was the only chaplain who had any conversation with him before his death. Two RC Chaplains called at the ambulance but one found him asleep and the other found him unconscious and then administered Extreme Unction.

He was a leader in the Nationalist Party but when he was wounded it was an Ulsterman who took him on his shoulders and carried him onwards safety till he too was wounded. Then the next to carry him were two Ulster stretcher bearers who carried him to our advanced Aid Post where an Ulster Chaplain and a doctor of Ulster Division ministered to him. And it was in an Ulster ambulance that he was affectionately cared for and tended till he was called away from earth. It is too much to hope for that his noble sacrifice for the cause of God and our Empire and the touching incidents surrounding his death may yet bear fruit – a better understanding and a greater sympathy between North and South in Ireland? God grant that it may!"

Major Redmond was buried by the nuns in the grounds of the Catholic Hospice in Locre (modern day Loker). The grave was later moved and today lies close to the path leading to Locre Hospice Cemetery and is cared for by the Commonwealth War Graves Commission.

WITNESS TO SLAUGHTER
Fred Percy Crozier defied orders to lead
his men out to No-Man's-Land.
(From A Brass Hat In No Man's Land,
published 1930)

WITNESS TO SLAUGHTER
A picture of what is believed to
be the site of Crozier's bunker
in Thiepval Wood, Somme,
from which he had to evacuate
the wounded before using as his
headquarters. *(Author)*

FOR THE SAKE OF IRELAND
Tom Kettle worried about
how nationalist Ireland would
remember him.
*(Reproduced by kind permission
of UCD Archives)*

THE FINAL FIGHTING
Beaumont-Hamel was the scene fierce fighting throughout the Battle of the Somme. It
had been one of the objective on 1 July but didn't fall to the British until 13 November
1916. *(A Popular History of the Great War, published 1933)*

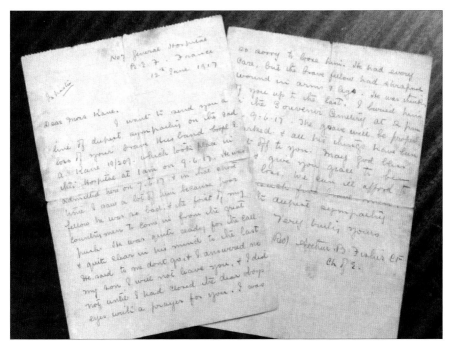

1917: WAR OF ATTRITION
Letter of sympathy sent to the widow of Corporal John Kane of the 15th Royal Irish Rifles, killed at Messines in June 1917. *(Courtesy of the Royal Ulster Rifles Museum)*

FIVE DAYS ADRIFT AT SEA
The *Bray Head* belonged the 'Head Line' Ulster Steam Ship Company. It became one of twenty-two ships sunk by U-44, with another two damaged and three taken as prizes.

KILLED BY A GERMAN MINE
A newspaper report of the tragedy that
occurred in Loughanebeg, County
Galway when nine fishermen were
killed by a mine explosion. Believing
they had found another 'barrel'
from a torpedoed ship they dragged
a live German mine ashore before
attempting to open it.
(From the Irish News)

FATAL TOYING WITH MINE.

County Galway Fishermen Blown to Pieces.

APPALLING COAST DISASTER.

Details came to hand on Saturday of a shocking tragedy which occurred at Serrighnabeg, about sixteen miles from Galway, on Friday afternoon, when eight persons were blown to pieces by a floating mine.

It seems that four men who were fishing in curraghs at noon saw a curious object in the water like a barrel, with handles on either side. They took the object in tow, and landed it on the shore without mishap. Six other men gathered round to see the strange object, and ultimately one of them proceeded to remove the screw from the mine. One, named Flaherty, warned the others of the danger, and hid himself behind a rock some distance away.

The man examining the mine persisted in his task, and in a few minutes there was a deafening explosion, which shook windows and houses twenty miles away. The only man who came out of the ordeal alive was Flaherty, and the eight other men were blown to pieces, their flesh and clothing covering the scene for a distance of 300 yards.

A boy going down towards the shore with a milk can was blown to pieces, and his body has not yet been recovered.

Dr. W. A. Sandys, of Galway, who was motoring near the place at the time, had his car lifted off the ground. Flaherty was rendered stone deaf by the explosion, and received a bad wound on the head. Some of the remains were found 300 yards away. The scene of the appalling occurrence was visited by crowds from Galway on Saturday. It is stated that

A FAMOUS MESSINES CASUALTY
Major William Redmond, brother of
John Redmond, the leader of the Irish
parliamentary party and himself an MP,
pleaded to be allowed to take part in the
Battle of Messines while serving with the
6th Royal Irish Regiment. He was buried
by the nuns in the grounds of the Catholic
Hospice in Locre.
(Courtesy of the Somme Museum)

Dear (1)
Mother a few lines
hoping to find you well
as this leves me at present
I am reting to David now
remember me to ahangaga
and little emma and all
about I might not see you
again but I hope to see
you all in heven but if
I am spared I hope soon
to bee home to see you

well tell all the neebours
I was asking for them
also frank and Emma
I wish them well and
hope if I am spared to
see them tell moses I was
asking for him and father
hope he has finished the
Drink so I think I will
draw to a close god bee
with you till we meet again
fondest love to all
from your loving son
W J Simpson

WOUNDED AT PASSCHENDAELE
William James Simpson, one of four brothers who enlisted with the Royal Irish
Fusiliers, wrote a letter home to his mother in which he warned 'I might never see you
again…' – a prediction that tragically proved to be true.
(Courtesy of the Royal Ulster Rifles Museum)

His brother, David, after recovering
from wounds inflicted at the Somme,
served in the Middle East with Sir
Edmund Allenby, who, conscious of the
symbolism involved, entered Jerusalem
on foot on 11 December 1917.
*(The Great War magazine, published
1915–1919)*

DEATH OF A TUNNELLING
HERO
John McCreesh worked on the
mines at Messines that were so
fundamental in the British taking
the ridge. A pre-war miner and so
exempt from military service, he
couldn't wait to get into uniform
as soon as the opportunity arose.
*(Courtesy of Amanda Moreno,
of the Royal Irish Regiment
Museums Group)*

DEATH OF A TUNNELLING HERO
The tunnellers lived in constant fear of
the enemy breaking in to their mine.
In this illustration British engineers
are listening for possible indications of
German counter-mining.
*(The Great War magazine, published
1915–1919)*

TANK GUNNER AT THE HINDENBURG LINE
The Battle of Cambrai, launched on 20 November 1917 across a 12 km wide front, rapidly overwhelmed a section of the Hindenburg Line that was feared to be virtually impregnable. The action was fierce and included, as depicted here, the fight for Bourlon Wood. *(A Popular History of the Great War, published 1933)*

TANK GUNNER AT THE HINDENBURG LINE
Cambrai saw the first mass use of tanks, changing the face of war forever. Here a British tank makes its way through the ruins of a French village.
(The Great War magazine, published 1915–1919)

AN IRISH ROVER
A company of the 25th Royal Fusiliers made up of the Legion of Frontiersmen under the command of Lieutenant Colonel Daniel Patrick Driscoll. They were an example of the odd assortment of people from across the globe who became involved in the war. (*The Great War magazine, published 1915–1919*)

WORLD'S GREATEST EXPLOSION
Some 2,000 people were killed and more than 9,000 injured in the explosion that followed the accidental collision of the departing *Imo* and the *Mont-Blanc*, which was making its way into Halifax harbour packed with 3,000 tons of explosives and munitions.
(*WG MacLaughlan, Library and Archives Canada C-019953*)

1918: THE GUNS FALL SILENT
Shortly after the signing of the Armistice, in November 1918, the Allied armies began crossing the Rhine, with the Cologne area allotted to Britain.
(A Popular History of the Great War, published 1933)

1918: THE GUNS FALL SILENT
Known as the 'iron harvest', the battlefields of the Western Front give up some of the buried hardware, including unexploded shells, hand grenades, rusting weapons and ammunition, to the plough each year. They are gathered up at the side of fields to be collected by the military for destruction. *(Author)*

1918: THE GUNS FALL SILENT
The dedication plaque on the ground floor of the Ulster Tower at Thiepval. The memorial was built on the old German front line at the Somme to commemorate the sacrifice of Ulstermen during the Great War. *(Author)*

1918: THE GUNS FALL SILENT
A Sword of Sacrifice stands in virtually every Commonwealth War Graves Commission cemetery around the world. *(Author)*

WOMAN WHO SERVED ON THE FRONTLINE

Flora Sandes joined the Red Cross in Serbia and was attached to the 2nd Infantry Regiment of the Serbian army. However, on the retreat to Albania she removed her Red Cross armband and became the only western European woman known to have served with a frontline unit during the war. *(From the City of Vancouver Archives)*

ABANDONED TO DIE

In early 1918 the Germans gambled everything on a last huge offensive with the aim of pushing the British out of the war. Reinforced by the divisions freed up by Russia's exit to the east, the German army had a superior numerical advantage – but it had to be deployed before American troops arrived in strength. Illustrated above is the fighting at Armentieres in April 1918 as envisaged by a war artist.
(The Great War magazine, published 1915-1919)

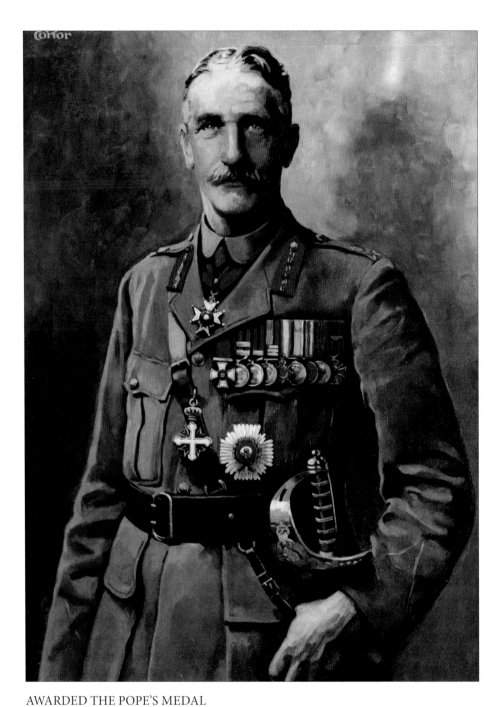

AWARDED THE POPE'S MEDAL
Major General Oliver Nugent commanded the 36th (Ulster) Division throughout the
majority of its active service.
(Courtesy of the Royal Irish Fusiliers Museum)

AWARDED THE POPE'S MEDAL
Major General Oliver Nugent's medals are now owned by the Museums
of The Royal Irish Regiment and include one awarded to him by the Pope
(inset) in recognition of his efforts to protect Catholic property in France.
(Courtesy of the Royal Irish Fusiliers Museum)

THE HEART OF A LION
Flight Sub-Lieutenant Robert Dickey was
an outstanding warrior of the skies and
emerged as one of the most decorated
pilots of the Great War. He accounted
for a Zeppelin and a U-boat among his
kills and was awarded the Distinguished
Service Cross and two bars.
*(The Great War magazine, published
1915–1919)*

AMERICAN MEDAL OF HONOR
WINNER
Joe Thompson was the only Irish-born
winner of the Congressional Medal
of Honor during the Great War. He
is buried in Beaver Falls Cemetery
and Mausoleum, Beaver County,
Pennsylvania.
*(Courtesy of Don Morfe, Medal of
Honor Historical Society)*

AMERICAN MEDAL OF HONOR
WINNER
Joe Thompson, born at Kilkeel,
County Down, was well-respected
in his adopted Pennsylvania both
as a highly successful sports coach
and heroic soldier serving with the
110th Infantry of the US Army in
the France.

RMS *LEINSTER* AND THE FIRST WRNS KILLED ON DUTY
This painting, entitled 'The Sinking of RMS *Leinster*', was executed by artist Simeon Hughes in 1918 and depicts the sinking of the vessel with the loss of 501 lives as it sailed between Dublin and Holyhead.
(Courtesy of the Trustees of the Holyhead Maritime Museum)

WORKING FOR THE GERMANS
Sir Roger Casement was a regular visitor to Limberg prisoner-of-war camp, where he attempted to persuade those from Ireland to sign up to his Irish Brigade. Some, like Pte John Mahony of the Royal Dublin Fusiliers, claimed to have been unimpressed by his efforts but still volunteered.
(The Great War magazine, published 1915–1919)

THE LAST TO DIE
A number of those who died of their wounds on 11 November 1918 are buried in Etaples cemetery. *(A Popular History of the Great War, published 1933)*

THE LAST TO DIE
A simple plaque was all that initially marked the spot where the Armistice of 11 November 1918 was signed. A more permanent memorial was erected in the clearing in the forest of Compiegne in 1922. The carriage in which Marshal Foch met the enemy delegation was also returned there but was towed away by the Germans during the Second World War and destroyed.
(A Popular History of the Great War, published 1933)

MILLIONAIRE FAMILY DEVASTATED BY WAR:
John Dunville

"It may be that when the eventful era arrives when our airmen drop bombs on Potsdam there may be an Ulsterman who will fling one missile with more precise aim, and dub it 'A remembrance of Holywood,'" wrote a *Belfast Telegraph* journalist in October 1917. The man he had in mind was John Dunville, head of the Dunville whiskey distillery and then serving in the Royal Naval Air Service. The thrust of the article was the need for reprisals on Germany for the spate of air attacks on the south of England and his conclusion was that the Holywood flier was ideally placed to undertake the task as, in 1908 while taking part in a balloon endurance race, he had flown over Berlin and Hamburg. But John Dunville had more reason to wish this paper dream could come true than simply his knowledge of the landscape. There is little doubt that the wish for revenge figured prominently in his thoughts in that autumn of 1917. Just months before he had lost a son on the Western Front while his eldest boy was still suffering from severe wounds inflicted by rebels during the Easter Rising.

John Dunville married in 1892 Violet Anne Blanche Lambart, the fifth daughter of Gustavus William Lambart, Deputy Lieutenant, of Beau Parc, County Meath. They had four children: Robert Lambart Dunville, John Spencer Dunville, William Gustavus Dunville and Una Dunville. The family lived at 46 Portland Place, London, with twelve servants: a butler, two footmen, a lady's maid, a cook, two nurses, two house maids, two kitchen maids and a hall boy. He had served as a lieutenant colonel in the 5th Leinster Regiment as a private secretary to the Duke of Devonshire.

A skilled polo player, cross-country runner and former master of Cambridge University Staghounds, his real passion was for ballooning and he was to win several competitions in the years leading up to the First World War. In 1908 he took part in the Coupe Aéronautique Gordon Bennett from Schmargendoft, near Berlin, in a balloon named *Banshee*, covering some 368 miles. In December that year, during another event, he landed near Stuttgart in Germany.

John Dunville took over as chairman of the family's whiskey company, first established early in the 19th century, in 1910 following the death of his father. In March 1915, he joined the Royal Naval Air Service, rising to the rank of wing commander by 1917. By then, however, tragedy had already struck twice.

Robert Lambart Dunville, his eldest son, had joined the 1st Life Guards as a second lieutenant on leaving Eton, transferring to the Royal Bucks Hussars on the outbreak of war. He had been due to be deployed to Gallipoli in April 1915 when he fell ill with acute appendicitis and, after initial treatment, was returned to England for preventative surgery. Posted to a home garrison, he was making his way to Kingstown at Easter 1916, to catch a boat for the return journey to barracks after a spell of leave, when his car was stopped at Castlebellingham by a group of rebels. Made to stand next to a group of police officers captured by the gang, he was shot in the chest and seriously wounded. One of the RIC officers died of his injuries. Robert Dunville, who was aged 23 at the time, never fully recovered and endured poor health the remainder of his life, dying at the young age of 38.

His second son, Second Lieutenant John Spencer Dunville, was also Eton educated and went straight into the army on the outbreak of war. In June 1915, he crossed to France with the 6th Inniskilling Dragoons in time for the Battle of Loos. In January 1916, he transferred to the 1st Royal Dragoons, and in June the following year was out in No-Man's-Land supervising a party of men cutting the enemy wire when they came under heavy fire. Despite being wounded, Dunville continued to command his troops and return fire, allowing the task to be completed. He died of his injuries the following day and is buried at Villers Faucon, France. His bravery was recognised by the posthumous awarding of the Victoria Cross, which was presented to his father John by King George V at Buckingham Palace in August that year.

John Spencer Dunville was buried at Villers Faucon in France, but there is a stone in Holywood Graveyard to commemorate him. The inscription on the memorial stone reads:

'To commemorate John Spencer Dunville, VC, 2nd Lieut. Royal Dragoons, second son of John and Violet Dunville; he gave his life for his country in the Great War and died of his wounds in France on 27th June 1917 aged 21 years, buried at Villers Faucon, was awarded the Victoria Cross for conspicuous bravery. Let those who come after see to it that his memory is not forgotten.'

Part of a ligustrum (privet) bush from his grave in France was planted next to the family grave in Holywood.

John Dunville ended the war as a temporary lieutenant colonel in the

Royal Air Force, being demobilised in 1919, For his war service he was made a Commander of the British Empire. He died in June 1929, with his son Robert becoming chairman of the distillery but just 19 months later, while on a visit to his wife's father in Johannesburg, South Africa, he took ill and died. Dunville & Co, no longer with a member of the family at the helm, was liquidated in 1936.

Second Lieutenant John Spencer Dunville, who died of his wounds, was awarded the Victoria Cross.
(*The Great War magazine, published 1915–1919*)

He is buried at Villers Faucon in France.
(*Author*)

HERO ON THE RUSSIAN FRONT:
Chief Petty Officer John McFarland

Chief Petty Officer John McFarland found himself a long way from home in 1917. The 36-year-old, a member of the Royal Naval Air Service, had already a lengthy career behind him before the outbreak of the war. As a solider he had fought during the Boer War and was quick to sign up again in 1914, eventually ending up in the Russian Armoured Car Division. This unit fought across Asia Minor, Austria, Rumania and, of course, Russia, against Germans, Austrians, Kurds and Turks from 1915–1918. In 1917, however, it was on the Galician front, a region that today straddles Poland and the Ukraine. Chief Petty Officer McFarland was one of more than 100 Irishmen in his squadron – a fifth of the total manpower – many of whom had been members of the Ulster Volunteer Force prior to the war. The Petrograd correspondent of the *Morning Post* related his story to the masses:

"Chief Petty-Officer McFarland was an Ulster Orangeman – a big man, and an old soldier of infinite resource and willingness. He had served, I believe, seven years with the 7th Dragoons, was all through the South African war, and when the Great War came was nearer forty than thirty. He was among the first even of that race who are always the first to rush where there is fighting. When I heard of him, he was serving with the naval armoured cars on the Romanian front, and so long as there was active work on hand McFarland was a tower of strength. When a car got bogged in a thin copse near the enemy's line, and well within range, it was McFarland who devised overalls of forest greenery to hide the derelict all day, and returning by night with planks and screwjacks, recovered her from No Man's Land under a heavy fire evoked by the motor's explosive efforts."

First day of July 1917 – exactly 12 months on from the opening day of the Battle of the Somme – was the beginning of a major offensive on the Galician front, and the chief petty officer had orders to lead the Russian infantry into action, along the line of the southern road to Brzezany, with his squadron of armoured cars. The previous evening he had taken part in a reconnaissance foot patrol, probing along the roadway to seek out possible obstructions. It had found the road blocked by a sandbag barrier, erected by the Russians as a check on the roadway, and instructions were issued for the picket to take it down. *The Morning Post* went on:

"At ten minutes to ten next morning the squadron of British naval armoured cars sped forward to lead the attack upon Brzezany. They came well within range of the enemy guns long before reaching the point where the sandbag barrier had been discovered the night before. When they came in sight of the spot they found to their horror that the sandbags still stood intact and that the enemy had evidently got the range of that point to a nicety, well knowing that there, if anywhere, they could catch anything moving. Volunteers were called for to clear away the barrier. Under a hail of Maxim bullets and shrapnel purposely concentrated by the German gunners on this marked range, McFarland stepped out among the first as always. The barrier was reached by crawling, without casualties, and provided comparative safety for the five gallant volunteers. It was the old soldier McFarland who suggested the cautious removal of the protective barrier in such wise as to protect the flanks of the road from enfilading fire, and to leave as much cover as possible in front till the last moment. By dashing out and in between the shrapnel bursts from the ditches on either side, these gallant men, ignoring the Maxim fusillade, gradually got all the bags away from a wide space in the centre of the road, leaving an ample fairway for the passage of the cars which were waiting, also under fire, some way behind."

It had taken three-quarters of an hour to clear the road, yet despite the heavy fire there had been no casualties among the group until they began withdrawing. A piece of shrapnel is said to have struck McFarland in the neck, killing him instantly. His body was taken back behind the lines so he could be given a soldier's funeral at Litjatin, with shots fired over his grave. His last resting place, however, along with those of four comrades, could not be found after the war and today he is remembered on the Poznan Memorial, in the Poznan Old Garrison Cemetery, Poland. The holder of the Distinguished Service Medal (DSM), he was awarded the medals of 2nd, 3rd and 4th Classes of the Order of St George (Russia).

FOOLING THE RECRUITING SERGEANT:
Private J Hutchinson

The legal age at which men could serve overseas was 19, but there were plenty younger who yearned to sign up. Over the course of the war it is estimated that some 250,000 boys and young men under this age volunteered and were accepted. Official policy allowed 18-year-olds to be trained, but not to fight. Recruiting sergeants, who were paid two shillings and sixpence for each new recruit, were the main line of defence to keeping boys out of the army, though often they played the role of co-conspirator to enlist under-age lads.

One such was J Hutchinson, who was born in east Belfast in 1901. In his unpublished memoirs, *The Early Reminiscences of a Royal Irish Rifleman 1917–1919*, he explains the efforts he had to make to get into the army at the age of 16:

"It was August 1917 and I was on holiday from work. So I went along to the old Town Hall in Victoria Street where the recruiting office was situated. I loitered outside and watched a stream of men come and go. Then I peeped in and discovered the office was empty except for the recruiting Sergeant, he sat at a table with a pile of papers in front of him and I heard him say 'Phew!' He'd had a busy morning. In I walked in Boys' Brigade manner, and stretching myself to full height, chin up, head erect, I knew the drill, I would make an impression.

'Well?' exclaimed the Sergeant as he eyes me in such a way I felt like melting through the floor. 'What can I do for you?' I told him that I wished to join the Royal Irish Rifles. A smile spread over his face for he was an RIR man himself. 'So you have picked your Regiment already, what age are you?' he asked sharply. I cleared my throat, there was a pause, 'nineteen,' I replied. By this time his face was transformed to a block of ice, I knew he didn't believe me. 'Tell that to the Marines sonny, I do admire your spirit and choice of Regiment, but you are wasting my time, I'm a busy man, come back in three years time, you should be ready by then'."

Disheartened but not defeated, he determined to try again a few days later. He recalled:

"Soon, I was in the wide main street of Ards town, and on the right-hand side I saw a row of low buildings, they were the County Council Offices and beside a door outside, was a board leaning against a wall with the magic words, 'Recruiting Office'. This board was my invitation card to Newtownards. I did not rush in but stood on the other side of the road until I cooled down, and watched how many entered the door. They were not hard to count, in a full hour no one entered. This was encouraging; did this prove my theory that some recruiting officers had more work than others? I would try a new tactic, no more walking into the office in a smart and soldierly manner.

So with a cunning engendered in the back streets of East Belfast, I waited. Presently, a silver-haired Sergeant came to the door and looked down the street. I moved in the opposite direction and crossed to the other side, then came to the recruiting board and looked at it indifferently for some time, there was a list of Irish Regiments needing men urgently, including the Royal Irish Rifles. I moved away as if I couldn't care less. I knew the Sergeant had his eye on me fixedly. When I had walked a few yards, he called me. I saw he was an elderly man and obviously an old soldier.

'Can I help you?' he asked in a quiet voice, 'I mean is there anything on the board you'd like explained, rates of pay and the different Regiments?' He wore the Royal Irish Rifles badge.

'No, I just read it out of curiosity,' I replied. 'I was not thinking of joining'.

'We need men, we have a lot of vacancies, young chaps like you are the type we need.'

'Oh I don't think that I'd pass, there are still medical tests, besides, I'm not out of a job,' I answered evasively.

'Come into the office,' he said invitingly, 'I'll give you a few tests to see if you are suitable.'

'I'd be wasting your time.'

'Not at all lad, it's my duty here.'

I entered the offices, knowing we were playing a cat-and-mouse game. He took my height. 'You are not too tall, but you pass this test and you are young enough to still grow,' he commented. He tested my eyes and I removed my boots for he wanted to check if I had flat feet. I had a small test in reading and writing. Presently, he filled in a form, my name and my age, I told him I was nineteen, he didn't flick an eye-lid when I told him, it was the jack-pot question but I survived it."

The army was not to be fooled, however, and while he got to sign up he was kept in Britain as an under-age soldier and was still in England when the war ended. He later joined the regular army and served during the Second World War.

East Belfast man J Hutchinson went to great lengths to join the army underage.
(*Courtesy of the Royal Ulster Rifles Museum*)

WOUNDED AT PASSCHENDAELE:
Private Moses Simpson

Moses Simpson was always a fighter and his experiences of war did not mellow him in the least. He and his three brothers had enlisted in the Royal Irish Fusiliers but fate had different paths in store for them. Along with William James, Moses was sent to the Western Front with the 9th battalion, part of the 36th (Ulster) Division, where, on the first day of the Battle of the Somme, the former was reported missing. His death was not confirmed until after the war's end. The third brother, David, was also sent to France, where he was attached to the Manchester Regiment for a spell before being assigned to the 2nd Royal Irish Regiment and ending up in an English hospital after being wounded in the right arm at the Somme on 3 September 1916. "There was a very big fight on at the time," he wrote to his mother with typical understatement.

Moses took part in the highly successful Battle of Messines of 7 June 1917, during which the 36th (Ulster) and 16th (Irish) divisions fought side-by-side, telling his sister Emma:

> "We have got the upper hand of the Germans out here now. In that last battle they were completely beaten. I am sure you all heard of the fine work of the Ulster Division and the South of Ireland men. There is no party work out here or there ought to be none at home.
>
> … If I get home soon, I have a German watch off a German I took prisoner, he gave it to me, he said 'Komerade don't shoot me', you would be sorry for them sometimes, when you get them they are that much scared. I have a wee German cap I must give it to you when I get home."

As training was stepped up ahead of the impending Battle of Passchendaele, Moses began showing his frustration at the lack of recruits coming forward among his former neighbours. "RJ Buckley is in the same platoon as me so that leaves Joe Allen, Joe Faugher, RJ and me in the one company," he told his mother on 24 July 1917.

> "It is very pleasant when there are some of the boys from your own country out here but it is nearly time some more of the boys round there were out. I think by appearance of things it is going to be rough out here again but I hope to pull through and get home."

Moses did survive the battle on 16 August, but was severely wounded. After initially being treated for injuries to his thigh and knee in an Australian field hospital in Belgium he was evacuated to the 5th Northern General Hospital in Leicester, England. "It was something terrible, I don't know how I got through without being killed," he wrote to his sister Emma.

"I got wounded at Ypres, the big battle that is going on so long. We had only 75 left out of the battalion, we got cut down as fast as we advanced. Very sorry to hear about poor J Allen, him and me stopped together but I am sorry to say there are hundreds for by him killed.
… I suppose round there is just going on as usual, the boys slinging about in the same old way, I don't think much about them… Don't be telling any of the people round there anything about the Battalion, tell them nothing. If they want to know anything, tell them to come out and see."

Moses went on in the same theme in a separate letter to his mother:

"It's not the same as a fight round Doyles with some of the boys. It would do me good to see a lot of the boys round there getting the life scared out of them. It will take them all to keep very quiet when I get home. I think I'm worse than the last time. I suppose my old friends the Coppers are all getting on all alright?"

After David Simpson had recovered from his wounds he was sent to Salonika. In January 1918 he told Moses: "I suppose you heard of us taking Gaza and Jerusalem and all them places. Old Johnnie Turk has to fly for it here, it is very hilly country this." David finished the war in Alexandria while Moses was still recovering at home. He wrote to him on 23 December 1918:

"Well the war is about over now and I am sure you are not sorry either, we are not in the firing line now. We are stopping outside Cairo a piece and we all expect to be home very shortly. I suppose you heard about the Turks getting beaten out here before the Germans chucked in."

Even at this stage the uncertainty over William James' fate remained, David writing:

"You heard nothing about W. James did you? I would like to hear about him, he might be living yet. I am very lucky since I came out here. Anyhow there were plenty of stunts but thank God I came through them alright."

A LOSS FELT ACROSS ALL RANKS:
Sergeant Richard Wolfe

The men of the 9th Royal Irish Fusiliers were not merely soldiers to Lieutenant Colonel Stewart Blacker. Having raised the battalion in September 1914, he viewed them almost as sons. It was with a heavy heart, therefore, that he picked up his pen on 2 September 1917, to write to the family of Sergeant Richard John Wolfe at Carrickblacker, Portadown, County Armagh, to express his sorrow after learning of his death the previous month at the Battle of Passchendaele:

> "Though no longer with them myself, I must write to tell you what a very high opinion I had of your son during the time he was with me. He was a splendid type of lad, brave as a lion, always ready for any job, no matter how dangerous, cheery, and no matter what the hardships, always with a smile, and sticking it to the end. I made him Scout Sergt and he did splendid work with the scouts, his old training at home stood to him. He took part in numerous raids and was a tower of strength. I always knew that when Dick was out all would go well and it did. I am sure he was doing more than his duty when he met his death and setting an example of coolness and bravery to all. We can ill spare such lads and I grieve with you in loss. He has gone over in excellent company with Lt. Col. Audley Pratt, to whom he was devoted and who, as you know, was killed the same day. He died a gallant soldier's death and in gallant company, one cannot ask for better when it comes to our own time. I am sure he would so have wished it, but his loss is hard to bear, I and all well know."

Richard Wolfe, born at Markethill, County Armagh, was an experienced gamekeeper who had been living and working at Cabra Castle, Kingscourt, County Cavan, at the time of his enlistment. A corporal at the opening of the Battle of the Somme on 1 July 1916, he was the battalion runner that day, carrying messages back and forth across No-Man's-Land. Despite such a perilous posting, he was one of the few from his battalion to emerge from the battle unscathed, a point he made to his mother in a letter written on 31 July: "It is very lonely now as all my old comrades are gone, some never to come back again."

On 12 October 1916, he won the Military Medal for his gallantry during an engagement at Petite Douve Farm, near Messines, Belgium. He was part of a large raiding party that encountered stronger than expected opposition while attempting to take the German strongpoint. Hand-to-hand fighting ensued, with both sides exchanging dozens of grenades. The raiders were eventually forced to withdraw as casualties mounted, with Sergeant Wolfe carrying some of the wounded out on his back. Lieutenant Colonel Audley Charles Pratt, of Enniscoe, Crossmolina, Couty Mayo, who had been second-in-command of Richard's battalion until promoted to lead the 11th Royal Inniskilling Fusiliers, wrote to his father to offer his congratulations on the award: "It is a medal which takes a deal of getting. Dick has brought credit to himself, to his family and to his regiment. How pleased you and Mrs Wolfe will be, I am proud of him too."

At Passchendaele on 16 August 1917, Sergeant Wolfe led the men of C Company in an attack on the heavily held enemy strongpoint at Langemarck, becoming one of some 477 casualties suffered by the 9th Royal Irish Fusiliers. Lieutenant Colonel Pratt also died that day, killed by a shell as he left his dug-out to go up to his battalion battle headquarters. His family, despite its loss, was quick to offer its condolences to the Wolfes. The lieutenant colonel's father, Joseph, writing on 8 September 1917, told them:

"I cannot tell you with what sorrow I saw in yesterday's *Irish Times* the name of your son Dick in the Roll of Honour. It went to my heart and grieved me as much as if he had been a near and dear relation. Colonel Audley was so attached to him and held him in such high esteem. He was indeed a gallant soldier. What I feel about my son you can equally do about yours, namely that he did his duty, did it well, and that it was in the performance of it that he has fallen. Our Heavenly Father makes no mistakes and you may believe as I do that all has been ordered for the best and in love. Although we cannot now see that that is so, we shall do so hereafter."

In a separate letter, the lieutenant-colonel's mother Madaline wrote:

"I was very sorry to hear from Mr Pratt this morning that Dick had been killed, you and Mrs Wolfe have my deepest sympathy. He was such a good son to you and liked by all. I know that he was a good soldier and

Colonel Audley thought very highly of him. He died fighting for his country and no one could have a better end."

Lieutenant Colonel Pratt, who was 43 when killed, lies in Ypres Reservoir Cemetery, Belgium, while Sergeant Wolfe, 21, is commemorated on the Tyne Cot Memorial.

Sergeant Richard John Wolfe has no known grave, being commemorated on the Tyne Cot Memorial in Belgium. *(Courtesy of the Royal Irish Fusiliers Museum)*

A SLOW AND CONTROVERSIAL DEATH:
Lance Corporal Richard Quinn

Like so many of his comrades, Lance Corporal Richard Quinn suffered a slow and agonizing death. His untimely end, however, wasn't on the battlefield amid the din and confusion of war but took place in public and in front of the wives of some of Belfast's more prominent citizens, sparking a public outcry and forcing the army to hold a military inquiry leading to an officer facing a court-martial.

Quinn, a 40-year-old former tramway conductor with Belfast Corporation, was based at Dundalk with the 17th Royal Irish Rifles in 1917. On 23 July he was admitted to the military hospital at Holywood, County Down, complaining of stomach pains. While his condition, diagnosed as gastritis, appeared to improve slightly over the coming weeks, there seemed to be an impression among some that he was "putting it on". On 19 September Quinn was transferred to the Central Hospital at Victoria Barracks in Belfast for further treatment. It was decided to transfer a number of patients to Londonderry to free up beds for more acute cases and Quinn was among those selected to travel on 24 September. That day his pains were particularly bad and he begged doctors, three of whom saw him, not to move him. According to a Sergeant Mabott, Quinn was twisting about in agony with beads of perspiration on his forehead yet Captain Robinson, one of the medics, was off-hand with him, threatening to have him arrested for play acting. Another witness heard him say: "Is that you rolling about again. If you don't get up I will put you in the clink."

The lance corporal was loaded into an ambulance and taken to the Midland Railway Station, where he lay in the buffet in obvious pain. The military transport officer on duty was so concerned that he phoned the hospital at Victoria Barracks, but the call was answered by Captain Robinson, who dismissed his concerns. On the train, Quinn was having convulsions, followed by bouts of sweats and cold, and vomiting. His comrades wrapped him in great coats and gave him sips of water but as the train approached Ballymena he passed away. A post mortem revealed he had died from acute pancreatitis. Lance Corporal Quinn was laid to rest at Dundonald Cemetery, east Belfast.

The military Court of Inquiry sat in the library of Victoria Barracks before Major PGW Eckford and Major RE McLean, both of the Royal Irish Rifles, and Captain JAL Wilson, Royal Army Medical Corps. The Quinn family, present throughout the proceedings, was represented by Councillor Thomas Alexander who, previously, had said at a City Council meeting:

"An inquiry into the circumstances under which this poor fellow was ordered to the train would be a lesson and a warning to such doctors and officials as were callously inclined to display a little more humanity and caution in their treatment of the wounded."

The inquiry had to be halted at one stage and Captain Robinson, against whom the most damaging allegations were made, summoned to attend so he could give his response which, perhaps typically, was dismissive and off-hand. By comparison, Lieutenant Colonel Wills, commander of the hospital, went out of his way to distance himself from the incident and, when the opportunity presented itself, made apparent his displeasure at Captain Robinson's actions. The Court of Inquiry concluded without making its findings public and it was several weeks before it was made known that the person "held most responsible" would face prosecution.

On 12 December, Captain JS Robinson, of the Royal Army Medical Corps, appeared before a court-martial at Victoria Barracks charged with neglect of duty for failing to take the appropriate action in that when contacted by the transport officer at the Midland Railway terminus warning about Quinn's condition he failed to report the fact to the orderly medical officer at the hospital. The prosecuting officer, Captain EV Longworth, told the court:

"It was well known that Quinn died a few hours later under the most distressing circumstances. Those facts were now notorious, and must be known to the members of that court. Captain Robinson, however, was not charged with failing to diagnose the disease from which Quinn suffered, and from which he subsequently died. Indeed, it was the opinion of the various medical men that that could not be made the subject of the charge, as Quinn had died of acute pancreatitis, a disease which gave no warning and which came on very suddenly."

The court-martial, with Brigadier-General HF Kays, commander of the 19th Infantry Brigade, as chairman, retired for just a few minutes before returning with a verdict of not guilty.

DEATH OF A TUNNELLING HERO:
Sapper John McCreesh

A random shell, fired blindly from far behind the German lines, took the life of John McCreesh on 16 October 1917, as he made his way back to barracks after a heavy day's work. It was an inglorious end for a man who had risked his own life time and again to save others.

McCreesh, from Camlough, County Armagh, was an unlikely soldier, standing at a little over 5ft in height, with only one good eye and, having been born in 1876, already over the enlistment age of 35. In 1914 he was living at Burnopfield, in County Durham, with his wife Bridget and daughter Josephine, and working as a miner, which as a reserved occupation meant he was not liable for military service in any case. Nonetheless, he had applied to join the army shortly after the declaration of war, hoping to find a place in the ranks of the Durham Light Infantry, but had been turned down flat. A second opportunity arose in early 1915, however, when the stalemate on the Western Front spawned a new type of warfare – underground.

The Germans had been first to employ what was a centuries-old technique when at Givenchy in December 1914 they had detonated 10 small mines under the British lines. Over the next three years it would become a common aspect of war, with those in the trenches living in fear that the very ground beneath their feet could erupt at anytime without warning. Initially the British, who blew their first mine at Hill 60 in February 1915, employed a combination of Royal Engineers and infantry labour. However, the decision was taken to recruit professionals to form Tunnelling Companies, with twenty in place by the end of 1915 with another added in 1916.

John McCreesh was accepted into the new unit and following basic training was sent to the 175th Tunnelling Company, arriving in France in June, 1915. The company was engaged at the time in constructing a 60-metre tunnel under a German strongpoint in the grounds of the Hooge chateau. It was detonated on 19 July, leaving a 40-metre wide and six metres deep crater. Sapper McCreesh had also worked on the middle section of the Loughnagar mine, exploded on 1 July 1916, at the beginning of the Somme offensive, leaving a huge crater that can still be visited today. He was later transferred to the 250th Tunnelling Company, where he worked on the tunnels being constructed under the German defences on the Messines Ridge. It would have been extremely dangerous work under any circumstances, but was made much more so by the fact that both sides were engaged in counter-mining, seeking to destroy the enemy's shaft with a camouflet, or even breaking in to a tunnel leading to ghastly hand-to-hand fighting with shovels and picks. A Mine Rescue School was established at Armentieres in 1915, and John McCreesh was selected to undergo training and over the coming months was to help pull from the earth many men who otherwise would never have seen the light of day again. On one occasion, at Petit Bois in June 1916, he was part of a team that dug for a solid week in a bid to rescue a dozen men trapped in a collapsed mine. In the event, only one was discovered alive.

The series of mines on Messines Ridge were detonated on 7 June 1917, and were fundamental in the British success that day. The largest of the explosions was at Spanbroekmolen, where more than 90,000 lbs of ammonal explosives were packed into the chamber below the German lines. All twenty-one mines were detonated at the same time, 3.10 am, with nineteen exploding. It was claimed the blast could be heard as far away as Dublin. At Spanbroekmolen the explosion was delayed by 15 seconds and the men of the 36th (Ulster) Division had already climbed out of their trenches and were making their way across No-Man's-Land when it detonated, with some injured and possibly even killed by the falling debris. Today the crater, which has filled with water, is known as the Pool of Peace.

After Messines the miners were largely deployed to other duties, including digging subways, cable trenches, saps and road building. On the day 40-year-old John McCreesh, who had been recommended for a Military Medal for his courageous mine rescue work, died he had completed his tasks for the day. Together with three fellow soldiers he was making his way along the St Eloi road when, as they passed through a crossroads, a German shell fell among them. Another sapper was killed outright and a third injured. In a letter of condolence sent to his widow on 19 October 1917, Adjutant JC Clutterbuck wrote:

> "The death of your husband inflicts a great loss upon this company, as apart from his excellent character and reliability, he was an expert in mine rescue work, in which he specialised. He always took a great interest in the work and had the whole subject at his fingertips. He recently delivered a lecture and gave a demonstration of the use of mine rescue equipment to the instructional staff of the Divisional Gas School."

McCreesh's remains lie today at Bedford House Cemetery, a mile south of Ypres, Belgium.

BATTERS AND PITCHERS DO BATTLE:
Baseball at Windsor Park

Sir Robert Liddell did not have the appearance of a natural sportsman, but then no-one on the famous turf of Windsor Park, the ground of Linfield football club in Belfast, looked quite at home that day. All suited up, he stood on a small mound of earth surrounded by what, to the overflowing terraces of fans, looked quite literally like something from another world. Drawing back his arm, the knight of the realm sent the little white ball through the air to be struck by what the local newspaper described as a "weapon that looked like a compromise between a policeman's baton and a swinging club," and the first baseball game to be played in the city for nearly 30 years was underway.

Following the outbreak of war in August 1914, the Ulster Volunteer Force had offered its entire medical organisation to the War Office – in effect providing a fully equipped hospital in which sick and wounded troops could be treated. A public appeal was made to provide the finance necessary for the running of the unit and a number of branch hospitals, with Sir Robert appointed honorary treasurer of the Ulster Volunteer Force Hospital Fund, one of his many charitable works in aid of servicemen. He took his position very seriously and actively fundraised, ensuring the UVF Hospital at Craigavon House, in east Belfast, not only operated throughout the Great War but laying the foundations for its continuing service up until the 1980s when it was superseded by the Somme Hospital, later renamed the Somme Nursing Home, which still provides care for former servicemen today.

So it was on the afternoon of 31 October 1917 that he found himself at the centre of things as the charity fundraiser between a team of American soldiers and Canadian servicemen got underway. The game had been the talk of the city for the past week and the curious came in their droves to watch. Belfast Corporation even dropped the tram fare to just a penny to ensure those attending had change to drop into the collection boxes being jangled at the entrances to the ground by "pretty and persuasive collectors".

The *Belfast Telegraph* reported:

"At two o'clock the teams appeared for a preliminary practice – a strangely costumed group, the drab monotony of whose garb made it difficult to distinguish the Yankees from the Canadians. The distinguishing flags on the left breasts were an aid to those who were favoured with the nearer view, but to the vast body of spectators these were not discernible. The preliminaries showed remarkable wrist flexibility on the part of the fielders, who seldom failed to hold. After the inevitable cinema camera formalities the men got ready for the more serious business of the day."

The Americans batted first with the Canadian pitcher taking the place of Sir Robert after the first ceremonial ball had been thrown. It was another player, however, to the rear of the batter, who captured the imagination of the Press writer:

"Immediately behind him stood the catcher (the equivalent to the wicket keeper), a strangely envisaged gentleman with padded breastplate who appeared prepared for all contingencies – whether to survive a gas attack, settle a swarm of bees, or accept a deep sea diving contract."

Among the crowd on the terraces was a contingent of soldiers from a reserve battalion of the Royal Irish Rifles, who had been allowed to attend by their colonel, and a group of American sailors, the latter possibly the only spectators in the ground with any real understanding of the game. The newspaper, which estimated that not one in 100 in attendance had ever visited America let alone witnessed a baseball game, reported that while the batter appeared to be at a disadvantage, after a few balls had been struck the spectators began to develop a better grasp of the game:

"The man with the weapon, however, was not always at the mercy of the pitcher, and when at times he scored a stroke and ran to the first base, the spectators, who at first were silent and mystified, began to 'tumble' to the meaning of the field movements. When an innings or two had elapsed, and some great catches had been brought off and some lightning returns to bases made, their interest became more lively, and the intervals between the bursts of applause became shorter. Mr F Hamilton, with speaking trumpet, made timely announcements as to the progress of the game, and contributed in no small measure to the general understanding as to the fortunes of the day."

The game, like all good friendly contests, ended in a draw, five a piece, with the UVF Hospital the real winner while the morale of everyone received a boost. The group of American and Canadian players, who had been entertained like sporting royalty on their visit, left the next day to carry out similar fixtures across Great Britain.

Sir Robert Liddell made an unlikely baseball player but was an active and effective fundraiser for the Ulster Volunteer Force Hospital Fund of which he was honorary treasurer. *(From the Northern Whig)*

WHEN LUCK RUNS OUT:
Lieutenant Harden Scott

As Lieutenant David Harden Scott took off for a routine patrol on 12 November 1917, he probably considered himself to be a lucky man. Two years before the one-time infantryman had escaped what must have appeared to be certain death as his plane had plunged thousands of feet after a clash with the enemy. Not only had he survived that incident unhurt, but he was still flying all these months later when so many of his contemporaries had perished – the life-expectancy of an airman during the Great War was usually measured in days or weeks at best. Luck, however, is a fickle companion, and his was about to run out.

Major J Cunningham, commanding officer of the 65th Squadron, Royal Flying Corps, told his parents:

> "He was on a patrol with five others. They had just crossed the line to do their patrol, and the first shell shot at them from the German anti-aircraft guns hit your son's machine, completely wrecking it. It was cruel luck, for it is only once in many thousand or even million that a direct hit is obtained."

Harden Scott was just 21 when he was killed at the controls of his Sopwith Camel aircraft yet had already three years service under his belt. The Camel, a single-seat plane, had only been introduced that year and, though difficult to handle, was considered at the time to be one of the more superior craft in the skies. Before the war Scott had attended the Municipal Technical Institute in Belfast, going on to secure a job with the County Down Weaving Company. A member of the Queen's University Officers' Training Corps, he had enlisted in the 36th (Ulster) Division in October 1914, but a short time later was granted a commission, being posted to the 16th Royal Irish Rifles, the divisional pioneer battalion. He then spent a spell with the Army Cyclist Corps before his transfer to the Royal Flying Corps. In August 1916 came his near brush with death. Flying as observer with Second Lieutenant Herbert Turk at the controls, they came across a formation of seven enemy aircraft near Ligny-Thilloy, southwest of Bapaume in northern France, and immediately went on the attack, bringing one down. However, as the pilot turned to find another target the plane was riddled with machine-gun fire that shot away the rudder controls. The aircraft went into a nosedive, falling 5,000 feet before Lieutenant Turk managed to regain some control and, despite the machine still "turning," he landed it safely. Both men were able to walk away from the incident uninjured and each received the Military Cross for their actions.

In his letter to Lieutenant Scott's father, Matthew, the railway stationmaster at Ballynahinch, County Down, Major Cunningham added:

"We all loved him. No one could help that. He was always so bright and cheery and the whole squadron will miss him terribly. My deepest sympathy goes out to you both, and I am more sorry than I know how to express to have to write such painful news."

The 65th Squadron, formed the previous year at Wyton, England, went on to claim 200 victories and produced thirteen flying aces with five or more kills. The Scott family later moved to Dufferin Avenue in Bangor. Their son lies in Pont-du-Hem Military Cemetery, La Gorgue, on the main road from La Bassee to Estaires.

Lieutenant Turk survived his lucky escape for just another three months. On 3 November 1916, he and another officer were killed when carrying out an experiment to see if messages could be picked up from a pole – some of the wires being used snagged the prop resulting in the plane crashing. The 27-year-old member of 11th Squadron had travelled from Queensland, Australia, to join the RFC. He had four confirmed kills to his name, just one short of officially becoming a flying ace.

TANK GUNNER AT THE HINDENBURG LINE:
William Galway

The Battle of Cambrai, launched on 20 November 1917, saw the first mass use of tanks, changing the face of war forever. At 6.20 am more than 1,000 British artillery guns opened up on the enemy lines with the first of the 476 tanks available moving forward in long waves. Overhead close to 300 planes kept the skies free of German aircraft. The three enemy divisions on the receiving end were rapidly overwhelmed and a section of the Hindenburg Line, feared virtually impregnable by many, had been taken along with 9,000 prisoners. All told, the advance had been about 7 kms on a 12 km wide front. For the first time since the war began, the church bells rang out in Britain to salute a great victory.

Around Flesquieres, however, it was a different story as fierce resistance by the German field artillery had halted the tanks in their tracks, with the supporting infantry of the 51st Highland Division too far behind to offer support. Just one tank, D51 and named *Deborah*, made it through the village before it too was knocked out by artillery fire, receiving five direct hits. On board was William Galway, a 25-year-old gunner. The vehicle commander, Second Lieutenant Frank Gustave Heap managed to get four of his crew out alive, though one may have subsequently died of his injuries. His courage won him the Military Cross.

However, among the other four crewmen who died was Gunner Galway. From Church View, Holywood, County Down, he was the son of a labourer. He had joined the Royal Irish Rifles and served with the 36th (Ulster) Division in the trenches before transferring to the tanks. William appears to have been the comedian of the crew, keeping his comrades amused in the noisy, fume-filled tank interior with his keen sense of humour. Second Lieutenant Heap, in a letter to the dead man's mother, Elizabeth, said:

"Your son was the life and soul of my crew, doing two men's work and cheering us all up. He kept us in shrieks of laughter right up to the moment of his death, and died with a laugh on his lips, like the true Irish gentlemen he was."

Gunner Galway and his dead comrades were initially buried alongside the wreck of their tank.

The following day the infantry recaptured Flesquieres but by then the first of substantial German reinforcements were arriving. The ringing of the church bells had been premature. On 30 November a major enemy counter-attack was launched and ultimately succeeded in winning back virtually all the ground lost ten days before. There were further major actions in the area during the German advance of March 1918, and the Allied drive to victory in September that year and somewhere along the way *Deborah* disappeared.

In 1998 the remains of a Mark IV Female tank, believed to be *Deborah*, were found on the edge of the village. The six-year search, led by local historian Philippe Gorczuynski, had been inspired by one old lady's fading childhood memories of a tank being pushed to the spot by Russian prisoners-of-war and buried in a huge hole. The tank clearly shows damage to the front, with at least one shell striking below the driver's compartment, but much of it was found to be in remarkably good condition. Most of the war material recovered from the site was German, leading some to believe it had been sunk in the ground late in the war as a ready-made bunker in which the enemy gunners could shelter from British artillery. The tank sat in a farmyard for a period after initially being recovered, but is now housed in a barn bought for the purpose and forms the centrepiece of a small museum housed nearby. It stands on a base of granite cobblestones that formerly graced some of the old streets of Cambrai.

Today the remains of Gunner William Galway lie in Flesquieres Hill British Cemetery, on the edge of the village, where they were re-interred after the war. Alongside him are the graves of three of the men who died in *Deborah*, with the fourth a short distance away in the same graveyard.

TOURING THE FRONT:
Trade unionist J McWhirter

On 20 November 1917, a deputation of influential business people from the munitions and shipbuilding sectors was taken on a tour of the Western Front battlefields to see something of the vast war machine it was feeding. Among their number was J McWhirter, vice-chairman of the Belfast branch of the Ship Constructors and Shipwrights' Association, who was suitably impressed with the gigantic scale of the military workshops. On the second day the group was taken up to the Messines Ridge, leaving their cars nearby and walking past the huge craters created by the detonation of British mines the previous June. "Judging by the elaborate care with which the dug-outs had been constructed, and by the extensive cabbage gardens planted by the Huns behind their lines, it was evident they had no intention of quitting the ridge so early, if at all," wrote Mr McWhirter in an account of his tour.

"We were much impressed by the ground pitted with mine and shell craters, by the mud and by the dirt and desolation of this part of the country from which the enemy had been driven. But we were able to form a very different estimate of the arduous work performed by our men in advancing over such ground, than by seeing it depicted by a black line moved forward an inch or so on the war map in our morning paper at home. Much the same conditions presented themselves on Vimy Ridge, on our way to which we motored through a beautiful undulating country. We admired the good French roads and the well-tilled fields, in which the peasant women were hard at work with old men and boys to 'keep the home fires burning'. What a contrast presented itself to us as we approached the country which had been occupied by the German, or which had been under their shell-fire. Here the farm houses, once happy homes, were demolished, and villages and churches in ruins, the very trees by the wayside blasted and dead as if struck by lightning.

We climbed to the top of Vimy Ridge, passing on our way through fields which had been fought over again and again by the French and by the British. From the crest we could see Lens and part of the rich coal producing district of France, which is still in the hands of the Germans. We had also pointed out to us Givenchy, Neuville-St-Vast, and Loos, scenes of many a hard-fought battle, the names of which have become historic. While on the Ridge we were within easy reach of the enemy shell and shrapnel fire, and although none was coming our way, it was advisable to wear the steel helmets provided for us."

The group then made its way to Ypres in Belgium, pausing to watch an aerial duel involving up to seven German planes that had crossed into the skies above the British lines.

"The anti-aircraft guns quickly opened fire and surrounded them with puffs of shrapnel, through which they continued to sail with apparent unconcern. Eventually when they were almost above our heads they were encountered by a small squadron of our machines, which quickly drove them back, and continued to chase them out of sight over the German lines. At this, the German guns opened fire to cover their retreat, and the simultaneous bursting of both enemy and British shrapnel over our heads caused a hasty scramble for tin hats amongst our party. The German shrapnel was easily distinguished by the black smoke cloud it emitted, 'to match their souls,' as a French poilu put it."

Arriving in Ypres they were immediately struck by the immense damage the "once prosperous and beautiful town" had sustained during the three years of conflict to date, though they quickly moved on: "We, however, did not remain long as the evening was falling, and the enemy were shelling a point quite near to the town," admitted Mr McWhirter.

"The fact that their fire might be directed towards us at any moment, added to the general desolation and unhealthiness of the place, made us glad to leave it and the war zone behind us. In conclusion, we may state we are all elated with a strong conviction of the great and lasting victory that is surely approaching, and while we gazed respectfully at some wooden crosses which indicate where some of our brave fellows have fallen into their last sleep, it reminded us forcibly that we at home must continue to put forth our greatest efforts to keep him going who has not yet fallen and while the honourable name of the British Empire is safe in their keeping that we in the munition factories and shipbuilding yards will strengthen and not weaken the efforts of our soldiers who are engaged in their great fight for freedom, liberty, and democracy."

AN IRISH ROVER:
Frontiersman Daniel Driscoll

Daniel Patrick Driscoll was a rare character who headed up a body of men of a similar ilk during the First World War. Most likely born in Limerick in May 1862, he was a true Irish rover who, despite his strong brogue, appears to have spent very little time in Ireland. After service in the Upper Burma Volunteer Rifles and the Indian Merchant Navy, serving on a number of ships as an engineer, he decided to go to South Africa to take part in the Boer War. Attached to the Border Mounted Rifles, he rose to the rank of captain. According to Australian war correspondent Alfred Hales, at the battle of Labuschagne's Nek Driscoll was "the first man to gallop into the Boer laager before the fight had ceased". An excellent scout, he was given permission to form the Driscoll's Scouts in 1900, which grew in strength to more than 400 men. The unit was disbanded in July 1902. Hales described Driscoll as a "typical Irishman":

"...of dauntless daring, with a heart of iron, and a face to match. Strangely enough, the captain does not pride himself a bit on his pluck, but he thinks a deuce of a lot of his beauty. As a matter of fact, he has the courage of ten ordinary men, but he would not take a prize in a first-class beauty show... Yet if you want to know if Driscoll can shoot, just go to Burmah, where for ten years he held the position of captain in the Upper Burmah Volunteer Rifles. That was where I heard of him first, as the most deadly rifle and revolver shot in all the East. The Boers know him now as the prince of rifle shots and the king of scouts. He is standing in the wintry sunlight just in front of my tent as I am writing, one hand on the bridle of his horse, rapping out Dutch oaths with a strong Cork accent to a n_____ who has not groomed his pet animal properly. The n_____ is very meek, for past experience has told him that Irish blood is hot, and an Irishman's boot quick and heavy."

Driscoll remained in South Africa for a number of years. In 1907 he left for England, where he joined the Legion of Frontiersmen, shortly afterwards being appointed commandant for London and later overall commander. In 1914 he volunteered the services of about 100 Frontiersmen to fight as a unit in France then, when that was rejected, suggested their services could be used in East Africa. When this was accepted by the War Office, Driscoll launched a recruitment campaign, quickly signing up some 1,200 volunteers to form the 25th Royal Fusiliers. The battalion arrived in Mombasa in May 1915. Its ranks included an odd assortment of people from across the globe, including a 63-year-old game hunter, former French Foreign Legion members, a lighthouse keeper, palace footman, Texan cowboys, circus acrobats and clowns, and a 27-stone American.

Robert Dolbey, in his 1918 book *Sketches of the East Africa Campaign*, described them as "soldiers of fortune". He wrote:

"Of the most romantic interest probably are the 25th Royal Fusiliers, the Legion of Frontiersmen. Volumes might be written of the varied careers and wild lives lived by these strange soldiers of fortune. They were led by Colonel Driscoll, who for all his sixty years, has found no work too arduous and no climate too unhealthy for his brave spirit. I knew him in the Boer War when he commanded Driscoll's Scouts, of happy, though irregular memory; their badge in those days, the harp of Erin on the side of their slouch hats, and known throughout the country wherever there was fighting to be had. The 25th Fusiliers, too, were out here in the early days, and participated in the capture of Bukoba on the Lake. A hundred professions are represented in their ranks. Miners from Australia and the Congo, prospectors after the precious mineral earths of Siam and the Malay States, pearl-fishers and elephant poachers, actors and opera singers, jugglers, professional strong men, big game hunters, sailors, all mingled with professions of peace, medicine, the law and the clerk's varied trade. Here two Englishmen, soldiers of fortune or misfortune, as the case might be, who had specialised in recent Mexican revolutions, till the fall of Huerta brought them, too, to unemployment; an Irishman there, for whom the President of Costa Rica had promised a swift death against a blank wall. Cunning in the art of gun-running, they were knowing in all the tides of the Caribbean Sea, and in every dodge to outwit the United States patrol. Nor must I forget one priceless fellow, a lion tamer, who strange to say, feared exceedingly the wild denizens of the scrub that sniffed around his patrol at night."

The Frontiersmen were constantly involved in the pursuit of the German forces throughout 1916 but the real enemy was the unhealthy climate, which took a hefty toll on the men. The following year the greatly depleted unit fought at Ziwani, Tandamuti and Narunyu, having to survive for five days against overwhelming odds until it was able to withdraw under darkness. Later that year the 25th Fusiliers battalion was disbanded.

Driscoll, who received the Order of St Michael and St George and the Croix de Guerre for his war efforts, returned to East Africa where he purchased land and grew coffee until his death on 6 August 1934.

Lieutenant Colonel Daniel Patrick Driscoll was a true 'wild rover'. *(From the Belfast Telegraph)*

WORLD'S GREATEST EXPLOSION:
Private John Murphy

The biggest explosion of the First World War took place thousands of miles away from any fighting. On the morning of 6 December 1917, the Norwegian ship *Imo* was leaving Halifax harbour after unloading its war supplies. The port was a hive of activity as one of Canada's main points from which troops were embarking for Europe and where the wounded arrived for hospital care. And, of course, munitions were constantly on the move.

On this particular morning, the French ship *Mont-Blanc*, packed with 3,000 tons of explosives and munitions, was slowly making its way into the harbour. At 8.45 am, the two ships, the *Imo* and *Mont-Blanc*, collided, causing onboard fires. Just 21 minutes later, the *Mont-Blanc*'s cargo of explosives detonated, creating what was claimed to be the largest man-made explosion the world had ever known at the time and wiping out some six square kilometres of the city. Windows in buildings some 75 kilometres away were broken and the shock waves felt more than 300 kilometres distant. Some 2,000 people were killed and another 9,000 injured by debris. The blast caused a tsunami, with waves up to 18 metres high swamping the town and sweeping the remains of the *Imo* on to the shoreline at Dartmouth, across the inlet from Halifax. Elsewhere, fire swept through the streets of the largely wooden buildings.

Among those passing through Halifax on the day of the explosion was County Tyrone man John Murphy from Ballinderry. He had been living in Chicago when the United States entered the war and had immediately volunteered to join the US army only to be rejected as being over the maximum age of 35. Not to be denied, he decided to travel home to enlist and was awaiting a boat in Halifax in December 1917. Together with other prospective recruits, he was undergoing some basic training when the tragedy struck. The roof of the building collapsed, injuring a number of those inside. After helping to dig his comrades from the rubble, Murphy joined others who made their way into the ruined city to help in the rescue work. They found bodies everywhere and others suffering horrendous wounds, including many blinded by flying glass.

The *Belfast Telegraph*, which interviewed Murphy, reported:

"The men, together with those who survived the shock, quickly got to work, and the horrible sights which faced them among the debris made even those who had been in the worst carnage of the fields of France and Flanders sick. A barber's establishment was discovered in ruins, and when the debris was sorted it was found that the barber had been shaving a soldier when the awful crash came and had cut his throat. The soldier was lying dead in the chair, and alongside him lay the lifeless remains of the barber. One whole family of fourteen members were found in the debris of their home, every one a lifeless piece of clay. A sugar refinery was turned into a mass of wreckage, and six days later, when it was possible to secure a passage into the basement, a man was found who had kept himself alive by eating the sugar. Unfortunately he passed away soon after his discovery.

The day following the disaster brought one of the worst blizzards seen for years, and the thermometer dropped to 25 below zero, and it can be imagined how difficult the work of the rescuers in such conditions. Private Murphy was in one of the morgues and he says it was extremely pathetic to see survivors passing amongst the mangled remains looking for those who were near and dear to them. One little girl identified her mother's head, the only portion of the body which was found. Every available building which was not damaged, or only slightly so, was turned into a hospital, and the doctors and nurses worked for days and nights together without thinking of sleep. Thirty hours from the awful calamity occurred brought two Red Cross trains with full hospital equipment, nurses, and doctors, from Boston, and in a short space of time two large temporary hospitals were in full swing. Pieces of the ill-fated munitions ship were found everywhere, and her anchor, a massive piece of steel, was found three miles away from where the collision occurred, a testimony to its awful force. Private Murphy says never till his dying day will he forget the awful scenes of Halifax."

Dear lady, living in sad Courtrai,
Ulster has heard of you today -
Living alone, as your friend doth tell,
Near the old church on which ne'er fell
The curse that sped the blasting shell;
Where the air was vile with German breath,
And life seemed an endless game with death,
Babes hushed - the while - with hated breath.
Tho' many friends had hurried away,
Yet you stayed on while the foe held sway,
And lived to see him steal away.

Elizabeth B King, Belfast, dedicated to Miss Mary Cunningham,
found living at Courtrai after the German withdrawal

1918

THE GUNS FALL SILENT

The end of Germany's war in the East meant a major enemy assault on the Western Front was not only inevitable, but likely to fall sooner rather than later, with even the newspapers talking openly about the coming offensive for weeks beforehand. The British army, starved of men due to political disagreements and differences of opinion over the conduct of the war, was undergoing a major reform. Infantry divisions, formerly made up of four battalions per brigade, were reduced to three each, or nine in total compared to the former twelve. The men thus freed up were used to bring the remaining fighting units up to strength or incorporated into labour battalions employed to improve the totally inadequate defences behind the Allied frontlines.

It was too little, too late however, for on 21 March 1918 the Germans launched their spring offensive. Taking advantage of an early morning mist, and proceeded by a five hour bombardment that targeted the heavy gun positions as well as command and communication centres before switching to the front lines, the assault troops of three German armies rapidly overran the British positions on the Somme. That evening the British forces began a withdrawal that by the end of 22 March would see a 40 mile gap opened in the line. All available reserves were thrown into the battle as appeals were made for French help.

On 26 March, at a hastily arranged conference at Doullens, it was decided that for the first time the British army would operate under the overall command of the French, and hence resolve the problems caused by a lack of coordinated action. It was not until 28 March, however, that the British enjoyed a victory of sorts, as artillery and machine-gun fire inflicted a terrible price on the Germans forces at the First Battle of Arras, though even here some ground had to be given up. On 4 April a determined attack aimed at taking the city of Amiens was halted by the Allies at Villers-Bretonneux.

Opposite: A service of thanksgiving, celebrating the fact the Germans had been driven back from the city, was held at Amiens Cathedral in August 1918. Note the heavily sandbagged walls to protect the building from enemy shelling. *(From A Popular History of the Great War, published 1933)*

Though the fighting would continue for days to come, the line held with only minor withdrawals. At the end of April the Germans launched a fresh attack at Villers-Bretonneux, which saw the first tank verses tank battle in history. The town fell but that evening Australian troops conducted a brutal night attack to retake it.

At about the same time German attempts to force a breakthrough in Flanders were drawing to a close. Launched on 9 April against British troops holding Givenchy and Armentieres, it had also proved remarkably successful initially. Eight German divisions stormed a 12-mile front, rapidly making progress as a Portuguese division holding the centre of the line at Neuve Chapelle crumbled. The British divisions on each flank, along with rapidly arriving reserves, managed to plug the gap by mid-afternoon. The fighting continued until 29 April, and while more ground had to be given up, including the Messines Ridge and the gains at Passchendaele the previous year, the line held.

In the midst of the intense land activity, the Royal Navy launched raids on Zeebrugge and Ostend aimed at denying their use as German submarine bases for attacking Allied shipping. On 23 April, some seventy-five ships, supported by infantry who were landed to attack the shore batteries, launched the assaults. Old ships, full of concrete, were sunk in the entrances to the ports and other antiquated vessels filled with explosives detonated to destroy infrastructure. However, despite being hailed as a huge success, the raids did little to hinder German activities.

A final German attempt to break the Allied line was launched at the Aisne on 27 May, focusing on the Chemin des Dames Ridge, lost the previous year. British troops, sent to the sector to recuperate from their participation in the earlier fighting, were in the front trenches and suffered considerably. However, despite an initial breakthrough that took them to within 90 km of Paris, this German assault also ground to a halt on the Marne after just more than a week. The tables had now turned. The German army was exhausted and short on supplies while the worldwide influenza pandemic that was to claim millions of lives had found its way to the trenches. With thousands of American troops arriving each week, the Allies turned towards offensive operations of their own.

On 18 July, the French, British, American and Italian troops, supported by tanks, counter-attacked at the Marne, advancing five miles on the first day. The Germans were thrown into retreat and by the beginning of August virtually all of their gains had been lost. The Allies now faced the formidable Hindenburg Line, a series of linked strong points running from the coast to Verdun, up to 15 kms deep, built using forced labour and huge quantities of concrete, steel and barbed wire. On 18 September, the British successfully attacked the forward outposts of the line, advancing three miles. Eleven days later, on 29 September, tanks, infantry, artillery and aircraft worked in concert to finally break the line in four days of fighting. Other breaches followed and the Germans were forced into retreat. Chased by the Allies, they continued to withdraw throughout October. The German government fell, being replaced with a more moderate administration that began negotiations towards an Armistice on 7 November. Kaiser Wilhelm II abdicated two days later, fleeing the country. At 11.00 am, on 11 November 1918, following an agreement signed earlier that day in a railway siding at Compiegne, north of Paris, the guns finally fell silent. The British army finished the war at Mons where four years previously it had first encountered the Germans.

On 9 August 1919, Belfast held its formal peace celebrations. Up to 30,000 men and women, some still serving but most having been discharged in the months before, marched through the city. Lord French, who had commanded the British Expeditionary Force when it had first crossed to France and was then Lord Lieutenant of Ireland, took the salute on a specially constructed platform below the statue of Queen Victoria in the grounds of the City Hall. To the east of the building, four soldiers stood with bowed heads at the corners of the temporary cenotaph, while on the west side stood a victory column bedecked with bunting.

The Armistice of 11 November 1918 was, on paper, a temporary halt to the war, though in reality the Germans had no more fight left in them. On 28 June 1919 – five years to the day after the assassination of Austrian Archduke Franz Ferdinand at Sarajevo – the representatives of the new regime in Germany signed the Treaty of Versailles in the Hall of Mirrors, at the Palace of Versailles, on the fringes of Paris, bringing the Great War officially to an end.

DODGING THE GERMAN BOMBS:
Selby Clough Herring

The first significant German air raids of the war were carried out on 19 January 1915, when the towns of Yarmouth and Kings Lynn were bombed from airships with the loss of four lives and sixteen injured. London, which was to emerge as the main target over the coming years, was first targeted in May of that year. Such attacks continued at an average of two raids a month into 1917, when the Zeppelins were supplemented, then largely replaced, by heavy bomber aircraft. A public blackout was introduced in 1916 and, such was the terror felt, some 300,000 Londoners routinely took shelter in the underground railway stations, while the German raiders ranged further and further afield, even reaching as far as Scotland. Though the first bombing of England by a German aircraft had taken place in December 1914, it was not until the end of 1916 that planes were used in significant numbers and by 1918 one ton bombs were being dropped. Overall, some 1,413 people were killed and another 4,822 injured in air attacks over mainland Britain.

Many Irish service personnel and volunteers, of course, passed through England, and London in particular, including Selby Clough Herring, Commandant of City of Belfast Red Cross. In 1918 she wrote of her experiences while spending a couple of weeks in the Red Cross Voluntary Aid Detachment Hostel in the capital.

"There is also a pathetic as well as a humorous side in the case of the girl who has left home and bade good-bye to all near and dear to her, facing risks and dangers that in times of peace would have been unheard of. A few nights ago one member said 'Good-bye, Superintendent; I hope I shall return,' not knowing whether a bomb would drop her way or not. An air-raid is an experience that fills one with overpowering emotions, and my experience in the last raid was somewhat interesting. You don't know what is going to happen. You hear one crash near and another nearer, and you wonder if you are the next to go under. You know that every crash means something to some soul. In the recent raid I was awakened by the booming of guns.

I sat up in bed and called out to my chum at the end of the room – 'There is an air raid on'. She said 'Yes,' and we jumped out of bed, scrambling into anything we could find. She knocked and gave the warning to the girls on our floor, and I found myself flying up into the attic, calling out to those up there, along with another VAD.

Very soon we were all downstairs, in wonderful apparel. Some were fortunate to have on shoes and stockings and others were with bare feet, some ready for walking and many clad in eiderdowns, dressing-gowns, and all manner of headgear. No one became hysterical, but displayed courage, and their calm serene looks were a credit to them. There they were, standing, sitting, reclining as the case might be; others curled up in blankets on couches and floor. One lady came down with her little case and said in a matter of fact voice, 'I will just write a few letters'. Another girl put her head on my knee, and as I had given one or two funny verses by way of a cheer-up, I too settled down to write to friends. In the midst of guns firing and bombs dropping one VAD came in and said. 'I hope ladies, you all have your uniform permits.' Then tea was a wonderful help, and set us all talking, and so we each had a nice hot cup of that which cheers but not inebriates, and there we were until 6.30 am, when the call came – 'squad dismiss,' and we all wended our way to bed for an hour.

Sometime afterwards the call 'All clear' rang out, and our minds were at rest for a bit. A remarkable thing was when a VAD came to me in the morning and said, 'Mrs Herring, don't you know me?' She was a member from Belfast, who had been in City of Belfast R2 for a short time, and she was on her way to the front. The night of the air-raid was her first from Belfast. I can assure you it was a comfort to see someone from her native soil."

WOMAN WHO SERVED ON THE FRONTLINE:
Flora Sandes

Just eight days after the declaration of war, Flora Sandes left England for Serbia as part of a St John Ambulance group. She was, however, an unlikely nurse though she was eventually to find her true vocation as the only western woman to serve as a soldier on the frontline. She was born in Yorkshire to an Irish family in 1876, her father Samuel having previously served as the rector of Whitchurch in County Cork. When she was still a child they moved to Suffolk and later to Surrey. A tomboy by nature, the hard drinking chain-smoker had learned to drive and ride a horse, and enjoyed shooting.

Arriving in Serbia in August 1914, the 38-year-old joined the local Red Cross and was attached to the 2nd Infantry Regiment of the Serbian army. However, on the retreat to Albania she removed her Red Cross armband and went to see the military commander:

"When the 'commandant' of the regiment, Colonel Militch, laughingly took the little brass figure '2' off his own epaulettes, and fastened them on the shoulder-straps of his 'new recruit,' as he called me, it seemed a 'fait accompli,' and official sanction came when we reached Bitol before going into Albania. There Colonel Militch took me with him to Colonel Vasitch, the commandant of the division, and he told me that, though I could even then get back to Salonique by the last train leaving that night, it would be better for the Serbs if I joined the army and went through Albania with them, as the simple peasant soldiers already looked upon me as a sort of representative of England, and a pledge, and if I stuck to them it would encourage them, and strengthen their belief that in the end England would help them."

Flora was no token soldier, however, but was thrown into the thick of the fighting. Seriously wounded by a grenade during the Serbian advance on Bitola in 1916 – with shrapnel embedded in her back, shoulder and knee and her right arm broken and badly lacerated – she was left unfit to return to frontline service. Though promoted to sergeant major, and awarded Serbia's highest military honour, the Order of the Karađorđe's Star, she was forced to return to her former role of running a hospital.

In early 1918 she returned to England on leave with the intention of raising funds for a charity she had established to provide comforts for Serbian soldiers. Interviewed by the Press, she said:

"I went out to Servia [sic] in August, 1914, being one of the first to go to the help of that little nation. I went there as a nurse, and took part in the memorable retreat. After that terrible retreat I joined the regimental ambulance, but, being cut off from the ambulance, I asked permission to join the Servian [sic] Army as a private, and was accepted. For two years I have taken part in all the fighting, and was badly wounded at the taking of Hill 1212. On this occasion a hand-grenade exploded near me, and I sustained 24 wounds. It was at Hill 1212 that I witnessed magnificent acts of bravery. My company, which was in advance of the main body, was outnumbered by the Bulgarians. When I fell wounded I ordered the men to fall back, but they refused point blank, saying, 'We are not going unless we can take you.' One of the officers crawled through the snow, dragging me along, while the men remained behind and fought a gallant rearguard action until I was carried into safety. The next day, when our troops attacked and occupied the Bulgarian trenches, they found a number of our men who had been taken prisoner. Everyone lay dead in the trench with the throat cut from ear to ear. That is the Bulgar way of dealing with prisoners."

At the war's end Flora remained in the Serbian army, being the first foreigner to be made an officer, and retired in 1922 at the rank of captain. She married five years later, her husband being a White Russian twelve years her junior who had been her platoon sergeant, and set up home in Belgrade. During the Second World War she was, aged 65, briefly arrested by the Gestapo and on release had to report to a German officer once a week for the rest of the war. In 1945 Flora returned to Britain, and passed away at Ipswich in November 1956.

LIVING A DOG'S LIFE:
Bally Shannon

While Irishmen and women were doing their 'bit' in the cause of freedom, an unlikely recruit was making a name for himself among friend and foe alike. Evacuated from the Western Front to the United States late in the war, he came to the attention of the *New York Sun* in early 1918. It reported:

"Bally Shannon, a big soldier of France, who is convalescing here has a record which for all sorts of adventure far surpasses that of any other survivor of the Hun's fire who has come over to write or lecture about his war experiences. For several good reasons Bally Shannon will do neither. He can neither read nor write; besides he is dumb.

For to be perfectly plain and direct in the second paragraph, the hero whose praises were here to be sung is a dog, a war dog and one of the finest specimens of a little known species that have ever come to America. There are but three of his breed in this country. Mrs James McLain owns one of these, and Campbell Thompson has two others. The breed is the Irish wolfhound, famous but always uncommon throughout the long and troubled history of Ireland. This kind of dog has ever achieved and merited distinction, but perhaps the breed, if aware of it, would cherish highest the fact that a place has always been reserved for the Irish wolfhound on the Irish flag. If you look in the right-hand corner of this flag, in the big dog raised on his haunches you will have a perfect picture of Bally Shannon."

The article went on:

"Bally is only a month or two over 24 months old, and for 13 of these months he was a soldier. In the second year of the war his master, who had him in training for a police dog, took him from Dublin to France. Bally took to the life like a true Irishman – the harder the knocks, the more desperate the fighting, the better he liked it. What he didn't care for was the enforced marches in retreat. For six months or so Bally served his master and the French troops, a faithful messenger. He weighs about 170 pounds, but for a big fellow he is splendidly lithe and sinuous and able to get very easily where a man dared not follow. They say that when the regiment to which he justifiably belonged was ordered to Ypres, Bally was the happiest and lightest hearted member of it. This proves that even a dog does not know what is coming to him. For Ypres was destined to be a dangerous if not fatal field to Bally.

In the first action in which he was employed a heavy cannon thrown off its carriage rolled over on Bally and crushed him to the earth. There the Huns found the dog and seeing that it was still alive they carried him into their lines. For the first time in his military career Bally was a prisoner, helpless and apparently near death. At least the Germans so considered him and the next day they thrust the crippled animal back into the French lines. There at least he might die among friendly faces. But Bally wasn't to be so quickly killed. A surgeon examined him and a nun took an X-ray of his bent and contused ribs. They were not broken, and as his master was returning to Ireland to nurse a shattered arm he took the dog along to get well in his native land.

Bally's worst adventure was to come and shortly. Off the coast of Ireland the ship was torpedoed by a submarine and but three of those on board escaped with their lives, a sailor, a New York man named Maloney and Bally. The three supported themselves in the water by clinging to a plank, and when they were finally picked up and put ashore in Ireland Mr Maloney was so penetrated with admiration of the superb courage displayed by the dog that, there being nobody else to claim him, he adopted the animal as his own and brought him to New York.

That was last May. Bally, still almost unable to walk, was taken by his new master up to Central Park, and put in charge of Tom Hoey, who has been shepherd there for a score of years. For seventeen of these Lady Dale, an Airedale, has assisted Tom. It is a question which was the more pleased by Bally's advent, Tommy Hoey, or Lady Dale. Both welcomed the Irish wolfhound heartily, but with Lady Dale it was a case of love at first sight. Since then Bally has lived in what ought to seem like a canine paradise. The shepherd, acting for Mr Maloney, doctored and fed him medicine and food most calculated to restore his strength, while Lady Dale saw to it that in his exercise he should see all her favourite haunts in the Park. A safe and pleasant life, Bally ought to be content to lead it, but he isn't. 'The dog's that restless at times,' said Tom Hoey. 'that I fair believe he wants to be going back to the wars'."

WAR CORRESPONDENT TURNED SOLDIER:
Martin Donohoe

Martin Donohoe led an extraordinary life, much of it spent abroad in the world's most troubled countries and war-torn regions. Born in Galway in 1869, he moved to Australia where he served for a spell in the New South Wales Lancers. Settling in Sydney, he found a job in the machine room of the *Evening News*, later being moved to its literary department. Shifting to London, he found a job with the *Daily Chronicle*, becoming its foreign and war correspondent. Over the years he covered events in South Africa, the Japanese war with Russia of 1904, the Turkish and Portuguese revolutions in 1909 and 1910 respectively, the Italian-Turkey conflict and 1912–13 war between the Balkan States. As he modestly put it in his 1919-published book *With The Persian Expedition*:

"For the past twenty years, as Special Correspondent of the *Daily Chronicle*, I have been privileged to be present at most of the world's great upheavals, both military and political. From July 1914, on, for some eighteen months, I followed the fortunes of the Entente armies in the field as a war chronicler, first in Serbia, next in Belgium, and afterwards in Italy and Greece… But I was not happy, because I felt I was not doing my 'bit' as effectively as I might; so I followed the example of millions of other citizens of the Empire and joined the army. Detailed to the Intelligence Corps, I was sent first to Roumania [sic], then to Russia."

In 1918, having escaped from the 'Red Terror' in Petrograd, he was part of the force, commanded by General Dunsterville, that was sent to Persia, via Bagdad, to bring peace to a region where there was no clear cut enemy or natural friend. It was, as Donohoe put it, "a very mixed-up and complicated business". And even for a man who had seen so much of the world already, it was an eye-opener. He recorded:

"Who has not heard and read of Bagdad, of its former glory and its greatness? I set foot in it for the first time on March 20th, 1918, the day after the arrival of our little party at Hinaida Transit Camp on the left bank of the Tigris. As I tramped across the dusty Hinaida plain towards the belt of palm groves which veils the city on the east, I had visions of Haroun al Raschid, and fancied myself coming face to face with the wonders of the 'Arabian Nights'.

It was with something of a shock, then, that on entering the city I encountered khaki-clad figures, and saw Ford vans and motor lorries tearing wildly along the streets. In the main thoroughfare, hard by British Headquarters, a steam roller was travelling backwards and forwards over the freshly metalled roadway, completing the work of an Indian Labour Corps; farther on, a watering cart labelled "Bagdad Municipality" was busily drowning the fine-spun desert dust that had settled thickly on the newly born macadamized street. Here was an Arab cafe, with low benches on the inclined plane principle like seats in a theatre, where the occupants sipped their Mocha from tiny cups, or inhaled tobacco-smoke through the amber stem of a hubble-bubble, watching the passing show, and betimes discussing the idiosyncrasies of the strange race of unbelievers that has settled itself down in the fair city which once had been the pride of Islam. Truly a city of contrasts! Cheek by jowl with the Arab cafe was an eating-house full of British soldiers. The principal street runs parallel with the river and, as one proceeded, it was possible to catch glimpses of pleasant gardens running down to the water's edge and empowering handsome villas gardens where pomegranates, figs, oranges, and lemons grew in abundance.

The Oriental readily adapts himself to changing circumstances, and unhesitatingly abandons the master of yesterday to follow the new one of today. Already traces of the Ottoman dominion were being obliterated. The Turkish language was disappearing from shop signs to be replaced by English or French, with, in some cases, a total disregard of etymology, such choice gems as "Englisch talking lessons", "Stanley Maude wash company" (this over a laundry), "British Tommy shave room", showing at all events a praiseworthy attempt to wrestle with the niceties of the English language.

Bagdad as I saw it in the first days following my arrival struck me as a place whose remains of faded greatness still clung about it. No one could deny its claim to a certain wild beauty which age, dirt, and decay have not been able wholly to eliminate. The glory of the river scene is unsurpassable. To see Bagdad at its best one must view it from the balcony of the British Residency (now General Headquarters). Here, as you look down upon the river, the old bridge of boats connecting with the western bank is on your right, and handsome villas where flowers grow in profusion, the residences of former Turkish officials or wealthy citizens, adorn the foreshore. The river is broad and majestic, and strange craft dot its surface."

ABANDONED TO DIE:
Major John Brew

On 21 March 1918, the Germans gambled everything on a last roll of the dice. That morning they launched Operation Michael, or Kaiserschlacht, with the aim of pushing the British out of the war. Vastly reinforced by the divisions freed up by the exit of Russia to the east, the German army now had a substantially superior numerical advantage – but it had to be deployed sooner rather than later as the American troops were beginning to arrive in strength. The British had recently extended their lines, taking over miles of defences from the French. The new front was poorly constructed with no second or third lines prepared in most places. Preceded by an intense artillery barrage that concentrated on the back areas of the British front, disrupting communications and targeting the opposing artillery, the German infantry surged forward. Exploiting gaps in the line, and leaving strong points to be mopped up later, the German army was able to advance some 40 miles before finally being halted just outside the city of Amiens. The British, forced into full retreat, was forced to agree to a joint command, with the French Marshal Ferdinand Foch appointed as overall supremo. A huge number of men were taken prisoner and complete divisions, including the 16th (Irish) and 36th (Ulster), were all but destroyed, each losing over 7,000 in dead, wounded and missing.

The 9th Royal Irish Fusiliers, under the command of Major John Brew, staged a fighting retreat. The major, from Portadown, County Armagh, had enlisted as a private in September 1914, being commissioned on 1 December of that year. By April 1916 he had risen to captain and served as second-in-command of the battalion. He was seriously wounded at the Battle of the Somme on 1 July 1916, but returned to the front as a major. By 25 March 1918, the 9th RIF had fallen well behind the rest of its division, forcing the men to undertake a 30-mile forced march to reach its position in the new line at Erches with the Germans close behind. Soon battle was joined again and the decision was taken that a further withdrawal should take place after dark. Lieutenant Colonel Furnell, who had been commanding the 1st Royal Irish Fusiliers, writing to Major Brew's widow after the war, recalled:

"We went to tell the General who was on our right what our intentions were, when the General Staff Officer No 1, Col. Green of the Ulster

Division, arrived and said he would take your husband and myself to see our own Brigadier in his motor; we went and saw the Brigadier but upon returning in the motor, drove into an advance party of the Germans who opened fire and bombed the car. Col. Green was wounded and we were all captured. After being searched we were being marched back to the German Headquarters by an escort, when some Germans who evidently mistook us for British troops opened fire on us; your husband was walking alongside me and was hit. I ran over towards the men who were firing thinking they were our own troops as things were rather mixed up and it was dark. However, I discovered they were Bosche as they fired at me when I was a few yards from them. I then went back to your husband who was lying on the road. I found he had been hit through the lung and as Col. Green and the motor driver were already wounded it was impossible to move him without help from the Bosche which they refused to give any and only beat us with the butts of their rifles when we asked them to move your husband.

We moved him to the side of the road and made him as comfortable as possible, he couldn't speak much, the Bosche were trying to hurry us on all the time so didn't have much chance of doing anything and said goodbye to your husband and he was able to shake hands with me. When we reached German Headquarters Col. Green, who spoke German, told the German Commanding Officer about your husband and they told him they would send out for him but one can never believe a Bosche. There was one of our doctors also a prisoner and I asked him about your husband. He said the best thing that could happen was for him to remain where he was as it was a frosty night and that might stop the bleeding. I never heard what happened to your husband afterwards and I didn't meet anyone who had met him in a German hospital but heard when I was released that he had died."

AWARDED THE POPE'S MEDAL:
Major General Oliver Nugent

When Major General Oliver Nugent stepped down as commander of the 36th (Ulster) Division in May 1918, he left France with an honour that no other could rival – a medal from the Pope. The silver token, bearing an inscription from Benedictus 15th, stands in marked contrast to the other awards earned by the old warrior, including three Masonic Jewels, one of which was regimental, the Order of Savoy; the Distinguished Service Order and Bar, Indian General Service Medals, Queen's South Africa medal with clasps, a Coronation medal of 1911, the 1915 Star, British War Medal and Victory Medal from 1914–18, the French Croix de Guerre, the Italian Order of Saints Maurice, and KCB.

The son of a major-general, Nugent, from County Cavan, attended Harrow and Sandhurst before being commissioned into the Royal Munster Fusiliers. By the age of 30 he had made captain and was serving in India with the King's Royal Rifle Corps, being mentioned in dispatches a number of times and being presented with the Distinguished Service Order for gallantry by Queen Victoria. During the Boer War he fought in Natal and Talana as a major, but was severely wounded and taken prisoner. Prior to the First World War he enjoyed a period of home service that included his appointment as Deputy Assistant Adjutant General at army headquarters in Dublin and ADC to King Edward VII and then King George V. In 1914 he was given command of the Humber Defences until May 1915, when he was sent to France as commander of the 41st Infantry Brigade.

In October 1915, Nugent was given command of the 36th Ulster Division, taking over from Major General Sir Charles Herbert Powell who was considered "too old" and lacking adequate recent experience to take the division overseas. Nugent was a tough and competent commander who was to see his men through all the major battles of the Western Front. He took a no-nonsense approach and, although a unionist himself, put military demands ahead of politics, resulting in him clashing with those who saw the Ulster Division as an extension of the campaign against Home Rule. His men, for the most part, had been recruited from the ranks of the Ulster Volunteer Force, raised to resist Home Rule. Virtually Protestant to a man, they were more than a little bemused to find themselves in Catholic France. A handful failed to treat their new surroundings, and particularly the churches, with due respect – earning the wrath of their commanding officer who made it known to the entire division in no uncertain terms that he would not tolerate such anti-Catholic sectarianism. His actions reached the ears of the Pope through senior army chaplains, and the pontiff responded by awarding Nugent, a member of a plantation family and himself associated with the UVF before the war, with a silver medal.

Knighted after the Great War, Sir Oliver spent his retirement years working for the welfare of former soldiers and promoting the building of the Ulster Memorial Tower at Thiepval, France. It was officially opened on 19 November 1921, by Sir Henry Wilson, from County Longford, who had been Chief of the Imperial General Staff during the war. Sir Henry, who stood in for Sir Edward Carson at the last moment after illness prevented him travelling, was murdered by two IRA men outside his London home in June 1922. The Field Marshal, who was returning after unveiling a war memorial, was in ceremonial dress and attempted to draw his sword to fend off his attackers.

General Nugent died in 1926, with his medals being passed on to his daughter. For 30 years it was believed they had been lost when she had been involved in a car crash in the 1970s but were later discovered in a box, along with 78 records, at her home following her death. In 2010 they were purchased jointly by the Inniskillings Museum, Enniskillen, the Royal Ulster Rifles Museum in Belfast, the Royal Irish Fusiliers Museum in Armagh and the Royal Irish Regiment Museum with the help of grant aid from the Northern Ireland Museums Council and the Northern Ireland War Memorial Trust.

THE HEART OF A LION:
Flight Sub-Lieutenant Robert Dickey

What Robert Frederick Lea Dickey lacked in stature, he more than made up for in courage and fighting spirit, emerging as one of the most decorated pilots of the Great War. He was credited with shooting down a Zeppelin and sinking a U-boat. In the space of six months he was awarded the Distinguished Service Cross and two bars and twice mentioned in dispatches. Throughout the course of the war, only 10 officers were awarded a second bar to the DSC, seven of them members of the Royal Naval Air Service.

Robert Dickey was born at Londonderry in July 1895, where his father was a professor at McCrea Magee College. He enlisted in the Royal Naval Air Service in April 1915, being appointed as a Petty Officer Mechanic. Following training as a pilot, he was posted to RNAS Felixstowe as a sub-lieutenant flying Curtis H12 flying boats on submarine hunting patrols. It was in air-to-air combat, however, that he claimed his first kill. Along with Canadian Flight Lieutenant Basil Deacon Hobbs, he spotted Zeppelin L43 south-west of Terschilling as he returned to base on 14 June 1917. Climbing above the enemy craft before diving at 140 mph, Dickey fired two bursts from his Lewis gun, just 15 rounds in total. However, as the plane came round a second time they spotted that the incendiary bullets had set the escaping gas alight and moments later the airship exploded, ripping in half and plunging into the water. Dickey was awarded the DSC and Hobbs the DSO for their exploits though their success went unreported at the time. L43 had carried out the only Zeppelin raid on Nottingham during the war, with three civilians killed and eight injured, and that too had gone unreported until after the Armistice.

On 17 June the same pilots attacked an enemy seaplane and on the 28th of that month spotted their first submarine, dropping three 100 lbs bombs on it, for which Dickey was awarded a bar to the DSC. On 12 July he attacked another Zeppelin escorting enemy destroyers but it climbed to 13,000 feet to escape the seaplane.

On 3 September, Hobbs and Dickey bombed a U-boat then ten days later spotted another, dropping two 230 lb bombs, one of which exploded next to the conning tower. Within minutes oil and wreckage came to the surface. It was not until 28 September, however, that they were given credit for sinking a submarine, UC-6. In his flying log, Dickey, who was awarded a second bar to his DSC for this action, noted:

"Before we left we were told hostile submarine was 25–30 miles S. of North Hinder. We went to N. Hinder and set a course S. and when on this course after 20 minutes, the W/T operator received (indications of) a hostile wireless. These signals got stronger and at 8.30 we sighted a hostile submarine in full buoyancy. We attacked and dropped one 230 lb bomb which got a direct hit on tail. Before bomb hit he fired one shell at us which went 25 feet in front of us and burst above us. We turned to drop the other bomb and saw three more hostile submarines and three destroyers, escorted by two seaplanes. Destroyers and subs all opened fire on us with shrapnel but we managed to drop our second bomb which fell 15 feet in front of the same submarine. Submarine sank with a large hole in tail and made a large upheaval in water. We got a photograph."

The UC-6, a minelayer U-boat, had been commissioned in June 1915. It undertook 89 patrols and is credited with sinking 54 ships.

Shortly afterwards Dickey went on sick leave, not returning to duty until March 1918. In June, while flying off the coast of Holland, he suffered engine trouble and set down his flying boat. As he attempted repairs he came under fire from an enemy destroyer, forcing him to flee into Dutch waters and leading to him been interned, though he was allowed to return to the UK in August due to ill health.

After the war Dickey was granted a permanent commission as a Flight Lieutenant in the Royal Air Force, serving until 1924. On the outbreak of the Second World War he returned to the services, being appointed to Gosport on home defence duties as a lieutenant in the Royal Navy Volunteer Reserve.

JUST FEET FROM FREEDOM:
Major John Morrogh

John Morrogh had a fascinating life. Born in Cape Town on 2 February 1884, he was from a well-to-do Irish family with his father, also John, from Douglas, County Cork, and one-time MP for South East Cork, having made his money through investing in a diamond company in South Africa. Commissioned into the Royal Irish Regiment, John junior spent a decade in India. In April 1912 he took what has been claimed to be the last photograph of the *Titanic* as the ship passed Crosshaven, County Cork, after leaving Queenstown. Following the declaration of war he fought in many of the battles of the early months of the conflict until May 1915, when he was wounded, a bullet striking him on the cheek and lodging in his respiratory tract. One of his brothers, Frank, was killed with the Royal Munster Fusiliers the following month in Gallipoli, and several others served throughout the war. In April 1916, Major Morrogh was serving with a reserve battalion in Dublin when the uprising began on Easter Monday. On the Thursday of that week he commanded a group of snipers that from an advantage point on O'Connell Street inflicted casualties on the rebels in the General Post Office, including James Connolly, and captured the republican flag being flown from the top of the building.

During the enemy spring offensive of 21 March 1918, the Germans overran the Royal Irish Regiment's trenches at Ronsoy, on the Somme front. The major's company, facing an enemy division, held out for most of the day before finally being forced to surrender. Now a prisoner of war, he was taken to Holzminden Camp, where he was invited to take part in what was to prove the only mass escape of the war. Using a couple of broken knives, forks and spoons as their only tools, a group of men had already spent months scraping out a narrow tunnel under the foundations of the barracks and out towards a field of beans growing some 50 yards away. On the night of 21 July 1918, after nine months of tunnelling, they were ready to go. Major Morrogh was number 22 on the list of officers waiting their turn to escape and lay anxiously in his bed to be called. His rucksack, containing a tin of bully beef, ship's biscuits, chocolate, tea, cigarettes, compass, torch, maps and matches, along with his 'civilian' outfit of khaki sweater, flannel trousers and marching boots, was tucked away nearby. At 12.45 am he was summoned to the tunnel only to discover that someone had become stuck and so there was a delay. When the all clear was given, he launched himself into the tunnel, pushing his kit bag ahead of him, though not before shaking hands with a corporal of his regiment who had got out of bed to see him on his way and wish him luck. Halfway along, sweating profusely, covered in dirt and terrified, Major Morrogh suddenly found his way blocked by the feet of another escaper who was trying to crawl back out! After his human blockage moved on he came across another obstacle, a large stone that had fallen from the roof. Impossible to get past it, he had to inch forward, pushing the boulder ahead of him with his rucksack until he was able to move it back into its original place. After two hours of crawling, he felt the fresh air on his face and after a last scramble he was out of the tunnel, relieved but exhausted.

Major Morrogh planned to walk the 160 miles to the Dutch border but first had to swim the River Weser, stripping naked to do so as he needed to keep his clothes and equipment dry. The fast flowing waters carried him some 150 yards downstream, making it a struggle to reach the far bank. Despite his best efforts, his clothes and rucksack were soaked through. After 14 days walking, most of these accompanied by two fellow escapers he had met up with on the road, he was just five miles away from the German-Dutch border. The following night they set out for the frontier, swimming the Ems canal and making it as far as the Ems River. There his luck ran out for he literally bumped into the German sentries just 500 yards short of the border.

Major Morrogh, dirty and ragged, and having lost two stone in weight in just two weeks, was eventually taken back to Holzminden, where he spent six weeks in solitary confinement in the cells. In total 29 officers had escaped, with 10 making it to safety. Of those recaptured, the major had spent the longest time at liberty. For their escape bid, the men were all sentenced to six months in a fortress prison though the war ended before they could serve their time.

Major Morrogh returned to Ireland after the war but his role in the Easter Rising had not been forgotten and he was forced to leave for England to avoid being murdered by the IRA. The family then moved to Uruguay and later Argentina. He returned to England following the outbreak of the Second World War to volunteer for service. Major Morrogh died on 7 December 1954.

THE LAST OF THE BRAVE:
James Crichton and Martin Moffatt

James Crichton was not a man to brag about his achievements. Comments made to a cleric friend in his adopted home of New Zealand gives no hint of his heroics:

> "I expect to go to England soon. I got a very slight wound crossing the Canal du Nord; in fact so slight that I did not think I would get away from the regiment. I got it about 7.00 am and I carried on with it till about 5.00 pm before I got the doctor. And then I had to swim across a river as six of us got cut off from the company. But I got out and so did the others. Everything was going well. We had the Germans on the run alright."

The incident he is describing took place as the British pursued the Germans across the Canal de Nord, one of the last natural barriers to an Allied advance. A more accurate account of his day was published in the *London Gazette* on 15 November 1918. It read:

> "On 30 September 1918, at Crevecoeur, France, Private Crichton, although wounded in the foot, stayed with the advancing troops despite difficult canal and river obstacles. When his platoon was forced back by a counterattack he succeeded in carrying a message which involved swimming a river and crossing an area swept by machine-gun fire. Subsequently he rejoined his platoon and later undertook on his own initiative to save a bridge which had been mined. Under close fire he managed to remove the charges, returning with the fuses and detonators. Though suffering from a painful wound, he displayed the highest degree of valour and devotion to duty."

His courage that day earned him the Victoria Cross. Crichton was born at Carrickfergus, County Antrim, on 15 July 1879, making him 39-years-old – considerably older than virtually all his comrades in arms – when he risked his life to prevent the enemy destroying a bridge. He had joined the army as a young man, serving during the Boer War with the Cameron Highlanders. Crichton had later sailed for New Zealand, settling in Auckland where he worked as a linesman in the Telegraph Department. He re-enlisted in the New Zealand forces on 22 August 1914, and with his past experience was rapidly promoted, reaching the rank of warrant officer in the Army Service Corps. He embarked for Egypt with the New Zealand Expeditionary Force in October, 1914, and served in Gallipoli from October to December 1915. In April 1916, he arrived on the Western Front. Working behind the lines, however, wasn't to his taste and in May 1918 he relinquished his rank to transfer to the 2nd Auckland Infantry Regiment as a private.

After his heroics on 30 September, Crichton was prevented from returning to his platoon by his company officer, who ordered him back to his own lines where he insisted in acting as a stretcher-bearer until, despite his protests, he was made to seek medical treatment himself.

James Bell Crichton, who stood at just 5ft 4ins tall, was later promoted to sergeant but did not see further action as he was still receiving treatment for his wound when the war ended and was discharged from the army the following year as unfit for active service, returning to his former job. He died on 22 September 1961, aged 82, and is buried in Waikumete Memorial Park Soldiers' Cemetery, near Auckland.

Martin Joseph Moffat, from Sligo, served in the Connaught Rangers for a spell before being transferred to the 2nd Leinster Regiment. Born in 1884, he was also a few years older than most of his comrades as the war entered its final months. Moffatt was part of a working party that had been crossing open ground at Ledeghem, Belgium, on 14 October when it came under fire from a nearby house. While the others took cover, Moffatt rushed the building despite the sustained rifle fire, tossing grenades as he ran. Working his way to the rear of the house, he burst in, killing two Germans and taking another 30 prisoner. After the war he returned to Sligo to become a harbour policeman. Moffatt, who received his Victoria Cross at Buckingham Palace the following June, died in 1946 in a drowning incident. He had been the last Irish VC winner on the Western Front.

AMERICAN MEDAL OF HONOR WINNER:
Major Joseph Thompson

Even before the Great War, Joe Thompson had a reputation of being the "fighting Irishman". Born at Kilkeel, County Down, he was only 18 years old when he arrived in America. Embracing his new life and culture, he excelled at sport, initially making a name for himself in college basketball. American football, however, proved to be to his liking to such an extent that he captained the University of Pittsburgh team, the Panthers, during the 1904–05 season and, after qualifying from its law school, went on to coach the team successfully for a number of years. Thompson, a practicing lawyer, also turned to politics, and represented the Republican Party in the Pennsylvania State Senate from 1913–1916.

Joe Thompson joined the United States Army in 1917, and was sent to France the following year where he served as a major in the 110th Infantry, part of the 28th Division. His unit was involved in the Meuse-Argonne offensive, part of an Allied campaign designed to stretch the Germans, already in retreat, to the limit. Launched on 26 September 1918, the attack saw the largest commitment of US troops of the war. The 28th Division, largely made up of men from Pennsylvania National Guard, had earned the nickname of the "Iron Division" from General John Pershing following its part in holding back the German offensive at Chateau-Thierry that summer. However, it made little initial progress at the Meuse in the face of stiff opposition, though did manage, after three days of fighting, to take Apremont. On 1 October, the Germans launched a counter attack on the lightly defended town. Major Joe Thompson moved along his line, encouraging his men to hold their ground. Then, having repulsed the attack, he led them forward in an assault of their own on the German lines. They were accompanied by a number of tanks which, one by one, were knocked out of the battle until just the one was left. Major Thompson, ignoring the heavy machine-gun fire coming from the enemy lines, left his cover and time and again led the tank forward, acting as spotter to direct its fire. Under his direction, the tank knocked out an enemy machine-gun post, allowing the US infantry to advance and take the line. According to the citation for the Medal of Honor he was later awarded, the only one during the Great War to be given to an Irish-born soldier:

"Counter-attacked by two regiments of the enemy, Major Thompson encouraged his battalion in the front line of constantly braving the hazardous fire of machine-guns and artillery. His courage was mainly responsible for the heavy repulse of the enemy. Later in the action, when the advance of his assaulting companies was held up by fire from a hostile machine-gun nest and all but one of the six assaulting tanks were disabled, Major Thompson, with great gallantry and coolness, rushed forward on foot three separate times in advance of the assaulting line, under heavy machine-gun and anti-tank gun fire, and led the one remaining tank to within a few yards of the enemy machine-gun nest, which succeeded in reducing it, thereby making it possible for the infantry to advance."

Thompson, who went on to become a Lieutenant Colonel in the American Reserve Corps, was presented with his Medal of Honor by Major General Charles Muir on 14 December 1922. That same year he had become the Pennsylvania State Commander of the American Legion. During his service Thompson, who had settled in Beaver Falls, Pennsylvania, had been wounded a number of times and on 1 February 1928, he passed away from associated complications. In America today he is better remembered for his sports achievements than his war service and in 1971 was inducted into the National Football Foundation's College Football Hall of Fame and, six years later, to the Beaver County Sports Hall of Fame.

At least four other Great War recipients of the Medal of Honor during the Great War were of Irish descent: Sergeant Michael Donaldson, of the 165th Infantry Regiment, repeatedly risked his life at Landres-et-Saint-Georges on 14 October 1918, to rescue six wounded men; William Donovan, who during the Second World War was to head the Office of Strategic Services, precursor to the Central Intelligence Agency, commanded a battalion of the 165th Regiment and was awarded the Medal of Honor for his service also at Landres-et-Saint-Georges on 14–15 October 1918; Sergeant Richard O'Neill, also of the 165th regiment, received his medal for an assault on the German lines at Ourcq River on 30 July 1918, when he continued to command his detachment despite being wounded several times; and Private Michael Perkins, of the 101st Regiment, who bombed his way into an enemy pill box at Belieu Bois on 27 October 1918, and, armed with a knife, engaged in vicious hand-to-hand combat with those inside, killing and wounding a number of Germans and taking twenty-five prisoners and seven machine-guns. Perkins, wounded in the fight, was killed the following day by artillery fire as he was being transferred to hospital.

A HELPING HAND:
Miss Mary Cunningham

They were the "idle rich," with no jobs and never any need to work as they came from some of the wealthiest families in Ireland. Yet the well-to-do ladies, like their more humble neighbours, rolled up their sleeves and got on with helping the war effort in whatever way they could. With millions of men away to war, women took over many of the roles from which they had formerly been excluded, earning good money and asserting their claim to equality of treatment. Others, of a higher social standing, concentrated on attending to the sick and needy. One such was Mary Cunningham, a 50-year-old spinster in 1918, who could have spent the entire war enjoying the comforts of the family home in Glencairn, west Belfast, where she was waited on hand and foot by servants. Yet most days of the week she donned an apron over her fine clothes and got on with helping others – serving up cups of tea and biscuits to troops passing through the railway stations, providing the necessities of life to the victims of German U-boat attacks, assisting in one of a number of hospitals, organising entertainments for wounded soldiers, raising funds for comforts for those at the front, and meeting every hospital train that arrived in Belfast.

The Cunninghams had arrived in Ireland from Scotland during the plantation, and had made their wealth through the importation and manufacture of tobacco from the West Indies. Mary's father, Josias Cunningham, owner of Glencairn House and the surrounding 100-acre estate, established a stockbrokers business in Waring Street in the middle of the 19th century. It continued under his name until 1991, when it merged with another concern. The family, which also owned the *Northern Whig* newspaper, was staunchly unionist, allowing the Ulster Volunteer Force to parade and train in the estate grounds and to store arms in one of its properties, Fernhill House.

For two years Miss Cunningham had been an organiser, deputy president and controller of the Great Northern Railway's sailor's and soldiers' buffet. Mary also supplied food and clothing to those brought ashore from ships sunk by enemy action. Both operations were conducted out of York Road railway station, initially from a large room and, towards the war's end, from a converted passageway. Mary told a *Belfast Telegraph* reporter:

"When the military authorities took over the room I and the railway company were at a loss to know where they could find the further space, and as they recognised the value of the work they considered it imperative that some place must either be given up or made, and as I already knew the amount of traffic this important station dealt with, the smallest space to them must have been a great sacrifice. Finally, I got this passage – an exit from the station to the goods yard not more than 5ft wide and 14ft long."

The corridor had been lined with shelves packed with crockery, while tea and coffee urns sat on a gas stove next to a family-sized kettle. In the centre was a large dining table and chairs capable of catering for up to 16 people at once. In another room were stored coats, suits and hats, with boots, socks and underclothing kept nearby as emergency supplies for those rescued at sea. "I may have a telephone message at any time, and if required, load up cars with garments and other things, and go immediately to the help of these poor fellows, many of whom have only their shirts on when rescued," said Miss Cunningham. "They simply seem too surprised to speak, and many have been seen with tears in their eyes. Surely no better form of gratitude." Miss Cunningham was assisted in the venture by her sister, Mrs Ferguson, being joint treasurers for the Torpedoed Crews Fund, while another sister, Miss Lallie Cunningham, looked after the catering arrangements at the docks for the Sailors' and Soldiers' Service Club, Waring Street.

Mary, who had helped in the formation of the 109th Field Ambulance for war service, was also commandant and demonstrator for the St John Ambulance Association; worked several days a week at the Donegall Road Hospital and the Victoria Barracks Hospital; sat on a committee that provided comforts for the men of the 9th Royal Irish Rifles, initially recruited from west Belfast, and for members of the Fire Brigade on active service; helped Forth River National School in its efforts to raise war funds; and took to do with organising entertainments at the Randalstown Scottish Camp, which cared for convalescing soldiers. Mary had met every hospital train that had arrived in Belfast so that, with the help of her Voluntary Aid Detachment, she could supervised the distribution of refreshments to the wounded.

BREAKING THE LINE:
Charles Brett

Charles Brett, from Belfast, was just 17 when he applied for, and was granted, a commission in the 6th Connaught Rangers in October 1914. Four years later he was commanding a company of the Rangers, then part of the 66th Division, at the Second Battle of Le Cateau, which ran from 8–12 October 1918, and formed part of the storming of the highly-fortified German Hindenburg Line. In his account of his service days he recorded:

"We were told that the Germans were holding the last of their prepared trenches and that we might expect to get into open country if we were lucky. There was no sleep for anyone that night, and next morning just before dawn we set off behind a very heavy barrage, in company with four tanks. The tanks were a great help to us, as they drew fire from the enemy who were so busy shooting at the tanks that they paid little attention to us (the tanks were all knocked out before we had gone far) so we had a fairly easy job putting the Germans out of their trench and getting out into the open country beyond. Our first objective was a village called Serain, about a mile behind the German line. On our way there, we passed several batteries of German field guns which they had tried to get away; the horses they had brought up to pull out the guns had been caught by our shell fire and killed or dreadfully wounded, many were screaming pitifully. Alas, we could do nothing to put them out of their misery. I hope that some of those who followed us did."

Held up by their own artillery until Brett was able to pass a message on by signaling a reconnaissance aircraft, they took the village which was "full of terrified civilians and also several German snipers, who gave trouble till they were found and liquidated." He continued:

"We then went on to the next village. I really cannot describe the events of that day and the following two days. It was a nightmare. We advanced across muddy open fields, under continued shellfire (which was not heavy) from village to village, coming suddenly on a concealed machine-gun or hidden snipers, who killed or wounded some of our people before they could be dealt with. In those three days we went fifteen miles from our starting point near Serain, and landed up under a slight ridge on the other side of which was a descent to the valley of the river Selle, and the town of Le Cateau whose outskirts were about a quarter of a mile further on. Here we arrived about 11.00 am, and here we stuck, as the Germans were holding Le Cateau in some strength."

Having advanced further than the troops on either side, they were constantly shelled by the enemy, causing horrendous casualties: "I will never forget the look of horror on the face of one of my men, as a splinter of a shell disemboweled him, in the second or moments before he died," he wrote.

"Another had one of his legs almost amputated just at his knee, and I with my penknife severed the few scraps of flesh and sinew which held it together before tying him up and sending him back (where I wonder?) on a stretcher."

Brett's company came under sustained German artillery fire and was forced to dig in. About 3.00 pm orders arrived for the battalion to attack Le Cateau and two hours later, as it was getting dusk, he led his men forward on to the roadway. After they had gone about 100 yards the German guns opened up on them with the rear platoons taking heavy casualties. Brett, along with another officer and six men made it into the town. Under machine-gun fire, they made their way towards their objective, the town's railway line, where they discovered the iron rail bridge had been blown up:

"On top were several Germans with the machine-gun. We climbed up and disposed of them. Having done so we looked down into the roadway on the German side of the bridge, and saw below us fifty to a hundred German soldiers standing and looking up at the top of the bridge to see what it was all about. As I have said it was pretty dark but one could see the serried rows of white faces looking up. At my command we all leaped down among them, killed and wounded several and captured two. It was well for us that they were very poor class troops, because all the rest turned tail and fled and we were left in the roadway with two prisoners."

With no sign of reinforcements, Brett decided to withdraw and, guided by one of the prisoners, they managed to cross back over the river using what remained of a demolished foot bridge and staggered back to the holes they had dug previously. Brett added: "When I woke next morning I found there was something with me in the hole, and it turned out to be the leg I had cut off the evening before, with its boot and puttee complete."

Charles Brett survived the war and went on to enjoy a successful career as a solicitor in Belfast. He died in 1988 at the age of 91.

Charles Brett was only 17 years old when commissioned into the 6th Connaught Rangers. *(Courtesy of the Somme Museum)*

RMS *LEINSTER* AND THE FIRST WRNS KILLED ON DUTY:
Josephine Carr

Josephine Carr was just 19-years-old and heading off on the first real adventure of her life. From the Blackrock Road area of Cork, she had jumped at the opportunity of joining the Women's Royal Naval Service. Only officially created in November 1917, the WRNS aimed to train women to work in clerical roles on shore, freeing up men to go to sea. Josephine, who had qualified as a clerk and shorthand typist, boarded the Royal Mail Ship *Leinster* on 10 October 1918, on the way to her new posting. Operated by the City of Dublin Steam Packet Company, the RMS *Leinster* regularly sailed between Kingstown, modern day Dun Laoghaire, just south of Dublin, and Holyhead in Wales. Shortly before 9.00 am the ferry left Carlisle Pier to make its way out into Dublin Bay and the rough seas beyond. On board were some 771 passengers and crew. It was less than an hour out when it came under attack from a German U-boat. The first torpedo fired passed harmless in front of the *Leinster*, but a second struck it on the port side. The ship attempted to return to port but was struck again, this time on the starboard side, and sank within minutes. Officially 501 lives were lost, though the actual casualty toll is believed to be higher.

Josephine Carr was with a party of WRNS from Cork that included 30-year-old Cora Daly, of Blackrock, who only two days previously had married Major Louis Daly, and Maureen Waters, aged just 20, from Ballintemple, and Miss Barry. The women had found seats in the reading room of the steamer and Josephine had remained there while Maureen went out on deck. Miss Waters had been close to the bow of the ship when the first torpedo struck and along with Mrs Daly and Miss Barry had made her way to the top deck: "I then saw Cora get into a lifeboat, screamed at Miss Barry, and in we got, and were swung down," she wrote a few days later in a letter home.

"On our way we saw Louis on the bridge waving and smiling at us. I cried then, but stopped immediately to console poor Cora. We reached the water; no one let the ropes go, so were tied to the sinking ship, and our oars were tied to the seats with rope. It was awful. A man yelled for penknives. I remembered mine was in my coat pocket. Miss Barry also had hers, so I tell you we were not long in passing them to the men, and they cut the oars loose, also the ropes which tied us to the ship. Just then, the second torpedo came on our side. How we were not swamped then and there God alone knows. I saw half the *Leinster* go up into the air, and volumes of water, and thought we would get it all down over us, but we didn't. I then looked behind, and the ship was standing upright almost, propeller in the air, and we were hardly three yards away. I just prayed as I never did before, and buried my head in Cora's lap, never even hoped to be saved. Needless to say, our boat was crammed, and we had only three oars left; all the others broke. To see the crowds of unfortunate people struggling in that awful sea was terrible. We had a very clear-headed man who took command of our boat, and he was splendid. We got clear of the wreckage, and hauled Captain Birch into our boat, but his eye was out, and one leg broken."

After approximately 90 minutes the first rescue ships, including several destroyers, arrived at the scene. Miss Waters' ordeal was far from over, however:

"The getting on board was the worst of all. She came close to us and there was a desperate rush to grab ropes or a sailor's hand. Cora said 'Oh, my God, we're swamped and looked round quickly. The destroyer washed over on to us. It was terrible, I know I went right under and thought I was never coming up again. But I did, and was between the destroyer and our boat, hanging on with one hand, and just my legs inside the gunwale of our boat. Three times I had a sailor's hand, but not securely enough, and three times I went down. After the second time I went under I saw Cora being hauled up. Then a man saw me going down between boats, and gave me a tug onboard our lifeboat. A wave came, and I made a desperate grab at the same sailor's hand, and with my other grabbed the rope round the deck part of the destroyer, and there I hung. I nearly lost consciousness, and I faintly heard 'One, two, three – haul,' and I was pulled on board. Three sailors cut the lifebelt off, and worked my arms and made me drink rum. I knew I was conscious all the time."

Miss Barry and Major Daly were both rescued, though the latter sustained severe leg injuries. The U-boat responsible, UB-123, never made it home. On 19 October 1918, it struck a mine and was lost along with all 36 crew members. Josephine Carr was the first 'Wren' to die on active service. Her body was never recovered and today she is commemorated on the Plymouth Naval Memorial.

WORKING FOR THE GERMANS:
Private John Mahony

John Mahony was born at Ennis, County Clare, in 1891. He had worked as a clerk and later head porter at the Milton Malbay railway station in Clare before joining the Royal Dublin Fusiliers in 1906. He landed in France with the British Expeditionary Force on 23 August 1914, and three days later was wounded and taken prisoner. Moved to Limburg Camp in Germany in December 1914, he volunteered to join Roger Casement's Irish Brigade. By 1918 the Germans had long lost interest in employing the Irishmen as a fighting force and in October sent them to Munich with false papers to fend for themselves. Mahony eventually handed himself over to the authorities, and gave a detailed statement of his war:

"In the first week of December all the Irish at Doberitz were sent to Limburg-in-Lahn. At Limburg I stayed till June 1916. I saw Casement in March 1915. I speak Irish. Casement did not know Irish. There were about 3,000 Irish at Limburg. The priest, Nicholson, spoke to me when I was sick. He told me that I should be built up. When the occasion arose I could be taken to Ireland to fight. I asked the conditions. He said he would give me a pamphlet to read and said everything would be correct. A few days later I received a pamphlet which promised different things. I told Nicholson that he must understand that while serving the King I would not fight against him, but I would be willing to return to Ireland with the Germans in case of an invasion. My intention was to get home, but not to fight. I have been present when Father Nicholson celebrated Mass."

Mahony claimed that he opted to join the Irish Brigade as he was ill – he was still suffering from 'fits' after being wounded in the head and shoulder – and thought he might get the chance to escape. As a sign of his commitment, he pointed out that he had refused to volunteer for a German scheme to send the Irish Brigade to Egypt as a machine-gun section. "I want to have nothing to do with the Sinn Féin question in any way. But if my services are longer required in His Majesty's services I am willing to take up arms and fight against the King's enemies. I would rather not return to Ireland," he added.

Mahony said the whole camp had been brought before Casement at Limburg, section by section, and questioned.

"I agreed to join. Casement told me to stay under the doctor's care till I was better. For two years after this date I suffered from fits and on two occasions I nearly died. In June 1916, fifty-six of us were sent to Zossen. After a week in the stone barracks where I had fits I went to hospital in the Halbmond Lager where I remained for three weeks. I joined the others in the Halbmond Lager. After a few months we were transferred to a little hut built for us in the Arbeitskommando at Zossen. We then had permission to wear the special uniform which I wore until I reached Danzig. I was appointed to the rank of corporal by Casement, the order coming from Bohm. I remained a corporal until we were asked to volunteer for Egypt in January 1916. I was questioned in the office at Zossen by Casement and Captain Monteith, Keogh, Dowling and Quinlisk were also there. I was asked would I volunteer to go to the east to fight against our enemy. I replied and said that I joined the Irish movement in case of a German invasion of Ireland. I made it clear on doing this that I would not volunteer to take up arms in any respect to fight against His Majesty's Forces in any part of the world. I was therefore told to remove my stripes as corporal. I remarked that I did not want them but wanted to return to a prisoners' camp and to be left alone. Casement said I must stay till the end of the war. I took my stripes off. I asked the Commandantur a week later about going to a prisoners' camp. I was told that we were all going to be sent to a prisoners' camp."

They were indeed sent to Danzig Troyl at the end of June 1916, where they were set to work as labourers, then in October 1918, were taken to Munich, where they were given false names and papers. Mahony, now calling himself Hans Harbeck and dressed in civilian working clothes, found a job as a gardener at a monastery before moving on to Tutzing, where he remained until March 1919 when he was again admitted to hospital.

"After leaving the hospital I returned to Tutzing for a fortnight. Then work ceased. I then worked for a Regetta Club on the lake, but returned to Munich before the Revolution. I fought for two days and two nights at the bridge beyond the Banhof where there was much fighting."

Mahony became aware that the Red Cross was inquiring about him and went to Berlin, ending up in the charge of the British Provost Marshall at Cologne.

HEROINE OF COURTRAI:
A second Miss Mary Cunningham

English war correspondent Philip Gibbs had seen more than enough war to last any man. But even he was surprised by his discovery in one recently liberated Belgium town on 21 October 1918:

"I went into Courtrai itself this morning. It has now been freed from the enemy. But it was not wholly a joyous entry, like that into Lille or Bruges, or other towns where civilian crowds have greeted any Englishman with cheers and embraces. The people here, 25,000 to 30,000 of them, have suffered too much to have any complete reaction yet… I found one old English lady in the city, or rather an Irish lady named Miss Mary Cunningham. She is an old lady of over seventy, who has lived in Courtrai for twelve years, at first in well-to-do circumstances, her father being a flax-spinner, but afterwards obliged to earn her living by teaching French and English to Flemish pupils. Even that failed her after the war, because, as it dragged on, English and French did not seem much good to people surrounded by Germans.

So Miss Cunningham is poor now, and lives in a tiny house opposite the cathedral, with a cooking-stove in her parlour, and not much to cook on it, poor soul. But she received us as a great lady of the old school with most beautiful dignity, undisturbed by 'noises without', ominous crashes close at hand, and sounds of breaking glass. She made only one remark showing that she noticed these things. 'Do you mind shutting the door, my dear? I don't like those bombs coming in.' I noticed that 'bombs,' as she called German shells, had already broken the front part of her little parlour, and she was very close to the danger-point of hostile shell-fire range by the belfry of Courtrai.

She did not say much about the war, except when she spoke of the Germans as highway robbers; but her mind went back to Ireland and old friends there, and her old people. Her grandmother was a Miss Kimmins (sic), the sister of President Wilson's great-grandmother. She told us that as a passing thought, but I was startled by her words and thought how queer it was that I should be sitting with President Wilson's cousin in a little front parlour of Courtrai, with Germans not far away and the city under shell-fire."

His report sparked huge interest in Ireland, with the Editor of the *Belfast Telegraph* requesting Mr Gibbs return for a second interview. He reported on 1 November:

"I had a quite interesting chat with Miss Mary Cunningham at Courtrai this morning. It was her 78th birthday, and I found her in her little apartment beside St Martin's Church talking with three young Belgian boys who had been her pupils in the first year of the war, and had called to pay their respects to the old lady. Miss Cunningham told me that her father, Bernard Cunningham, was a native of Ballyshannon, Co Donegal; her mother, Jane Miskimmin, was born at Carrickfergus, but the Miskimmin family lived at Doagh. Her uncle, James Miskimmin, died at Monkstown on 20 September 1887, at the age of 75; her mother died at the residence of James Miskimmin on 2 October 1887, aged 73, and was buried at Doagh. Miss Cunningham's great grandmother, Nancy Miskimmin, had a sister Sally, who married Malcolm Wilson, a farmer of Islandmagee, from whom, she says, President Wilson is descended'."

Following German occupation Miss Cunningham, born at Vouziers, in the Ardennes area of France, had applied to the Courtrai authorities for relief from a fund for distressed British subjects but had been refused on the grounds that she was of French nationality, which the old woman indignantly denied. "She told me that in the winter of 1915–16 frequently she went to bed after drinking a little grated nutmeg in warm water – absolutely without food," said the war correspondent.

"For days at a time she lived wholly on potatoes. Some old friends helped her as best they could, but often she was nearly on the verge of starvation. She is really a very wonderful old lady. I will try to recall some of her conversation. 'When the British began bombing,' she said, 'I didn't feel afraid. Sometimes my little pupils would be frightened, but I told them it was all right, and I said to myself, "I can't complain, it's the British!" But when the windows began to fall in I went to the far side of the room (the room is not more than seven feet wide) and hid behind the stove (the stove is hardly bigger than a top hat). There I would wait until the business seemed to be finished. My windows were broken, but some friends put up paper, and strips of boards to keep out the rain, and I went on teaching English as long as pupils would come to me. But there's very little light (as a matter of fact, her room is in absolute darkness when the door is closed), and some kind soldiers have promised to try and find me new panes of glass. The soldiers won't let me starve. The day before yesterday I went up to one of their places, and they gave me what I call 'Bull Beef', and that big pitcher full of fine stew. I did enjoy that dinner, the finest I have had for years. I wouldn't have given it up to a King'."

English war correspondent Philip Gibbs discovered Miss Mary Cunningham had remained in her Courtrai home throughout the war. *(From the Belfast Telegraph)*

THE LAST TO DIE:
Final deaths on the Western Front

The Armistice that brought an end to the horror on the Western Front was signed at 5.10 am in a railway carriage on a siding outside Compiegne, north of Paris, to come into affect at the symbolic time of 11.00 am – meaning the end of hostilities would be at the 11th hour of the 11th day of the 11th month of 1918. The delay was to allow word to be passed to the combatants of both sides. Overall, some 863 Commonwealth soldiers died that day, most from injuries sustained in earlier fighting and some, no doubt, after the fighting had officially come to an end. Some estimates put the total death toll among the opposing armies on 11 November 1918, as in excess of 11,000.

Private George Edwin Ellison, of the 5th Royal Irish Lancers, is listed by the Commonwealth War Graves Commission as being the last British soldier killed. The 40-year-old had been on patrol on the outskirts of Mons, in Belgium, where the first shots of the war had been fired, when he was killed at 9.30 am on 11 November 1918, just 90 minutes before the Armistice was due to come into effect. However, while he was serving in an Irish regiment, Private Ellison, a pre-war regular who had been on the army reserve when called up again, was actually a Yorkshire man. A trawl though the death records for 11 November, throws up the names of Irishmen who died that day. They include: Corporal Robert John Johnston, of the 15th Royal Irish Rifles, who was the 23 year old son of Richard and Emma Johnston from the Ligoniel area of Belfast. He is buried at Terlincthun British Cemetery, on the northern outskirts of Boulogne; Private L McCarthy, who had served with the 16th Machine Gun Corps, and was from Coolbawn, Ballinspittle, Kinsale, County Cork. He also lies in Terlincthun; Belfast man William Irwin, also buried at Terlincthun, was aged 30 and a member of the 2nd Royal Irish Rifles; Private Frank McKeown was just 19 years old and serving with the 15th Highland Light Infantry. Although living in Glasgow he had been born at Cushendall, County Antrim, and today lies in Etaples Military Cemetery, Pas de Calais; Robert Connor, of Lower Gardiner Street, Dublin, was a private in the 2nd Machine Gun Corps. Aged 22, he is buried at St Sever Cemetery Extension, Rouen; Sergeant William Morrissey, who also lies at Rouen, was 34 years old and a member of the Army Services Corps based at 1st Base Remount Depot. He left behind a widow, Henrietta, at Albert Place, Fermoy, County Cork; Private James Murray, of the 9th Royal Inniskilling Fusiliers, was from Muff,

County Donegal, though had been living with his wife Isabel at Culmore, Londonderry. The 36 year old is buried at Les Baraques Military Cemetery, Sangatte; Thomas John O'Toole, 31, was from Castlecaulfield, County Tyrone. Serving with the 12th/13th Northumberland Fusiliers when killed, he lies in Mont Huon Military Cemetery, Le Treport; and Gunner D Keating, from Cork, served with V/V1 Corps Heavy Trench Mortar Battery of the Royal Garrison Artillery. The 38-year-old is buried at Awoingt British Cemetery near Cambrai.

The last French soldier to die, Augustin Trebuchon from the 415th Infantry Regiment, was killed at 10.50 am as he took word of the Armistice to his comrades in the front line. Eight minutes later Canadian George Lawrence Price, of the 2nd Canadian Division, was killed at Mons, becoming officially the last Commonwealth solider to be killed. The Americans suffered the most Allied casualties on 11 November 1918, as they had ordered their commanders to pursue the war right to the last minute. The United States' last soldier to be killed was Private Henry Gunter, who was of German extraction. He is said to have fallen virtually as the guns fell silent.

The war, and the political waves it created through Europe and beyond, had not nearly claimed its last victims, however. The Commonwealth War Graves Commission lists more than 55,000 names of those who died after the Armistice up to the end of 1919, almost 14,500 for 1920, and 10,500 for 1921, many from wounds inflicted during the war, others from the continued fighting as new nations or governments took shape, and countless others from the influenza epidemic that began sweeping the world in 1918, ultimately resulting in the deaths of an estimated 50 million people.

NOTES ON SOURCES

The journals, diaries, letters and published memoirs of those who served or experienced first-hand the Great War form the backbone of this work. In addition, the newspapers of the day, particularly before the imposition of tougher censorship, proved invaluable, in particular the *Belfast Evening Telegraph, Belfast News Letter, Galway Express, Irish News and Belfast Morning Post, Irish Times, Kildare Observer, and The Northern Whig*. The following books, while being by no means an exhaustive list, provided some of the stories but proved more useful when compiling the introduction passages and informed the general background against which the individual stories are set:

Bingham, Commander The Hon Barry, VC, RN, *Falklands, Jutland and the Bight,* John Murray, London, 1919

Brett, Charles, *Charles Brett MC: An Irish Soldier*, edited by Erskine Holmes, The Somme Association, Newtownards, 2007

Callwell, Major-General Sir CE, KCB, *Experiences of a Dug-Out 1914–18*, Constable & Company Limited, London, 1920

Canning, WJ, *A Wheen of Medals: The History of the 9th (Service) Bn. The Royal Inniskilling Fusiliers (The Tyrones) in World War One*, published by the author, 2006

Crozier, FP, *A Brass Hat in No Man's Land*, Cedric Chivers, Bath, 1968 (First published by Cape, London, 1930)

Denman, Terence, *A Lonely Grave: The Life and Death of William Redmond*, Irish Academic Press, Dublin, 1995

Doherty, Richard, & Truesdale, David, *Irish Winners of the Victoria Cross*, Four Courts Press, Dublin, 2000

Donohoe, Major MH, *With the Persian Expedition*, Edward Arnold, London, 1919

Dungan, M, *Irish Voices from the Great War*, Irish Academic Press, Dublin, 1995

Falls, Cyril, *The History of the 36th (Ulster) Division*, Constable, London, 1996 (First published by McCaw, Stevenson and Orr, Belfast, 1922)

Fisher, J, *Man on the Spot: Captain George Gracey and British policy towards the Assyrians, 1917–45*, Middle Eastern Studies, Vol 44 No2 p215–35, 2008

Grayson, Richard S, *Belfast Boys: How Unionists and Nationalists Fought and Died Together in the First World War*, Continuum, London, 2009

Jeffrey, Keith, *Ireland and the Great War*, Cambridge University Press, Cambridge, 2000

Johnstone, Tom, *Orange, Green and Khaki: The Story of the Irish Regiments in the Great War, 1914–18*, Gill and Macmillan, Dublin, 1992

Keegan, John, *The First World War*, Pimlico, London, 1999

MacDonagh, Michael, *The Irish at the Front*, Hodder and Stoughton, London, 1916

Macdonald, Lyn, *Somme*, Macmillan, London, 1983

MacIntyre, Ben, *A Foreign Field*, HarperCollinsPublishers, London, 2001

Middlebrook, Martin, *The First Day on the Somme*, Pengiun, London, 1971

Middlebrook, Martin, *The Kaiser's Battle, 21 March 1918: The First Day of the German Spring Offensive,* Pengiun, London, 1978

Mitchell, Gardiner S, *Three Cheers for the Derrys! A History of the 10th Royal Inniskilling Fusiliers in the 1914–18 War,* Yes! Publications, Derry, 1991

Moore, Steven, *The Irish on the Somme: A battlefield guide to the Irish regiments in the Great War and the monuments to their memory*, Colourpoint Books, Newtownards, 2016 (First published by Local Press Ltd, Portadown, 2005)

Moreno, Amanda, & Truesdale, David, *Angels and Heroes: The Story of a Machine Gunner with the Royal Irish Fusiliers, August 1914 to April 1915*, Royal Irish Fusiliers Museum, Armagh, 2004

Orr, Philip, *The Road to the Somme: Men of the Ulster Division tell their story*, Blackstaff Press, Belfast, 1987

Orr, Philip, *Field Of Bones: An Irish Division at Gallipoli*, The Lilliput Press, Dublin, 2006

Perry, Nicholas, *Major General Oliver Nugent and the Ulster Division, 1915–1918*, Sutton Publishing, Stroud, 2007

Pollock, John, *Kitchener*, Robinson, London, 2001

Sandes, Flora, *Autobiography of a Woman Soldier: A brief record of adventure with the Serbian Army 1916–19*, HF&G Witherby, London, 1927

Stoker, Henry, *Straws in the Wind,* Herbert Jenkins Limited, London, 1925

Taylor, James W, *The 1st Royal Irish Rifles in the Great War*, Four Courts Press, Dublin, 2002

Taylor, James W, *The 2nd Royal Irish Rifles in the Great War*, Four Courts Press, Dublin, 2005

Van Emden, Richard, *Boy Soldiers of the Great War*, Headline, London, 2005

INDEX